TEACHINGS OF PRESIDENTS OF THE CHURCH

HAROLD B. LEE

Published by
The Church of Jesus Christ of Latter-day Saints
Salt Lake City, Utah

Your comments and suggestions about this book would be appreciated. Please submit them to Curriculum Planning, 50 East North Temple Street, Floor 24, Salt Lake City, UT 84150-3200 USA. E-mail: cur-development@ldschurch.org

Please list your name, address, ward, and stake. Be sure to give the title of the book. Then offer your comments and suggestions about the book's strengths and areas of potential improvement.

Contents

Introduction

Harold B. Lee, eleventh President of the Church and an Apostle for over three decades, bore humble witness from a full heart "that God lives, that Jesus is the Redeemer of the world."[1] With conviction born of years of service he said, "My humble prayer is that all men everywhere may understand more fully the significance of the atonement of the Savior of all mankind, who has given us the plan of salvation which will lead us into eternal life, where God and Christ dwell."[2]

The journey home to our Father in Heaven was a central focus of President Lee's teachings to the members of the Church. He exhorted each of Heavenly Father's children to "gain for himself that unshakable testimony which will place his feet firmly on the pathway which leads surely toward the glorious goal of immortality and eternal life."[3]

"The most important message that I can give to you and to all the world is to keep the commandments of God," said President Lee, "for thereby you can qualify yourselves to receive divine guidance while you live here on the earth, and in the world that lies ahead be prepared to meet your Redeemer, and to gain your exaltation in the presence of the Father and the Son."[4]

The First Presidency and Quorum of the Twelve Apostles have established the series *Teachings of Presidents of the Church* to help Church members deepen their understanding of gospel doctrines and draw closer to Jesus Christ through the teachings of the prophets in this dispensation. This book features the teachings of President Harold B. Lee, who said:

"The laws of God given to mankind are embodied in the gospel plan, and the Church of Jesus Christ is made responsible for teaching these laws to the world."[5]

"Let there be burned into your souls those lessons that shall keep you always with your eye fixed upon the eternal goal, so that you won't fail in life's mission, so that, whether your life be short or long, you shall be prepared when the day comes to go into the presence of Him whose name you bear as a member of the Church of Jesus Christ in these latter days."[6]

Each chapter in this book includes four sections: (1) a question that briefly introduces the focus of the chapter; (2) the "Introduction," which illustrates the messages of the chapter with a story or counsel from President Lee; (3) "Teachings of Harold B. Lee," which presents important doctrines from his many messages and sermons; and (4) "Suggestions for Study and Discussion," which encourages personal review and inquiry, further discussion, and application to our lives today through questions.

How to Use This Book

For personal or family study. This book is intended to enhance each member's understanding of gospel principles taught powerfully by President Harold B. Lee. By prayerful reading and thoughtful study, each member may receive a personal witness of these truths. This volume will also add to each member's gospel library and will serve as an important resource for family instruction and for study in the home.

For discussion in Sunday meetings. This book is the text for Melchizedek Priesthood quorum and Relief Society Sunday meetings. Elder Dallin H. Oaks taught that the books in the series *Teachings of Presidents of the Church* "contain doctrine and principles. They are rich and relevant to the needs of our day, and they are superb for teaching and discussion." Teachers should focus on the content of the text and related scriptures. As Elder Oaks explained, "A gospel teacher is not called to choose the subject of the lesson but to teach and discuss what has been specified."[7]

Teachers should draw from the questions at the end of the chapter to encourage class discussion. Reviewing the questions before studying President Lee's words may give additional insight into his teachings.

The Sunday meetings should concentrate on gospel principles, personal examples that teach these principles, and testimonies of the truth. When teachers humbly seek the Spirit in preparing and directing the lesson, all who participate will be strengthened in their knowledge of the truth. Leaders and teachers should encourage class members to read the chapters before they are discussed in Sunday meetings. They should remind class members to bring their books to their meetings and should honor class members' preparation by teaching from President Harold B. Lee's words. When class members have read the chapter in advance, they will be prepared to teach and edify each other.

It is not necessary or recommended that members purchase additional commentaries or reference texts to support the material in the text. Members are encouraged to turn to the scriptures that have been suggested for further study of the doctrine.

Since this text is designed for personal study and gospel reference, many chapters contain more material than can be fully addressed in Sunday meetings. Therefore, study at home becomes essential to receiving the fulness of President Lee's teachings.

This prophet of God knew the way back home to our Father in Heaven, and he gave direction to all who would listen: "If you will listen and put into practice what you have heard, you will be led to that glorious place called not just happiness but joy. Joy means when you have lived such a life that you are ready to enter into the presence of the Lord."[8]

Notes

1. Address at dedication of Westwood Ward meetinghouse, Los Angeles, California, 12 Apr. 1953, Historical Department Archives, The Church of Jesus Christ of Latter-day Saints.
2. "To Ease the Aching Heart," *Ensign,* Apr. 1973, 5.
3. *Stand Ye in Holy Places* (1974), 319.
4. In Conference Report, Mexico and Central America Area Conference 1972, 120.
5. *The Teachings of Harold B. Lee,* ed. Clyde J. Williams (1996), 19.
6. *The Teachings of Harold B. Lee,* 627.
7. In Conference Report, Oct. 1999, 102; or *Ensign,* Nov. 1999, 80.
8. Address at youth conference in Billings, Montana, 10 June 1973, Historical Department Archives, The Church of Jesus Christ of Latter-day Saints, 17.

Historical Summary

This book is not a history, but rather a compilation of gospel principles as taught by President Harold B. Lee. However, in order to put the teachings in a historical framework, the following list is provided to summarize some of the milestones in his life that have most immediate relationship to his teachings.

1899, March 28:	Harold Bingham Lee born to Samuel Marion and Louisa Emeline Bingham Lee, Clifton, Oneida County, Idaho.
1907, June 9:	Baptized by Lester Bybee, Clifton, Idaho (8; numbers in parentheses show Harold B. Lee's age).
1912, fall:	Enters the Oneida Stake Academy, Preston, Idaho, with schoolmate Ezra Taft Benson (13).
1916, summer:	Enters Albion State Normal School, Albion, Idaho (17).
1916–17, winter:	Teaches at the Silver Star School, near Weston, Idaho (17).
1918–20:	Principal of the district school at Oxford, Idaho (18–21).
1920–22:	Missionary, Western States Mission, Denver, Colorado (21–23).
1923, summer:	Attends the University of Utah. He later finishes his degree by correspondence courses and extension classes (24).
1923, November 14:	Marries Fern Lucinda Tanner in the Salt Lake Temple (24).
1923–28:	Principal of the Whittier and Woodrow Wilson Schools, Salt Lake City (24–29).

1930, October 26: Set apart as president of the Pioneer Stake, 1930–37 (31).

1933, November 7: Elected to the Salt Lake City Commission; serves from 1933–37 (34).

1935, April 20: First Presidency assigns Harold B. Lee to work out a program of relief for the needy (36).

1936, April 18: Called as managing director of the Church security plan (later changed to Church welfare program) (37).

1939, April 16: First storehouse on Welfare Square is completed in Salt Lake City (40).

1941, April 6: Sustained a member of the Quorum of the Twelve Apostles (42). Ordained on April 10, 1941.

1954: Holds servicemen's conferences in Japan, Korea, Okinawa, Philippines, and Guam (55).

1958, August: Tours South Africa and the Holy Land (59).

1960, March 27: Organizes the first stake in Europe at Manchester, England (60).

1961, September 30: At the direction of the First Presidency, announces plan for correlating all Church programs (62).

1962, September 24: Death of Fern Lucinda Tanner, wife of Harold B. Lee (63).

1963, June 17: Marries Freda Joan Jensen in the Salt Lake Temple (64).

1965, August 27: Death of Maurine Lee Wilkins, daughter of Harold B. Lee (66).

1970, January 23:   Sustained as President of the Quorum of the Twelve Apostles and First Counselor to President Joseph Fielding Smith (70).

1972, July 2:   Death of President Joseph Fielding Smith (73).

1972, July 7:   Ordained and set apart as President of the Church (73).

1972, August 25–27:   Presides over area general conference in Mexico City (73).

1972, September 20:   Organizes the Jerusalem Branch at the Garden Tomb (73).

1972, October 5:   Worldwide welfare services program announced (73).

1972, October 6:   Sustained as President of the Church in a solemn assembly (73).

1972, December 14:   International Mission of the Church organized (73).

1973, March 8:   Organizes first stake on Asian mainland at Seoul, Korea (73).

1973, August 24–26:   Presides at the area general conference in Munich, Germany (74).

1973, December 26:   President Harold B. Lee dies in Salt Lake City (74).

1973, December 31:   End-of-year statistics: 3,321,556 members; 630 stakes; 4,580 wards; 108 missions; 17,258 missionaries; 15 temples.

The Ministry of Harold B. Lee

The following account of the life of President Harold B. Lee, written by Elder Gordon B. Hinckley, then a member of the Quorum of the Twelve, was published in the *Ensign* in November 1972 ("President Harold B. Lee: An Appreciation," 2–11). The article helped Church members become better acquainted with President Lee, who had recently become President of the Church.

"The story of Harold B. Lee, President of the Church, can be told in a few skeletal lines: *Born March 28, 1899, in Clifton, Idaho, the son of Samuel Marion and Louisa Emeline Bingham Lee, one of six children. Educated in the local school, the Oneida Academy at nearby Preston, the Albion State Normal School in Albion, Idaho, and later at the University of Utah. Began a teaching career at the age of 17, served as a school principal at 18, and later as principal of two schools in Salt Lake County, Utah. Married Fern Lucinda Tanner November 14, 1923. She passed away September 24, 1962. Married Freda Joan Jensen June 17, 1963.*

"*Managed Foundation Press, Inc., 1928–33. Served as Salt Lake City Commissioner 1933–37, when he became managing director of the Church welfare program. Named a member of the Council of the Twelve April 6, 1941, President of the Council of the Twelve and first counselor in the First Presidency January 23, 1970, and ordained and set apart as President of the Church July 7, 1972.*

"Such are the beads on the thread of his life. But that life is worthy of a more lengthy telling.

"As towns and cities go, Clifton is ever so small, and off the main line. But as the years pass, it will become better known as the birthplace of the eleventh President of the Church.

"President Lee's father, Samuel Marion, had come to Clifton from another country town, Panaca, in southern Nevada.

Samuel's mother (President Lee's grandmother) had died when he was eight days old, and the premature baby was so small that a finger ring could be slipped over his hand and onto his arm. He had to be fed with an eye dropper. His mother's sister lived in Clifton, and at the age of 18, the boy moved north to live with her family.

"There he met dark-haired, dark-eyed Louisa Bingham. They were married in the Logan Temple. The home they established and to which their six children came was 'out on the string, about three miles north of the store.' The store, incidentally, was the one commercial institution of the town. The string was the dirt road—dusty in summer, snow-clogged in winter, and miry muddy in the spring and fall. . . .

"Here, barefoot, overall-clad Harold grew, a boy among country boys. There was swimming in Dudley's Pond, but not on Sunday. The father was in the bishopric, the mother in the [Young Women organization]—and Sunday was sacred. It was in a similar pond, on Bybees' farm, that Harold B. Lee was baptized.

"Money was dreadfully scarce in those days. The farm produced generously but grain and potatoes brought little. The father augmented the family income by contracting for custom grain cutting, drilling wells, and building irrigation canals. But the Lee children did not know they were poor. The home and the Church provided entertainment opportunities. The jewel of the house was the piano. A Scottish lady, who knew how to rap knuckles at the sound of a wrong note, taught him how to play.

"Harold was particularly adept on the piano. It is interesting to note that a love for music, cultivated in those early days, later found expression when he served as chairman of the Church Music Committee. . . .

"A pony cart, usually driven by the mother, took the children the two miles to and from school. It afforded little shelter when the January wind whipped down from the north, and mud was a problem when the bottom thawed out of the road. But that was life in Clifton. As President Lee has commented, 'We had everything money could not buy.' And among these were some tremendous compensations. The air was clean and clear, with

President Harold B. Lee

something almost sweet in the taste of it. The water was like rippling glass, and it was easy to see the glistening stones at the bottom of the creek. The stars at night stood out like people and animals in the sky—and boyish minds conjectured on what they saw. Summer rains were the manna that fell in that wilderness, bringing life to the land. Spring came with vast carpets of green where the plow had touched the soil, followed by the grain drill. Thundering, smoking steam engines fed power over long belts to threshing machines that produced sack after sack of wheat, oats, and barley. . . .

"When the grades of the local school were completed, the boys 'left home' to attend the Oneida Academy, the Church-operated secondary school in Preston a long fifteen miles away. Harold was then 13, and here he first met Ezra Taft Benson [who became the thirteenth President of the Church]. Then followed the Albion State Normal School, on the other side of Idaho. Here, at the age of 17, Harold B. Lee earned his teaching certificate. That was a proud day for him and for his family. The district board of education offered him a job as teacher in the little one-room Silver Star School, between Dayton and Weston, 'down the string' from Clifton. The salary was sixty dollars per month. He commuted the ten miles on horseback on weekends.

". . . Next year, the board named him principal of the Oxford School with four rooms. It was a great opportunity for an 18-year-old boy. He commuted the four miles each way on horseback daily, rain or shine, fair weather or foul. With cultivated musical talent and athletic ability in basketball, he identified himself with community activities in his spare time. It was in these days, when his father was bishop, that Harold had his first glimpse of the Church welfare program, as it later came to be known. Then as now, the bishop was responsible for the care of those in need. Bishop Lee ran his own storehouse, the commodities coming from his own pantry. In the night, the family would see him take a sack of flour, they knew not where, because confidences concerning those in trouble were to be strictly observed, lest there be talk with consequent embarrassment to those who needed help.

"Then as now, it was also the bishop's prerogative and responsibility to recommend young men for missions. Harold was now 21, having been teaching for four years. A call came from President Heber J. Grant to serve in the Western States Mission.

"In the locked files of the Missionary Department of the Church is a report to the First Presidency on Elder Lee. It is dated December 30, 1922, and signed by President John M. Knight. It gives the period of his service—November 11, 1920, to December 18, 1922. Then various questions are answered: 'Qualifications—As a speaker, "Very Good." As a presiding officer, "Good." Has he a good knowledge of the Gospel? "Very good." Has he been energetic? "Very." Is he discreet and does he carry a good influence? "Yes." Remarks: "Elder Lee presided over the Denver Conference with marked distinction from August 8th 1921 to December 18th 1922. An exceptional missionary." '

"There was in that mission at the same time a young lady from Salt Lake City, Fern Lucinda Tanner. She was regarded by her associates as bright, beautiful, and as a scripturalist of unusual ability. When Elder Lee was released, he returned to Clifton only briefly and then came to Salt Lake City to find and court the girl he had admired from a distance in the mission field. They were married in the Salt Lake Temple approximately eleven months after his return.

"To the marriage were born two beautiful daughters, Helen [later Mrs. L. Brent Goates] and Maurine [later Mrs. Ernest J. Wilkins]. The Lee home was a gathering place for the young people of the area. Sister Lee's gentle manner and adroit handling of difficult situations won the admiration of all who knew her. On one occasion she silenced two prominent men who were criticizing one of their associates, saying, 'In your efforts to be just, don't forget to be kind.' . . .

"The qualities that had made [Harold B. Lee] principal of two schools by the time he was 18 were again recognized. Furthering his education at the University of Utah, he was named principal, first of the Whittier School and then the Woodrow Wilson School in Salt Lake County. . . .

"He lived in Pioneer Stake following his marriage, where one Church assignment was followed by another. Then in 1929, he was named a counselor in the stake presidency. The following year he was called as stake president. He was then 31 years of age, the youngest stake president in the Church.

"Depression stalked the nation and the world. Stocks tumbled like tenpins. Credit dried up. Banks closed and millions of dollars of savings were lost. Unemployment rose catastrophically. With the work of years wiped out, men committed suicide. There were soup kitchens and bread lines. There was discouragement and tragedy. In Pioneer Stake more than half of the members were unemployed.

"Here was a challenge, a terrifying challenge, for the young stake president. He worried, he wept, he prayed, as he saw men, once proud and prosperous, reduced through unemployment to a point where they could not feed their families. Then came inspiration to establish a storehouse where food and commodities could be gathered and from which they could be dispersed to the needy. Work projects were undertaken, not only to improve the community, but, more importantly, to afford men an opportunity to work for what they received. An old business building was demolished and the materials were used to construct a stake gymnasium to provide social and recreational facilities for the people.

"Other stakes were engaged in similar projects, and in April 1936 they were coordinated to form what President Heber J. Grant first called the Church security program, now known as the Church welfare program.

"Harold B. Lee, the young leader of Pioneer Stake, was called to pilot the newly launched vessel through the troubled waters of those desperate and trying days. The problems were monumental. It was difficult enough to assemble farm properties to produce food and to create processing and storage facilities. Even worse to cope with was the attitude of people critical of what the Church was doing and who felt that welfare should be kept within the province of government.

"But with prayer and persuasion, with sweat and tears, and with the blessing of him whom he regarded as prophet, he traveled up and down the stakes of Zion, and the program took shape and grew and prospered.

"The vast resources of today's welfare program—productive farms by the score, processing plants and canneries, grain elevators and mills, and other projects scattered over much of America—are the lengthened and impressive shadow of those early efforts. While government relief programs are under constant attack, the Church program continues to win the plaudits of men the world over. Taxpayers have been saved millions of dollars because of the welfare burdens assumed by the Church. Profitable employment has been found for thousands of men and women, including many of the handicapped who have been afforded opportunity to earn what they need. Those who have participated as the recipients of this program have been spared 'the curse of idleness and the evils of the dole.' Their dignity and self-respect have been preserved. And those myriads of men and women who have not been direct recipients, but who have participated in the growing and processing of food and in scores of associated undertakings, bear testimony of the joy to be found in unselfish service to others.

"No one witnessing this program in its vast implications and in its tremendous consequences can reasonably doubt the spirit of revelation that brought it about and that has enlarged its practical power for good. To President Harold B. Lee, its first managing director and longtime chairman of the Church Welfare Committee, must be given credit for inspired direction. In his modesty he would disclaim that, and rightly so, for he would properly give the credit to the Lord. The Lord, in magnifying his servant, has recognized his devotion and his faith. . . .

"Having been tested in the fire of those trying pioneer days of the Church welfare program, Elder Lee was called to the apostleship by President Heber J. Grant and sustained a member of the Council of the Twelve on April 6, 1941.

"On the occasion of that appointment Elder John A. Widtsoe wrote editorially of his new associate: 'He is full of faith in the

Lord; abundant in his love of his fellow men; loyal to the Church and State; self-forgetful in his devotion to the Gospel; endowed with intelligence, energy, and initiative; and gifted with eloquent power to teach the word and will of God. The Lord to whom he goes for help will make him a mighty instrument in carrying forward the eternal plan of human salvation. . . . He will be given strength beyond any yet known to him, as the prayers of the people ascend to the Lord in his behalf.' (*Improvement Era,* May 1941, p. 288.)

"Honest words of recognition these, and words of prophecy.

"His story . . . is one of fidelity to the great sacred trust of an apostle, whose particular calling it is to be a special witness 'of the name of Christ in all the world.' [D&C 107:23.]

"In pursuit of that responsibility, he has traveled under assignment of the First Presidency to many parts of the earth, lifting his voice in eloquence, in proclamation of the divinity of the Redeemer of mankind.

"He frequently has quoted Paul's words to the Corinthians: 'For if the trumpet give an uncertain sound, who shall prepare himself to the battle?' (1 Cor. 14:8.) There has been nothing uncertain about the message of Harold B. Lee. Without equivocation, and with that certainty which comes of a sure conviction, he has borne testimony to the high and the low of the earth. . . . He has never blanched from his responsibility as a servant of God in bearing testimony of the truth. Missionaries have been motivated to more earnest endeavor, members of the Church have grown in resolution to live the gospel, investigators have been pricked in their hearts as he has voiced his testimony. He has not spared himself and has kept up a rigorous schedule even at the peril of his health. Those close to him have known that during a period of many months he was seldom without pain. . . . His acquaintance with illness has sharpened his sensitivity to the sufferings of others. He has been one to travel far and near to encourage and bless the Saints. There are those in many lands who with appreciation bear testimony of the miraculous power of the priesthood exercised in their behalf by this servant of the Lord.

"He has likewise been sensitive to the loneliness, to the fear, to the challenges facing men in military service. During the years of World War II, the Korean War, and the war in [Vietnam], he directed the servicemen's program of the Church. He has constantly expressed himself to his brethren on the need to give those in military service the full program of the Church, with all of the blessings and opportunities that flow therefrom. He has traveled over land and sea to meet with members of the Church in military service. In 1955, he visited Korea when that was still largely an armed camp, dressing in fatigues. . . . Those with whom he met will never forget his kindness, his concern, or his testimony of the overruling power of God in the affairs of men. He comforted them, he reassured them, he saved many from slipping into tragic situations.

"He has comforted the bereaved. From personal experience he knows the sorrow of the loss of loved ones. He was away from Salt Lake City attending a stake conference when his beloved companion hovered between life and death. Traveling through the night, rushing to her bedside, he arrived only to find her slipping away. Those close to him in the dark days that followed her passing sensed in some small measure the depths of sorrow through which he walked. That was in 1962. In 1965 his beloved daughter Maurine was taken in death while Elder Lee was in Hawaii on a Church assignment. She left four children.

"These searing experiences, difficult to bear, served to increase his sensitivity to the burdens of others. Those who have sustained similar losses have found in him an understanding friend and one whose own tested faith has become a source of strength to them.

"In 1963 he married Freda Joan Jensen, who has complemented his life in a remarkable manner. Educated and refined, she is at home in the best of society. She is a woman of unusual accomplishments in her own right. Trained as an educator, she taught school, then rose through various administrative responsibilities to serve as supervisor of primary education in the Jordan School District of Salt Lake County. She also served on the general board of the Primary Association. The home she has managed has been a haven of peace for her husband and a place of delightful hospitality to all who have been privileged to enter it.

"President David O. McKay, recognizing Elder Lee's thorough knowledge of the programs of the Church and his proven administrative skills, appointed him chairman of a correlation committee to coordinate the entire curriculum of the Church. Out of this came an exhaustive review of courses of instruction used over a period of many years, together with an analysis of all teaching organizations and facilities. The vast effort made under his direction has resulted in a correlated curriculum designed to impart knowledge of every phase of Church activity and doctrinc and to build spirituality in the membership. The strength of his leadership has been evident in this undertaking. His hand has been firm, his objectives clearly defined. The entire Church is the beneficiary of his service.

"With the death of President McKay and the succession in the presidency of Joseph Fielding Smith, Elder Lee became President of the Council of the Twelve and was chosen by President Smith to be his first counselor. While this necessitated relieving him of the chairmanships of some of his earlier activities, the same objectives were pursued under his general leadership. Programs were instituted to improve the proficiency of teachers throughout the Church. A bishop's training program was put into operation. The worldwide missionary program was strengthened. . . .

"When President Joseph Fielding Smith passed quietly from life unto death on the evening of July 2, 1972, there was no doubt in the minds of the members of the Council of the Twelve who should succeed him as President of the Church. On Friday morning, July 7, they met together in the sacred precincts of the Salt Lake Temple. In that quiet and holy place, with subdued hearts, they sought the whisperings of the Spirit. All hearts were as one in response to those whisperings. Harold Bingham Lee, chosen of the Lord, schooled from childhood in the principles of the restored gospel, refined and polished through thirty-one years of service in the apostleship, was named President of The Church of Jesus Christ of Latter-day Saints and Prophet, Seer, and Revelator. The hands of all present werc laid upon his head, and he was ordained as the anointed of the Lord to this high and incomparable calling.

"Sustained by the faith and prayers of the Saints throughout the world, he stands as the presiding high priest in the kingdom of God on earth."

President Harold B. Lee served as the Lord's prophet for 17 months and 19 days. During this period of change and expansion, President Lee oversaw the creation of the first stakes in Chile and on the Asian mainland in Korea. He presided over the first area conferences held in Mexico City, Mexico, and Munich, Germany. He extended the welfare services program of the Church worldwide. He died on 26 December 1973, at age 74.

Jesus Christ calling Peter and Andrew.
The Atonement of the Savior was necessary to make possible
the Father's plan of salvation. By following the Savior, each person can
safely complete his "journey through mortality to his ultimate destiny—
a return to that God who gave him life."

CHAPTER 1

The Way to Eternal Life

How can we achieve our ultimate goal—
a return to that God who gave us life?

Introduction

Throughout his ministry, President Harold B. Lee emphasized that the overarching purpose of the gospel of Jesus Christ is to enable us to return to the presence of our Heavenly Father. He often taught the importance of walking by faith until we reach our heavenly goal.

President Lee's ministry coincided with the courageous flights of the dawning space age in the 1960s and early 1970s. When an accident in 1970 forced the astronauts on the Apollo 13 spacecraft to return prematurely to earth from the regions of the moon, President Lee was impressed with the careful attention to instruction and the exacting performance required to bring the men safely home. He saw in this experience a likeness to the faith and obedience necessary to complete our journey through mortality to our heavenly home. In an October 1970 general conference address, he used the story of the Apollo 13 spacecraft, the Aquarius, to illustrate the importance of keeping to the path the Lord has planned for us to follow.

President Lee's messages continually emphasized that the ultimate goal of this mortal journey is to return to our Father in Heaven. These messages can help us strive to see that "every act of our lives, every decision we make [is] patterned toward the development of a life that shall permit us to enter into the presence of the Lord our Heavenly Father."[1]

In this chapter, President Lee outlines the path by which we can return in peace and safety to our Heavenly Father's presence.

Teachings of Harold B. Lee

How can we be guided to safety in these troubled times?

Some months ago, millions of watchers and listeners over the world waited breathlessly and anxiously the precarious flight of Apollo 13. The whole world, it seemed, prayed for one significant result: the safe return to earth of three brave men.

When one of them with restrained anxiety announced the startling information, "We have had an explosion!" the mission control in Houston immediately mobilized all the technically trained scientists who had, over the years, planned every conceivable detail pertaining to that flight.

The safety of those three now depended on two vital qualifications: on the reliability of the skills and the knowledge of those technicians in the mission control center at Houston, and upon the implicit obedience of the men in the Aquarius to every instruction from the technicians, who, because of their understanding of the problems of the astronauts, were better qualified to find the essential solutions. The decisions of the technicians had to be perfect or the Aquarius could have missed the earth by thousands of miles.

This dramatic event is somewhat analogous to these [troubled] times in which we live. . . . Many are frightened when they see and hear of unbelievable happenings the world over—political intrigues, wars and contention everywhere, frustrations of parents endeavoring to cope with social problems that threaten to break down the sanctity of the home, the frustrations of children and youth as they face challenges to their faith and their morals.

Only if *you* are willing to listen and obey, as did the astronauts on the Aquarius, can you and all your households be guided to ultimate safety and security in the Lord's own way. . . .

From the incident of the Apollo 13 . . . , I will now, in a few moments, undertake to outline briefly the wondrously conceived plan upon obedience to which the salvation of every soul depends in his journey through mortality to his ultimate destiny—a return to that God who gave him life. . . .

What are the purposes of our Heavenly Father's plan?

This plan is identified by name, and the overarching purpose is clearly set forth in an announcement to the Church in the beginning of this gospel dispensation.

More than a century ago the Lord declared:

"And even so I have sent mine everlasting covenant into the world, to be a light to the world, and to be a standard for my people, and for the Gentiles to seek to it, and to be a messenger before my face to prepare the way before me." (D&C 45:9.)

This plan, then, was to be as a covenant, which implied a contract to be participated in by more than one person. It was to be a standard for the Lord's elect and for all the world to benefit by it. Its purpose was to serve the needs of all men and to prepare the world for the second coming of the Lord.

The participants in the formulation of this plan in the premortal world were all the spirit children of our Heavenly Father. Our oldest scriptures, from the writings of the ancient prophets Abraham and Jeremiah, affirm also that God, or Eloheim, was there; his Firstborn Son, Jehovah; Abraham; Jeremiah; and many others of great stature were there.

All the organized intelligences before the earth was formed, who had become spirits, were there, including many great and noble ones whose performance and conduct in that premortal sphere qualified them to become rulers and leaders in carrying out this eternal plan. . . .

Under the Father's instruction and by Jehovah's direction, the earth and all pertaining thereto was organized and formed. They "ordered," they "watched over" and "prepared" the earth. They took "counsel among themselves" as to the bringing of all manner of life to the earth and all things, including man, and prepared it for the carrying out of the plan, which we could well liken to a blueprint, by which the children of God could be tutored and trained in all that was necessary for the divine purpose of bringing to pass, "to the glory of God," the opportunity of every soul to gain "immortality and eternal life." Eternal life means to have everlasting life in that celestial sphere where God

3

and Christ dwell, by doing all things we are commanded. (See Abr. 3:25.)

What are the foundation principles of the plan of salvation?

The plan embodied three distinctive principles:

First, the privilege to be given to every soul to choose for himself "liberty and eternal life" through obedience to the laws of God, or "captivity and death" as to spiritual things because of disobedience. (See 2 Ne. 2:27.)

Next to life itself, free agency is God's greatest gift to mankind, providing thereby the greatest opportunity for the children of God to advance in this second estate of mortality. A prophet-leader on this continent explained this to his son as recorded in an ancient scripture: that to bring about these, the Lord's eternal purposes, there must be opposites, an enticement by the good on the one hand and by the evil on the other, or to say it in the language of the scriptures, ". . . the forbidden fruit in opposition to the tree of life; the one being sweet and the other bitter." This father further explained, "Wherefore, the Lord God gave unto man that he should act for himself. Wherefore, man could not act for himself save it should be that he was enticed by the one or the other." (2 Ne. 2:15–16.)

The second distinctive principle in this divine plan involved the necessity of providing a savior by whose atonement the most favored Son of God became our Savior, as a "Lamb slain from the foundation of the world" (Rev. 13:8), as revealed to John on the Isle of Patmos. [The prophet Lehi] explained that the mission of the Son of God was to "make intercession for all the children of men; and they that believe in him shall be saved." (2 Ne. 2:9.)

We hear much from some of limited understanding about the possibility of one's being saved by grace alone. But it requires the explanation of another prophet to understand the true doctrine of grace as he explained in these meaningful words:

4

"For," said this prophet, "we labor diligently to write, to per-suade our children, and also our brethren, to believe in Christ, and to be reconciled to God; for we know that it is by grace that we are saved, after all we can do." (2 Ne. 25:23.) Truly we are re-deemed by the atoning blood of the Savior of the world, but only after each has done all he can to work out his own salvation.

The third great distinctive principle in the plan of salvation was the provision that "all mankind may be saved, by obedience to the laws and ordinances of the Gospel." (Article of Faith 3.) These fundamental laws and ordinances by which salvation comes are clearly set forth:

First, faith in the Lord Jesus Christ.

Second, repentance from sin, meaning the turning away from the sins of disobedience to God's laws and never returning again thereto. The Lord spoke plainly on this point. Said he: ". . . go your ways and sin no more; but unto that soul who sinneth [meaning, of course, returning again to the sins from which he has repented] shall the former sins return, saith the Lord your God." (D&C 82:7.)

Third, baptism by water and of the Spirit, by which ordinances only, as the Master taught Nicodemus, could one see or enter into the kingdom of God. (See John 3:4–5.)

This same teaching was forcibly impressed by the resurrected Savior to the saints on this continent, in what it appears likely was his final message to his disciples. The Master taught his faith-ful saints that "no unclean thing can enter into his kingdom; therefore nothing entereth into his rest save it be those who have washed their garments in my blood, because of their faith, and the repentance of all their sins, and their faithfulness unto the end.

"Now this is the commandment: Repent, all ye ends of the earth, and come unto me and be baptized in my name, that ye may be sanctified by the reception of the Holy Ghost, that ye may stand spotless before me at the last day.

"Verily, verily, I say unto you, this is my gospel. . . ." (3 Ne. 27:19–21.)

What are the blessings promised to those who are faithful?

If the children of the Lord, which includes all who are upon this earth, regardless of nationality, color, or creed, will heed the call of the true messenger of the gospel of Jesus Christ, as did the three astronauts on the Aquarius to the trained technicians at Mission Control in the hour of their peril, each may in time see the Lord and know that he is, as the Lord has promised. . . .

This promise of the glory which awaits those who are faithful to the end was plainly portrayed in the Master's parable of the Prodigal Son. To the son who was faithful and did not squander his birthright, the father, who in the Master's lesson would be our Father and our God, promised this faithful son: "Son, thou art ever with me, and all that I have is thine." (Luke 15:31.)

In a revelation through a modern prophet, the Lord promises to the faithful and obedient today: ". . . all that my Father hath shall be given unto him." (D&C 84:38.)

Or will we be like those foolhardy ones on the river above the Niagara Falls who were approaching the dangerous rapids? Despite warnings of the river guards to go toward safety before it was too late, and in complete disregard of the warnings, they laughed, they danced, they drank, they mocked, and they perished.

So would have been the fate of the three astronauts on the Aquarius if they had refused to give heed to the minutest instruction from Houston Control. Their very lives depended upon obedience to the basic laws which govern and control the forces of the universe.

Jesus wept as he witnessed the world about him in his day which had seemingly gone mad, and continually mocked his pleading that they come unto him along "the strait and narrow way," so plainly marked out in God's eternal plan of salvation.

O that we could hear again his pleadings today as he then cried out: "O Jerusalem, Jerusalem, thou that killest the prophets, and stonest them which are sent unto thee, how often would I have gathered thy children together, even as a hen gathereth her chickens under her wings, and ye would not!" (Matt. 23:37.)

O that the world would see in another parable to John the Revelator the sacred figure of the Master calling to us today as he did to those of Jerusalem:

Said the Master, "Behold, I stand at the door, and knock: if any man hear my voice, and open the door, I will come in to him, and will sup with him, and he with me.

"To him that overcometh will I grant to sit with me in my throne, even as I also overcame, and am set down with my Father in his throne." (Rev. 3:20–21.)

Here, then, is the plan of salvation as taught by the true church, which is founded upon apostles and prophets, with Christ, the Lord, as the chief cornerstone (Eph. 2:20), by which only can peace come, not as the world giveth, but as only the Lord can give to those who overcome the things of the world, as did the Master.

"Neither is there salvation in any other: for there is none other name under heaven given among men, whereby we must be saved." (Acts 4:12.) . . .

How can our actions each day move us forward toward eternal life?

In a recent meeting I listened to a young girl's heartwarming testimony. Her father was afflicted with what the doctors had pronounced was an incurable malady. To his wife one morning, this stricken father, after a night of pain and suffering, had said with great feeling, "I am so thankful today." "For what?" she asked. He replied, "For God's giving me the privilege of one more day with you."

Today I could desire with all my heart that all within the sound of this broadcast would likewise thank God for one more day! For what? For the opportunity to take care of some unfinished business. To repent; to right some wrongs; to influence for good some wayward child; to reach out to someone who cries for help—in short, to thank God for one more day to prepare to meet God.

Don't try to live too many days ahead. Seek for strength to attend to the problems of today. In his Sermon on the Mount, the Master admonished: "Take therefore no thought for the morrow: for the morrow shall take thought for the things of itself. Sufficient unto the day is the evil thereof." (Matt. 6:34.)

Do all that you can do and leave the rest to God, the Father of us all. It is not enough to say I will do my best, but rather, I will do everything which is within my power; I will do all that is necessary.[2]

Suggestions for Study and Discussion

- In what ways does our Father's plan of salvation show His great love for us?

- How does an understanding of the plan of salvation bring peace into your life?

- Why is agency necessary if we are to return to God? Why is the Atonement necessary? Why must we be obedient to gospel principles and ordinances?

- What might be some of the consequences of deviating from the path Heavenly Father has laid out for us to follow?

- What things sometimes cause people to lose sight of the goal to return to Heavenly Father's presence? What counsel could we give to family members and others who have lost their way?

- Why is it important to serve each day? to express gratitude each day? to repent and strive to overcome our weaknesses? How can doing each of these things help us prepare to meet God?

Notes

1. In Conference Report, Oct. 1946, 145.
2. In Conference Report, Oct. 1970, 113–17; or *Improvement Era,* Dec. 1970, 28–30.

Who Am I?

*How does knowing who we are help us
to receive eternal life?*

Introduction

"One day a young Sunday School teacher [came] to ask a rather interesting question that had been asked of her in her class the preceding Sunday," said President Harold B. Lee to a congregation of Saints. "She explained that they were talking about the life before this, and this life, and the next life, and a young Sunday School student had asked, 'The life before this came to an end when we were born into mortal life; this life comes to an end when we suffer mortal death; what shall be the end of the next life? Shall it be oblivion?' The young Sunday School teacher said, 'I don't have the answer.'

"As I thought about it I remarked that we do use words rather loosely when we speak of the 'life before this, and this life, and the next life,' as though we were a cat of nine lives, when as a matter of fact, we only have one life. This life we speak of did not begin with mortal birth. This life does not end with mortal death. There is something that is not created or made. The Scriptures called it 'intelligence,' which at a certain stage in the pre-existence was organized into a 'spirit.' After that spirit had grown to a certain stature it then was given the opportunity by an all-wise Father to come into another stage for its development. It was added upon, and after having lived its span and having attained to its purpose in mortality, another change took place. We go, not into another life in fact, but into another stage of the same life. There is something which was not created or made, and something which does not die, and that something shall live on forever."[1]

This chapter discusses our eternal identity and how our knowledge of this identity affects our lives.

Teachings of Harold B. Lee

How does knowing that we are spirit sons and daughters of Heavenly Father bless us?

Who are we? . . . The Apostle Paul wrote: "Furthermore we have had fathers of our flesh which corrected us, and we gave them reverence: shall we not much rather be in subjection unto the Father of spirits, and live?" [Hebrews 12:9] suggesting that all who live upon the earth who have fathers of the flesh likewise had a father of their spirits. . . . To Moses and Aaron . . . the Lord had said, "Separate yourselves from among this congregation, that I may consume them in a moment." His anger was stirred against these unrighteous people, but Moses and Aaron fell upon their faces and said, "O God, the God of the spirits of all flesh, shall one man sin, and wilt thou be wroth with all the congregation?" [Numbers 16:21–22.] Did you notice how they addressed him? The God of the spirits of all flesh. . . .

One of the oldest scriptures we have has come down to us in a miraculous way—we call it the Pearl of Great Price. One of the great books of that precious scripture is known as the book of Abraham. In that book . . . we find this:

"Now the Lord had shown unto me, Abraham, the intelligences that were organized before the world was; and among all these there were many of the noble and great ones;

"And God saw these souls that they were good, and he stood in the midst of them, and he said: These I will make my rulers; for he stood among those that were spirits, and he saw that they were good; and he said unto me: Abraham, thou art one of them; thou wast chosen before thou wast born.

"And there stood one among them that was like unto God, and he said unto those who were with him: We will go down, for there is space there, and we will take of these materials, and we will make an earth whereon these may dwell;

"And we will prove them herewith, to see if they will do all things whatsoever the Lord their God shall command them;

"And they who keep their first estate shall be added upon; and they who keep not their first estate shall not have glory in the same kingdom with those who keep their first estate; and they who keep their second estate shall have glory added upon their heads for ever and ever." [Abraham 3:22–26.]

Now there are several precious truths found in that scripture. In the first place, we have just a hint, just a flash of what a spirit is. A spirit, did you hear Abraham saying, was an organized intelligence. This is the first beginning we have in our understanding of what a spirit is. It is an organized intelligence that lived as a spirit before this world was. Now what does a spirit look like? What kind of a conception do you have of that spirit? Well, the Lord has given through the Prophet Joseph Smith, an inspired answer, a part of which reads as follows: "That which is spiritual being in the likeness of that which is temporal; and that which is temporal in the likeness of that which is spiritual." Now listen, "the spirit of man in the likeness of his person, as also the spirit of the beast, and every other creature which God has created." [D&C 77:2.]

All right, now, you see me here as a mature physical man. There is a part of me that you can't see with your physical eyes— that spiritual part of me that looks out through my eyes and gives me power of movement, and gives me a measure of intellect and intelligence. . . .

Now that is the first truth that we learn—that there was an organized intelligence that was called . . . a spirit. Here the Lord [Jehovah], who was that great illustrious spirit like unto God [the Father], came among those organized intelligences called spirits, and He said to them, We will make an earth whereon you as spirits may dwell, and you who live worthy here in the spirit world can go down upon that earth and be added upon. And so those spirits who kept their faith, shall I say, or were worthy, were permitted to come on the earth and have added to their spiritual body, a physical body here on this earth. . . . The fact that you and I are here on this earth with a physical body is an evidence that we were among those who kept our first estate; we passed the test and were permitted to come here. If we hadn't passed the test we wouldn't be here; we would be down with Satan trying to tempt the ones who had a body. . . .

Why must we be faithful in order to complete our foreordained missions on earth?

Having established our premortal identity, who we are—sons and daughters of a God before this world was, who is the Father of the spirits of all men who live in the flesh upon the earth—then we are prepared to proceed to the next answer to the query. From what I read you from the book of Abraham in the 23rd verse you heard Abraham being told that he was ordained or chosen before he was born. I wonder if you have thought of that. Moses was told the same thing. . . .

"And calling upon the name of God, [Moses] beheld his glory again, for it was upon him; and he heard a voice, saying: Blessed art thou, Moses, for I, the Almighty, have chosen thee, and thou shalt be made stronger than many waters; for they shall obey thy command as if thou wert God." [Moses 1:25.] That was to be his mission to be a great and powerful ruler. To Jeremiah, likewise, the Lord said, "Before I formed thee in the belly I knew thee; and before thou camest forth out of the womb I sanctified thee, and I ordained thee a prophet unto the nations." [Jeremiah 1:5.] Joseph Smith, making that plainer, said this to us: "Every man who has a calling to minister to the inhabitants of the world was ordained to that very purpose in the Grand Council of heaven before this world was." Then he said, "I suppose that I was ordained to this very office in that Grand Council." [*History of the Church,* 6:364.]

Here comes an ominous warning. Despite that calling, the Lord put it into the mind of the Prophet Joseph Smith and he has written it . . . , "Behold, there are many called, but few are chosen." In other words, . . . because we have our agency here, there were many who were foreordained to a greater work than they prepare themselves to do here. Now he said, "And why are they not chosen?" Then he gives two reasons why men fail of their appointments. First, "because their hearts are set so much upon the things of this world," and second, they "aspire to the honors of men, that they do not learn this one lesson—that the rights of the priesthood are inseparably connected with the powers of heaven." [D&C 121:34–36.][2]

Do not misunderstand that such a calling and such foreordination pre-determine what you must do. A prophet on this western continent has spoken plainly on this subject: "Being called and prepared from the foundation of the world according to the foreknowledge of God, on account of their exceeding faith and good works; in the first place being left to choose good or evil." (Alma 13:3.) . . . God may have called and chosen men in the spirit world or in their first estate to do a certain work, but whether they will accept that calling here and magnify it by faithful service and good works while in mortality is a matter in which it is their right and privilege to exercise their free agency to choose good or evil.[3]

How does knowing who we are influence our use of agency?

What else are we told we are? We are an independent free agent and some people think to do as we please, but that isn't quite correct. We do have our free agency, but now let me read you something about that. Will you mark down 2 Nephi 2nd chapter, verses 15–16. I tell you I think this was a great risk that our Father was taking to send us down here with the privilege of our agency to make a choice. Now in order to make our choice and thus gain our eternal rewards, there was something that had to happen to us. Now notice—here is a father explaining this very matter to his son: "And to bring about his eternal purposes in the end of man, after he had created our first parents, and the beasts of the field and the fowls of the air, and in fine, all things which are created, it must needs be that there was an opposition; even the forbidden fruit in opposition to the tree of life; the one being sweet and the other bitter." [2 Nephi 2:15.]

Now that is the way it ofttimes sounds, that the things that are forbidden are the things which are the most desirable, and the

Jesus Christ with children from around the world.
We are all spirit sons and daughters of Heavenly Father. If we accept the full blessings
of the Savior's Atonement, we can return to live with our Father and our Savior again.

things that are right for us are sometimes pretty bitter pills for us
to swallow, as we say. Now, in order to give man the chance to
choose, "Wherefore, the Lord God gave unto man that he should
act for himself. Wherefore, man could not act for himself save it
should be that he was enticed by the one or the other." [2 Nephi
2:16.] Now to be an independent thinking individual, we had to
have not only just the good but we had to have the evil in order

14

that we could choose between the two. Now you think about that for a moment. If everything were good in the world and there were none evil, would you be able to choose anything but good? If everything were evil in the world, if there wasn't any good to choose, could you choose anything else but evil? When you think about it for a moment, the only way there could be free agency in the individuals who live upon this earth is to have both the good and the bad and each one of us given the opportunity to choose for ourselves. . . . You see, free agency takes its chances. The Lord was willing to risk that in order that we might walk by faith and, as free, independent agents, choose the right.[4]

What is our eternal potential as children of God?

The purpose of life was to bring to pass immortality and eternal life. Now, immortality means to eventually gain a body that will no longer be subject to the pains of mortality, no longer subject to another mortal death, and no longer disillusioned, all these former things having passed away. To gain eternal life is the right to live in the presence of the Eternal One, even God, our Heavenly Father, and His Son, Jesus Christ. These are the two objectives for which all of us are placed upon the earth.[5]

We are here today preparing for immortality, "an interminable extent of time which is the true life of man." We are all great souls, because we came through a noble heritage. We have the right to become kings and rulers because of the roles we played in the spirit world before we came here. We were chosen to come forth in this day and time, and we are destined for immortality as are all the youth of this church. We too should "find all that is not eternal too short and all that is not infinite too small" for us to stoop to.[6]

Now let me read from the 132nd section of the Doctrine and Covenants. . . . "And again, verily I say unto you, if a man marry a wife by my word, which is my law, and by the new and everlasting covenant, and it is sealed unto them by the Holy Spirit of promise," and I shall skip a few words in order to give you the meaning, "it shall be done unto them in all things whatsoever my servant hath put upon them, in time, and through all eternity; and shall be of full force when they are out of the world; and they shall pass by the angels, and the gods, which are set there, to their exaltation and glory." Now listen to this: and shall have "a continuation of the seeds forever and ever." [D&C 132:19.]

The Prophet Joseph Smith said this meant that those who were married in the new and everlasting covenant and were true to their covenants, that after they passed through the resurrection they would be able to live together again as husband and wife and have what he calls here, a continuation of the seeds. Now what does that mean? Let me read you from another scripture: . . .

"In the celestial glory there are three heavens or degrees;

"And in order to obtain the highest, a man must enter into this order of the priesthood [meaning the new and everlasting covenant of marriage];

"And if he does not, he cannot obtain it.

"He may enter into the other, but that is the end of his kingdom"; now notice, "he cannot have an increase." [D&C 131:1–4.]

Increase of what? Increase of posterity. In other words, through obedience to His divine command, we here as human beings are given power to cooperate with God in the creation of a human soul here, and then beyond the grave to have eternal increase in a family relationship after this earth has concluded its work.

. . . Now speaking of those resurrected beings who had kept the covenant of holy marriage and had been sealed by the Holy Spirit of Promise: "Then shall they be gods, because they have no end; therefore shall they be from everlasting to everlasting, because they continue; then shall they be above all, because all things are subject unto them. Then shall they be gods, because they have all power, and the angels are subject unto them." [D&C 132:20.] . . .

. . . May we so live that all who are with us may see not us but that which is divine that came from God, and in that vision of what we are and may become, may we receive the strength to climb higher and upward, onward to that great goal of eternal life, I humbly pray in the name of the Lord Jesus Christ, amen.[7]

Suggestions for Study and Discussion

- What has strengthened your testimony that God is your Father?

- Why do people sometimes fail to fulfill the work they were foreordained to do here on earth?

- What is agency? Why is opposition necessary in the exercise of our agency?

- How does the knowledge of our eternal potential influence our daily behavior?

- What has given you strength as you have sought to "climb higher and upward, onward to that great goal of eternal life"?

Notes

1. Address at the funeral of Edwin Marcellus Clark, 5 Apr. 1955, Harold Bingham Lee Addresses (1939–73), Historical Department Archives, The Church of Jesus Christ of Latter-day Saints, 11.

2. "Who Am I?" address to Grant Stake Senior Aaronic School, 18 Feb. 1957, Historical Department Archives, The Church of Jesus Christ of Latter-day Saints, 4–7.

3. *Decisions for Successful Living* (1973), 168–69.

4. "Who Am I?" 9–10.

5. *The Teachings of Harold B. Lee,* ed. Clyde J. Williams (1996), 30.

6. *The Teachings of Harold B. Lee,* 73.

7. "Who Am I?" 11–12, 14.

The Lamb Slain from the Foundation of the World

*How does the Atonement of Jesus Christ
overcome the Fall of Adam and enable us to return
to the presence of the Father?*

Introduction

President Harold B. Lee taught that we must understand the Fall of man in order to understand the Savior's Atonement, which overcame the effects of the Fall and made possible eternal life. He said, "How vital . . . it is to understand the Fall, making necessary the Atonement—hence the mission of the Lord Jesus Christ."[1]

President Lee often testified of the divine mission of the Savior, without whom we could not be delivered from death and sin. He declared: "The Son of God . . . had the power to make worlds, to direct them. He came here as the Only Begotten Son to fulfill a mission, to be as a Lamb slain before the foundation of the world, to bring about salvation to all mankind. By giving His life He opened the door to resurrection and taught the way by which we could gain eternal life, which means to go back into the presence of the Father and the Son. That was who Jesus was in all His grandeur."[2]

This chapter discusses the Fall of Adam and Eve, the Savior's Atonement that overcame the effects of the Fall, and our responsibilities if we are to receive the full blessings of the Atonement.

This painting of the Savior was a favorite of
President Harold B. Lee's and hung in his office.

Teachings of Harold B. Lee

How did the Fall of Adam and Eve make the blessings of mortality possible?

Adam and Eve . . . exercised their agency and of their own volition had partaken of the fruit, of which they were commanded not to eat; thus they had become subject to the law of Satan. In that disobedience, God was now free to visit upon them a judgment. They were to learn that besides God being a merciful Father, he is also a just Father, and when they broke the law they were subject to the receiving of a penalty and so they were cast out of that beautiful garden. They were visited by all the vicissitudes to which mortals from that time since have been heir. They were to learn that by their disobedience they received the penalty of a just judgment. They were forced to earn their bread by the sweat of their brow, for now they had become mortals.

. . . Pain, misery, death, all now came in their wake, but with that pain, quite like our own experiences from that time to this, there came knowledge and understanding that could never have been gained except by pain. . . .

. . . Besides the Fall having had to do with Adam and Eve, causing a change to come over them, that change affected all human nature, all of the natural creations, all of the creation of animals, plants—all kinds of life were changed. The earth itself became subject to death. . . . How it took place no one can explain, and anyone who would attempt to make an explanation would be going far beyond anything the Lord has told us. But a change was wrought over the whole face of the creation, which up to that time had not been subject to death. From that time henceforth all in nature was in a state of gradual dissolution until mortal death was to come, after which there would be required a restoration in a resurrected state. . . .

. . . One of the greatest sermons, I suppose the shortest sermon ever preached by a person, was preached by Mother Eve. . . .

"Were it not for our transgression we never should have had seed, and never should have known good and evil, and the joy of our redemption, and the eternal life which God giveth unto all the obedient." [Moses 5:11.]

So should we, with Eve, rejoice in the Fall, which permitted the coming of the knowledge of good and evil, which permitted the coming of children into mortality, which permitted the receiving of joy of redemption and the eternal life which God gives to all.

And so Adam likewise, blessed with the gift of the Holy Ghost, "blessed God and was filled, and began to prophesy concerning all the families of the earth, saying: Blessed be the name of God, for because of my transgression my eyes are opened, and in this life I shall have joy, and again in the flesh I shall see God." [Moses 5:10.] . . .

May the Lord give us His understanding of the great boon that has thus come to us, and let us honor in our minds and in our teachings the great legacy which Adam and Eve gave to us, when through their experience by the exercise of their own agency, they partook of fruit which gave them the seeds of mortal life and gave to us, their descendants down through the generations of time, that great boon by which we too can receive the joy of our redemption, and in our flesh see God and have eternal life.[3]

How does the Savior's Atonement overcome the effects of the Fall?

The Lord God cast Adam out of the Garden of Eden because of his disobedience. He suffered spiritual death. . . . But behold I say unto you that the Lord God gave unto Adam the promise that he should not die the temporal death until He should send forth angels to declare repentance in the name of His Only Begotten Son that by his death, he might be raised to eternal life [see D&C 29:41–43]. . . . When Adam was driven out of the Garden of Eden, he suffered spiritual death, which is a separation of the close communion with the presence of the Lord.[4]

Why was the Savior sent into the world? The Master himself answered that question during his ministry when he said: "For God sent not his Son into the world to condemn the world; but that the world through him might be saved." [John 3:17.] . . .

Saved from what? Redeemed from what? Well, first, saved from mortal death through the resurrection of the dead. But in another sense we are saved likewise by his atoning sacrifice. We are saved from sin.[5]

To the Latter-day Saint, salvation means liberation from bondage and the results of sin by divine agency, deliverance from sin and eternal damnation through the Atonement of Christ.

I think there is no place where we have a finer discussion of the plan of the Atonement than in the writings of Jacob, as found in the Book of Mormon, 2 Nephi, the 9th chapter. I therefore call it to your attention and urge you to read carefully again and again that precious explanation: . . .

"O the greatness of the mercy of our God, the Holy One of Israel! For he delivereth his saints from that awful monster the devil, and death, and hell, and that lake of fire and brimstone, which is endless torment.

"O how great the holiness of our God! For he knoweth all things, and there is not anything save he knows it.

"And he cometh into the world that he may save all men if they will hearken unto his voice; for behold, he suffereth the pains of all men, yea, the pains of every living creature, both men, women, and children, who belong to the family of Adam.

"And he suffereth this that the resurrection might pass upon all men, that all might stand before him at the great and judgment day.

"And he commandeth all men that they must repent, and be baptized in his name, having perfect faith in the Holy One of Israel, or they cannot be saved in the kingdom of God.

"And if they will not repent and believe in his name, and be baptized in his name, and endure to the end, they must be damned; for the Lord God, the Holy One of Israel, has spoken it." [2 Nephi 9:19–24.] . . .

Herein is defined . . . individual salvation, which comes to each, dependent upon his own conduct and his own life. But we [also] have what we call "general" [salvation], that which comes upon all mankind, whether they are good or bad, rich or poor, when they have lived—it makes no difference. All have the blessings of the Atonement and the blessings of the resurrection given to them as a free gift because of the Savior's atoning sacrifice. . . .

These basic teachings, therefore, plainly set forth that by the atoning power all mankind may be saved, for as in Adam all die, even so in Christ shall all be made alive without exception. Even the sons of perdition who commit the unpardonable sin shall be resurrected along with all others of Adam's posterity. . . . We have that declaration in the Articles of Faith: "We believe that through the Atonement of Christ, all mankind may be saved, by obedience to the laws and ordinances of the Gospel." [Articles of Faith 1:3.][6]

How does having faith in Jesus Christ and being obedient allow us to receive the full blessings of the Atonement?

The essentiality of [the] knowledge of the Savior and his divine mission was impressed by the Master on one occasion when he said to the Pharisees who had gathered around him, as they usually did to try to embarrass or to entrap him, "What think ye of Christ?" [Matthew 22:42.] . . .

During his ministry there had been [those] not possessed of faith who had declared themselves about the Master. In his home country of Nazareth they had said in derision:

"Is not this the carpenter's son? is not his mother called Mary? and his brethren, James, and Joses, and Simon, and Judas? . . . And they were offended in him." [Matthew 13:55, 57.] . . .

In contrast, . . . his faithful followers such as Peter, the chiefest of the apostles declared: "Thou art the Christ, the Son of the living God" (Matt. 16:16)—and from his faithful Martha, "Yea, Lord: I believe that thou art the Christ, the Son of God, which should come into the world." (John 11:27.) And from another of his disciples after he had seen and handled the Risen Lord, Thomas impressed his testimony with these simple words: "My Lord and my God"! [John 20:28.] . . .

I am thinking now of two contrasting incidents. A dear friend received one of those fateful messages: "We regret to inform you that your boy has been killed in action." I went to his home, and there I saw the shattered family, possessed of all the things that money could buy—wealth, position, the things that the world would call honorable, but there they were with their hopes and dreams shattered around them, grasping for something that they had not lived to obtain and from that time on, seemingly did not obtain. The comfort which they could have known was not there.

I contrasted that with a scene I witnessed up in the LDS Hospital just about six months ago now, when one of our dear faithful mission presidents was there slowly dying. He was in extreme pain, but in his heart there was a joy because he knew that through suffering ofttimes men learn obedience, and the right to kinship with him who suffered beyond all that any of us can ever suffer. He, too, knew the power of the risen Lord.

Today we should ask ourselves the question, in answer to what the Master asked of those in his day, "What think ye of Christ?" We ought to ask as we would say it today, "What think we of Christ?" and then make it a little more personal and ask, "What think I of Christ?" Do I think of him as the Redeemer of my soul? Do I think of him with no doubt in my mind as the one who appeared to the Prophet Joseph Smith? Do I believe that he established this Church upon the earth? Do I accept him as the Savior of this world? Am I true to my covenants, which in the waters of baptism, if I understood, meant that I would stand as a witness of him at all times, and in all things, and in all places, wherever I would be, even until death?[7]

The Lord will bless us to the degree to which we keep His commandments. Nephi . . . said:

"For we labor diligently to write, to persuade our children, and also our brethren, to believe in Christ, and to be reconciled to God; for we know that it is by grace that we are saved, after all we can do." (2 Nephi 25:23.)

The Savior's blood, His atonement, will save us, but only after we have done all we can to save ourselves by keeping His commandments. All of the principles of the gospel are principles of promise by which the plans of the Almighty are unfolded to us.[8]

Each must do all he can to save himself from sin; then he may lay claim to the blessings of redemption by the Holy One of

Israel, that all mankind may be saved by obedience to the law and ordinances of the gospel.

Jesus also atoned not only for Adam's transgressions but for the sins of all mankind. But redemption from individual sins depends upon individual effort, with each being judged according to his or her works.

The scriptures make it clear that while a resurrection will come to all, only those who obey the Christ will receive the expanded blessing of eternal salvation. Speaking of Jesus, Paul explained to the Hebrews that "he became the author of eternal salvation unto all them that obey him." (Heb. 5:9.) . . .

My humble prayer is that all men everywhere may understand more fully the significance of the atonement of the Savior of all mankind, who has given us the plan of salvation which will lead us into eternal life, where God and Christ dwell.[9]

Suggestions for Study and Discussion

- How would you answer the question "What think ye of Christ?"
- Why is the Savior referred to as the "Lamb slain from the foundation of the world"? (Revelation 13:8).
- In what ways was the Fall both a blessing and a trial for Adam and Eve? How is it also a source of both joy and sorrow for us?
- What kinds of knowledge and understanding can be gained only by enduring the trials and struggles of mortality?
- What is spiritual death? How is spiritual death overcome?
- What blessings of the Atonement come to all mankind as a free gift? What must we do individually to enjoy all the blessings of the Atonement?
- What do President Lee's two stories about people who faced death teach about the importance of faith in Jesus Christ?
- What experiences in your life have strengthened your testimony of the Savior's Atonement?
- How does the Atonement "lead us into eternal life, where God and Christ dwell"?

Notes

1. "Fall of Man," address to Brigham Young University seminary and institute personnel, 23 June 1954, Historical Department Archives, The Church of Jesus Christ of Latter-day Saints, 6.

2. Youth devotional address given at Long Beach, California, 29 Apr. 1973, Historical Department Archives, The Church of Jesus Christ of Latter-day Saints, 24.

3. "Fall of Man," 15, 17, 19–20.

4. Address to Jordan seminary convention, 26 Feb. 1947, Historical Department Archives, The Church of Jesus Christ of Latter-day Saints, 4.

5. In Conference Report, Oct. 1956, 61.

6. "The Plan of Salvation," address to Brigham Young University seminary and institute personnel, 1 July 1954, Historical Department Archives, The Church of Jesus Christ of Latter-day Saints, 4–6.

7. In Conference Report, Oct. 1955, 54–56.

8. *Stand Ye in Holy Places* (1974), 246.

9. "To Ease the Aching Heart," *Ensign,* Apr. 1973, 5.

The First Principles and Ordinances of the Gospel

*How can we more faithfully live in obedience
to the first principles and ordinances of the gospel
and endure to the end?*

Introduction

To become pure and holy in life and character is the desire of all faithful Latter-day Saints. President Harold B. Lee taught that the way to purity and holiness is accepting the first four principles and ordinances of the gospel—faith in the Lord Jesus Christ, repentance, baptism, and receiving the gift of the Holy Ghost—and then enduring to the end in keeping all the commandments of God. He said:

"The laws of God given to mankind are embodied in the gospel plan, and the Church of Jesus Christ is made responsible for teaching these laws to the world. They are given by our Heavenly Father for only one purpose, that you who are governed by law might also be preserved by law and perfected and sanctified, or made holy by the same (see D&C 88:34). The greatest of all gifts of God to us is the gift of salvation in His kingdom."[1]

He also taught, "Knowledge of God and Jesus, His Son, is essential to life eternal, but the keeping of God's commandments must precede the acquisition of that knowledge or intelligence."[2]

This chapter will discuss how the first four principles and ordinances of the gospel and enduring to the end in righteousness lead us toward eternal life.

Teachings of Harold B. Lee

What is faith, and how does it direct us in our efforts to receive eternal life?

Faith applied to religion is its foundation principle and indeed the source of all righteousness that directs man in his efforts to gain eternal life in the world to come. It centers in God who by faith is recognized as the source of all power and all wisdom in the universe and who is the directing Intelligence of "all things visible or invisible that demonstrate his wisdom." By faith in God then, you too . . . can become attuned to the Infinite and by power and wisdom obtained from your Heavenly Father harness the powers of the universe and have them serve you in your hour of need in the solution of problems too great for your human strength or intelligence.

How may [we] develop this faith? The answer is by study, by work and by prayer. Paul the Apostle asked the question, "How shall they believe in him of whom they have not heard? and how shall they hear without a preacher?" (Romans 10:14.) We must answer, they cannot. So then faith can only come by hearing the word of God from preachers of truth. The preaching of the truth concerning God and his purposes has been compared to the sowing of a seed, which if a good seed will begin to sprout and grow in your hearts on these conditions: First, that it is planted in the rich, fertile soil of sincerity and real desire; second, that it is cultivated with diligent study and searching; and third, that it is watered by genial spiritual "dews" and warmed by rays of inspiration that come from humble prayer. The harvest from such planting comes only to that individual who acts upon the truths he has learned and reforms his life of sin and fills his days with purposeful conduct in keeping the commandments of God in whom he has faith, and in service toward his fellowmen.[3]

By faith the commandments of the decalogue from Mount Sinai are transformed from mere platitudes of a philosopher to the thundered voice of authority from on high, and the teachings of the prophets become the revealed word of God to guide us to our Celestial home. . . . By faith we would understand that whatever contributes in life to the standard of Jesus "Be ye therefore perfect, even as your Father which is in heaven is perfect" [Matthew 5:48] is for our good and our eternal benefit even though into that molding may go the severe chastening of an all-wise God, "For whom the Lord loveth he chasteneth, and scourgeth every son whom he receiveth." [Hebrews 12:6.][4]

Every child must learn that faith sufficient to perfection can only be developed by sacrifice and except he learns to sacrifice of his appetites and [physical] desires in obedience to the laws of the Gospel he cannot be sanctified and made holy before the Lord.[5]

Why is daily repentance necessary?

In order for good to blossom it must be cultivated and exercised by constant practice, and to be truly righteous there is required a daily pruning of the evil growth of our characters by a daily repentance from sin. . . .

Now what are the steps to be taken on this climb up the road of repentance in order to be worthy of God's forgiveness, through the redemption of the Master's atoning sacrifice, and the privileges of eternal life in the world to come? An all-wise Father, foreseeing that some would fall in sin and all would have need to repent, has provided in the teachings of his gospel and through his Church the plan of salvation that defines the clear-cut way to repentance.

First, those in sin must confess them. "By this ye may know if a man repenteth of his sins—behold, he will confess them and forsake them." (Doc. and Cov. 58:43) That confession must be made first to him or her who has been most wronged by your acts. A sincere confession is not merely admitting guilt after the proof is already in evidence. If you have "offended many persons openly," your acknowledgment is to be made openly and before those whom you have offended that you might show your shame and humility and willingness to receive a merited rebuke. If your act is secret and has resulted in injury to no one but yourself, your confession should be in secret, that your Heavenly Father who hears in secret may reward you openly. Acts that may affect your standing in the Church, or your right to privileges or advancement in the Church, are to be promptly confessed to the bishop whom the Lord has appointed as a shepherd over every flock and commissioned to be a common judge in Israel. He may hear such confession in secret and deal justly and mercifully, as each case warrants. . . . Following confession, one in sin must show forth the fruits of his repentance by good deeds that are weighed against the bad. He must make proper restitution to the limit of his power to restore that which he has taken away or to repair the damage he has done. He that repents thus of his sins and altogether turns away therefrom, to return no more to a repetition thereof, is entitled to the promise of a forgiveness of his sins, if he has not committed the unpardonable sin, as it was declared by the Prophet Isaiah, "Though your sins be as scarlet, they shall be as white as snow; though they be red like crimson, they shall be as wool." (Isaiah 1:18.)[6]

Let's face it. All of us have done something that we ought not to have done, or we have neglected to do things we should have done. All of us then have made mistakes, and every one of us needs to repent. The old devil would have you believe that if you have made one mistake, why don't you just keep on making mistakes? That is Satan trying to tell you that there is no chance to come back. But you must turn your face towards the rising sun, and through repentance turn from the thing you have done that is wrong and never go back again thereto. The Lord said, "Go [thy way] and sin no more; but unto that soul who sinneth [meaning again] shall the former sins return, saith the Lord your God" (D&C 82:7).[7]

Now, if you have made mistakes, make today the beginning of a change of your lives. Turn from the thing that you have been doing that is wrong. The most important of all the commandments of God is that one that you are having the most difficulty keeping today. If it is one of dishonesty, if it is one of unchastity, if it is one of falsifying, not telling the truth, today is the day for you to work on that until you have been able to conquer that weakness. Put that aright and then you start on the next one that is most difficult for you to keep. That's the way to sanctify yourself by keeping the commandments of God.[8]

Why is baptism a necessary preparation to meet God?

When we went into the waters of baptism we entered into a covenant with the Lord that we would do all within our power to keep God's commandments, with the understanding that the Lord's promises would be given to us and His glory would be added forever and ever, and that we would let our lives be so ordered that we would serve as witnesses of God in all places even until death. [See Mosiah 18:8–10.] It was that covenant we made when we were baptized members of this Church.[9]

Baptism by immersion for the remission of sins . . . is for those who have attained the age of accountability, a necessary preparation to meet our God. It is by this means that you become "the children of God by faith in Christ Jesus. For as many of you as have been baptized into Christ have put on Christ," (Galatians 3:26–27) or in other words through baptism have received "the power to become the sons and daughters of God." [See Mosiah 5:7.] It is through this medium that you may apply to yourselves the atoning blood of Christ, that you may receive forgiveness of your sins, and your hearts be purified. [See Mosiah 4:2.] To be worthy of such a forgiveness after having been baptized, you must humble yourselves and call on the Lord daily and walk steadfastly in the light of the teachings of the gospel. . . .

. . . Only those who repent and are baptized for the remission of their sins will lay full claim to the redeeming blood of his atonement.[10]

The Savior Himself was baptized by John the Baptist, as He said, "to fulfil all righteousness." (Matthew 3:15.) If it be so with Him, what about ourselves? Nicodemus was told: "Except a man be born of water and of the Spirit, he cannot enter into the kingdom of God." (John 3:5.) The Master left no doubt as to the why of the baptism which He taught.

"And no unclean thing can enter into his kingdom; therefore nothing entereth into his rest save it be those who have washed their garments in my blood, because of their faith, and the repentance of all their sins, and their faithfulness unto the end." (3 Nephi 27:19.)

That was why Peter admonished his hearers, "Repent, and be baptized every one of you in the name of Jesus Christ for the remission of sins, and ye shall receive the gift of the Holy Ghost." (Acts 2:38.) For through baptism by one having authority, the recipient may indeed figuratively wash his garments in the blood of the Son of God, who atoned for the sins of all who receive Him and come in at the door of the sheepfold, by baptism. "But if they would not repent," the Savior declared in plainness, "they must suffer even as I." (D&C 19:17.)[11]

How does the Holy Ghost guide us to the presence of the Lord?

Every baptized member has hands laid upon his head or her head and the elders, after confirming him or her a member of the Church, said, "Receive the Holy Ghost." Then they may have repeated the words that the Master spoke to His disciples when He told them about the Comforter or the Holy Ghost, which was to come: It will bring all things to your remembrance. It will teach you all things. It will show you things to come. [See John 14:26; 16:13.] And so if I were confirming you a member of the Church, I would confer upon you the gift of the Holy Ghost, which shall be a lamp to your feet and a guide to your path, which shall teach you all things and bring all things to your remembrance and show you things to come.[12]

The Lord says: "And this is my gospel—repentance and baptism by water, and then cometh the baptism of fire and the Holy Ghost, even the Comforter, which showeth all things, and teacheth the peaceable things of the kingdom." (D&C 39:6.)

When a man has the gift of the Holy Ghost, he has that which is necessary to reveal to him every principle and ordinance of salvation that pertains unto man here on the earth.[13]

It is the ideal thing to say that when one is baptized of the water and receives the blessings of the Spirit by the laying on of hands, that this is a new birth. It is a new birth because he has been brought from that spiritual death into the presence of one of the Godhead, even the Holy Ghost. That is why we say unto you "Receive the Holy Ghost" when you are confirmed. That gift is given to the believer who is faithful and lives to claim that blessing, the right to the communion with one of the Godhead to overcome that spiritual death.[14]

Baptism by immersion symbolizes the death and burial of the man of sin; and the coming forth out of the water, the resurrection to a newness of spiritual life. After baptism, hands are laid upon the head of the baptized believer, and he is blessed to receive the Holy Ghost. Thus does the one baptized receive the promise or gift of the Holy Ghost, or the privilege of being brought back into the presence of one of the Godhead; by obedience and through his faithfulness, one so blessed might receive the guidance and direction of the Holy Ghost in his daily walks and talks, even as Adam walked and talked in the Garden of Eden with God, his Heavenly Father. To receive such guidance and such direction from the Holy Ghost is to be spiritually reborn.[15]

In the basic principles of the gospel—faith, repentance, baptism, and the receiving of the Holy Ghost, by which power all things can be revealed—we will begin to understand what the Prophet Joseph Smith possibly meant when he said on one occasion when asked why this church was different than all other churches—because we have the Holy Ghost. [See *History of the Church,* 4:42.] Having that power by which all things can be revealed, therein the fulness of the gospel of Jesus Christ can be established.[16]

How can we endure to the end?

What are the laws and the way by which we receive [the blessing of celestial glory]? Well, we have the first principles and ordinances of the Gospel—faith, repentance, baptism, and the Holy Ghost; and in the kingdom of God there are laws which teach us the way to perfection. Any member of the Church who is learning to live perfectly each of the laws that are in the kingdom is learning the way to become perfect. There is no member of this Church who cannot live the law, every law of the gospel perfectly. All of us can learn to talk with God in prayer. All of us can learn to live the Word of Wisdom perfectly. All of us can learn to keep the Sabbath day holy, perfectly. All of you can learn how to keep the law of fasting perfectly. We know how to keep the law of chastity perfectly. Now as we learn to keep one of these laws perfectly we ourselves are on the road to perfection.[17]

You may ask me, how does one sanctify himself, and make himself holy so that he is prepared to walk in the presence of the Lord? . . . The Lord says this, "And again, verily I say unto you, that which is governed by law is also preserved by law and perfected and sanctified by the same" (D&C 88:34). What law? The laws of the Lord as contained in the gospel of Jesus Christ, the keeping of which laws and ordinances are the ways by which we are purified and made holy. The keeping of every law that the Lord has given us is one step closer to receiving the right to enter one day into the presence of the Lord.

He has given us in another revelation the formula by which we can prepare ourselves as the years pass. "Verily, thus saith the Lord: It shall come to pass that every soul who forsaketh his sins and cometh unto me, and calleth on my name, and obeyeth my voice, and keepeth my commandments, shall see my face and know that I am" (D&C 93:1). Simple, isn't it? But listen again. All you have to do is to forsake your sins, come unto Him, call on His name, obey His voice, and keep His commandments, and then you shall see His face and shall know that He is.[18]

This is the Lord's work and when he gives a commandment to the children of men, he provides a way by which that commandment can be realized. If his children will do all that they can to help themselves, then the Lord will bless their efforts.

. . . The Lord expects us to do all we can to save ourselves, and . . . after we have done all we can to save ourselves, then we can lean upon the mercies of the grace of our Heavenly Father. He gave his Son that through obedience to the laws and ordinances of the gospel we might gain our salvation, but not until we have done all we can do for ourselves.[19]

The Lord gives us, each one, a lamp to carry, but whether or not we shall have oil in our lamps depends solely upon each one of us. Whether or not we keep the commandments and supply the needed oil to light our way and to guide us on our way depends upon each of us individually. We cannot borrow from our

Church membership. We cannot borrow from an illustrious ancestry. Whether or not we have oil in our lamps, I repeat, depends solely upon each one of us; it is determined by our faithfulness in keeping the commandments of the Living God.[20]

All of the gospel principles and all of the gospel ordinances are but invitations to the learning of the gospel by the practice of its teachings. That's all they are—invitations to come and practice in order that you can know. . . . It seems clear to me that we might well say, we never really know any of the teachings of the gospel until we have experienced them one by one by living them. We learn the gospel, in other words, by living it.[21]

The greatest message that one in this position could give to the membership of the Church is to keep the commandments of God, for therein lies the safety of the Church and the safety of the individual. Keep the commandments. There could be nothing that I could say that would be a more powerful or important message today.[22]

Suggestions for Study and Discussion

- How can we develop greater faith in the Lord Jesus Christ? How does faith help us to live the commandments rather than treat them lightly? When has your faith in God enabled you to deal with "problems too great for your human strength or intelligence"?

- Why is confession important to the process of repentance? Why should we begin today to repent of our sins and change our lives, instead of waiting for another day?

- How do we "figuratively wash [our] garments in the blood of the Son of God"?

- According to President Lee, how does receiving the gift of the Holy Ghost help us overcome spiritual death? What can we do to more fully have the guidance of the Holy Ghost in our "daily walks and talks"?

- What does Doctrine and Covenants 93:1 teach about the importance of enduring to the end in keeping the commandments?

- How has living a particular gospel teaching helped you know that it is true?

Notes

1. *The Teachings of Harold B. Lee,* ed. Clyde J. Williams (1996), 19.

2. "'And This Is Life Eternal,'" *Relief Society Magazine,* Apr. 1950, 225.

3. *Decisions for Successful Living* (1973), 75–76.

4. "'Put on the Whole Armor of God,'" *Church News,* 30 May 1942, 8.

5. "For Every Child, His Spiritual and Cultural Heritage," *Children's Friend,* Aug. 1943, 373.

6. *Decisions for Successful Living,* 94, 98–99.

7. *The Teachings of Harold B. Lee,* 115.

8. *The Teachings of Harold B. Lee,* 82.

9. Address to Mutual Improvement Association, 1948, Historical Department Archives, The Church of Jesus Christ of Latter-day Saints, 5.

10. *Decisions for Successful Living,* 116, 118.

11. *Stand Ye in Holy Places* (1974), 316–17.

12. Address to youth conference in Billings, Montana, 10 June 1973, Historical Department Archives, The Church of Jesus Christ of Latter-day Saints, 4.

13. *Stand Ye in Holy Places,* 51.

14. Address to Jordan seminary convention, 26 Feb. 1947, Historical Department Archives, The Church of Jesus Christ of Latter-day Saints, 5.

15. *The Teachings of Harold B. Lee,* 95.

16. Address to new mission presidents' seminar, 29–30 June 1972, Historical Department Archives, The Church of Jesus Christ of Latter-day Saints, 5.

17. Address to district conference in Lima, Peru, 1 Nov. 1959, Historical Department Archives, The Church of Jesus Christ of Latter-day Saints, 6–7.

18. *The Teachings of Harold B. Lee,* 166; paragraphing added.

19. In Conference Report, Munich Germany Area Conference 1973, 7.

20. In Conference Report, Oct. 1951, 30.

21. "Learning the Gospel by Living It," address to 52nd annual Primary conference, 3 Apr. 1958, Historical Department Archives, The Church of Jesus Christ of Latter-day Saints, 3.

22. *Ensign,* Aug. 1972, back cover.

Walking in the Light of Testimony

How can the light of our testimony grow into a "brightness of certainty"?

Introduction

For more than 32 years, Harold B. Lee was a special witness of the Savior, Jesus Christ. He testified, "In all solemnity, and with all my soul, I bear you my testimony that I know that Jesus lives, that he is the Savior of the world."[1]

In speaking of how to gain a testimony, he said:

"I once had a visit from a young Catholic priest who came with a stake missionary from Colorado. I asked him why he had come, and he replied, 'I came to see you.'

" 'Why?' I asked.

" 'Well,' he said, 'I have been searching for certain concepts that I have not been able to find. But I think I am finding them now in the Mormon community.'

"That led to a half-hour conversation. I told him, 'Father, when your heart begins to tell you things that your mind does not know, then you are getting the Spirit of the Lord.'

"He smiled and said, 'I think that's happening to me already.'

" 'Then don't wait too long,' I said to him.

"A few weeks later I received a telephone call from him. He said, 'Next Saturday I am going to be baptized a member of the Church, because my heart has told me things my mind did not know.'

"He was converted. He saw what he should have seen. He heard what he should have heard. He understood what he should have understood, and he was doing something about it. He had a testimony."[2]

Teachings of Harold B. Lee

What is a testimony?

Testimony may be defined simply as divine revelation to the man of faith. The psalmist echoes the same thought: ". . . the testimony of the Lord is sure. . . ." (Psalm 19:7.) Paul, the apostle, declared ". . . no man can say [or know] that Jesus is the Lord, but by the Holy Ghost." (1 Corinthians 12:3.) The prophets have further taught that if you were to "ask with a sincere heart, with real intent, having faith in Christ, he will manifest the truth of it unto you, by the power of the Holy Ghost. And by the power of the Holy Ghost ye may know the truth of all things." (Moroni 10:4–5.) . . .

God lives! Jesus is the Savior of this world! The gospel of Jesus Christ as contained in fulness in the ancient and modern scriptures is true! These things I know by the witness of the Spirit to my spirit.[3]

Let me share with you an experience I had with one of our business executives. His wife and children are members, but he is not. . . . He said to me, "I can't join the Church until I get a testimony." I said to him, "The next time you are in Salt Lake, come in and visit with me." As we talked following our business meeting a few weeks later I said to him, "I don't know if you realize whether you have a testimony or not; or if you know what a testimony is." And so he wanted to know what a testimony is. I answered him by saying, "When the time comes that your heart tells you things your mind doesn't know, that is the Spirit of the Lord dictating to you." And then I said, "As I've come to know you, there are things that you know in your heart are true. No angel is going to tap you on the shoulder and tell you this is true." The Spirit of the Lord is as the Master said: "The wind bloweth where it listeth, and thou hearest the sound thereof, but canst not tell whence it cometh, and whither it goeth: so is every one that is born of the Spirit" (John 3:8). So I said to my friend, the business executive: "Now, remember that your testimony won't come in a dramatic way, but when it comes, the tears of gladness will water your pillow by night. You'll know, my beloved friend, when that testimony comes."[4]

I bear you my testimony that I know the Savior lives, that the most powerful witness you can have that He lives comes when the power of the Holy Spirit bears witness to your soul that He does live. More powerful than sight, more powerful than walking and talking with Him, is that witness of the Spirit by which you shall be judged if you were to turn against Him. But it is the responsibility of all of you, as well as my responsibility, to get that testimony established. We are constantly asked, just how does one receive revelation? The Lord said in a revelation to the early leaders, "I will tell you in your mind and in your heart by the Holy Ghost. It shall dwell within you. This is the revelation by which Moses led the children of Israel to the Red Sea and on across it." [See D&C 8:2–3.] When that Spirit has witnessed to our spirit, that's a revelation from Almighty God.[5]

[When Lazarus died, the Savior declared to Martha,] "I am the resurrection, and the life: he that believeth in me, though he were dead, yet shall he live: And whosoever liveth and believeth in me shall never die." Then He looked at Martha and He said, "Believest thou this?" And from the depths of this humble woman, something awakened and she said with the same conviction that Peter had said, "Yea, Lord: I believe that thou art the Christ, the Son of God, which should come into the world." [John 11:25–27.]

Where did she get that from? It didn't come from reading books. It didn't come from studying theology or science or philosophy. She had had a witness in her heart, just as Peter had. If the Master had replied, He would have said, "Blessed art thou, Martha, for flesh and blood did not reveal this to you, but my Father which is in heaven." . . . The most prized of all the things you can have is to have the witness in your heart that these things are true.[6]

Not many have seen the Savior face to face here in mortality, but there is no one of us who has been blessed to receive the gift of the Holy Ghost after baptism but that may have a perfect assurance of His existence as though we had seen. Indeed, if we have faith in the reality of His existence even though we have not seen, as the Master implied in His statement to Thomas, even greater is the blessing to those who "have not seen, and yet have believed" (John 20:29), for "we walk by faith, not by sight" (2 Corinthians 5:7). Although not seeing, yet believing, we rejoice with joy unspeakable in receiving the end of our faith, even the salvation of our souls (see 1 Peter 1:8–9).[7]

Can we sum it up and say then, that any person who has received a true testimony has received a revelation from the living God, or else he would not have the testimony? Anyone who has a testimony, then, has enjoyed the gift of prophecy, he's had the spirit of revelation. He has had the gift by which the prophets have been able to speak things pertaining to their responsibilities. . . .

The Lord help us all to strive to gain that testimony most vital in our preparation to know. When finally we get that one divine thought that Joseph Smith was and is a prophet and that the gospel is true, all the other seeming difficulties melt away like heavy frost before the coming of the rising sun.[8]

How do we prepare ourselves to receive a testimony?

[The Savior is] quoted as having said that ". . . the kingdom of God is within you." (Luke 17:21.) A more correct translation probably would have said, "The kingdom of God is among you or in your midst," but as I thought of that other statement, "The kingdom of God is within you," I recalled an experience that we had with a group of students from Brigham Young University . . . over in the Lion House, and there sixteen, representing sixteen foreign countries, were asked to stand and tell how they came to know about the gospel and accept it, . . . and to bear their testimonies. It was a most intensely interesting evening. We heard from young men and women from Mexico, Argentina, Brazil, the Scandinavian countries, France, and England. The story was the same. When they began to relate how they came to find the gospel, it was this: They were yearning for truth. They were seeking for light. They were not satisfied, and in the midst of their search, someone came to them with the truths of the gospel. They prayed about it and sought the Lord intensely, intently, with all their hearts, and came to receive a divine testimony by which they knew that this is the gospel of Jesus Christ. . . . So within the heart of everyone, every honest seeker after truth, if he has the desire to know, and studies with real intent and faith in the Lord Jesus Christ, the kingdom of God may be within him, or in other words, the power to receive it is his.[9]

At the root of the individual testimony must be a righteous, pure life, else the Spirit cannot witness as to the divinity of the mission of the Lord or of this work in our day.[10]

The first essential . . . in gaining a testimony is to make certain that one's personal spiritual "housekeeping" is in proper order. His mind and body must be clean if he would enjoy the indwelling gift of the Holy Ghost by which he could know the certainty of spiritual things.[11]

Conversion must mean more than just being a "card carrying" member of the Church with a tithing receipt, a membership card, a temple recommend, etc. It means to overcome the tendencies to criticize and to strive continually to improve inward weaknesses and not merely the outward appearances.[12]

Now when our missionaries go out, we say to those among whom they labor, "We are not asking you to join the Church just to put your name on the records. That is not our concern. We come to you offering you the greatest gift the world can give, the gift of the kingdom of God. This is here for you if you will only accept and believe." Now that is our challenge to the world. "We can teach you the doctrines of the Church of Jesus Christ and bear testimony of the divinity of the work, but the witness of the truth of what we teach has to come from your own searching."

We say to our people whom we teach, "Now, you ask the Lord. Study, work, and pray." This is the process by which people are brought into the Church, and it is the same way that from the beginning the honest in heart everywhere have been brought into the Church.[13]

As Jesus lifted up his eyes in prayer as "his hour was come," [see John 17:1] he gave expression to a profound truth that should be full of meaning to every soul: "And this is life eternal, that they might know thee the only true God, and Jesus Christ, whom thou hast sent." (John 17:3.) While this expression has deeper significance than I shall discuss here, I should like to take one thought from it. How can you know the Father and the Son? . . . We begin to acquire that knowledge by study. The Savior counseled us to "Search the scriptures; for in them ye think ye have eternal life: and they are they which testify of me." (John 5:39.) Therein will be found a history of God's dealings with mankind in every dispensation and the works and words of the prophets and those of the Savior himself as given "by inspiration of God," as the Apostle Paul said, "and is profitable for doctrine, for reproof, for correction, for instruction in righteousness: that the man of God may be perfect, throughly furnished unto all good works." (II Timothy 3:16–17.) Youth should let no day pass without reading from these sacred books.

But it is not enough merely to learn of his life and works by study. It was the Master who replied in answer to the question as to how one might know of him and his doctrine: "If any man will do his will, he shall know." (John 7:17.) Would you think an authority on science to be one who had never experimented in a laboratory? Would you give much heed to the comments of a music critic who did not know music or an art critic who didn't paint? Just so, one like yourself who would "know God" must be one who does his will and keeps his commandments and practices the virtues Jesus lived.[14]

The acquiring of knowledge by faith is no easy road to learning. It demands strenuous effort and a continual striving by faith. . . .

In short, learning by faith is no task for a lazy man. Someone has said, in effect, that such a process requires the bending of the whole soul, the calling up from the depths of the human mind and linking it with God—the right connection must be formed. Then only comes "knowledge by faith."[15]

What can we do to strengthen our testimonies?

[The Master said to Peter,] "Satan hath desired to have you, that he may sift you as wheat: But I have prayed for thee, that thy faith fail not: and when thou art converted, strengthen thy brethren" (Luke 22:31–32). Now, mind you, He is saying that to the chiefest of the Twelve. I am praying for you; now go out and get converted, and when you get converted, then go strengthen your brother. It means [we can become] unconverted just as well as we can become converted. Your testimony is something that you have today but you may not have it always.[16]

Testimony is as elusive as a moonbeam; it's as fragile as an orchid; you have to recapture it every morning of your life. You have to hold on by study, and by faith, and by prayer. If you allow yourself to be angry, if you allow yourself to get into the wrong kind of company, you listen to the wrong kind of stories, you are studying the wrong kind of subjects, you are engaging in sinful practices, there is nothing that will be more deadening as to take away the Spirit of the Lord from you until it will be as though you had walked from a lighted room when you go out of this building, as though you had gone out into a darkness.[17]

That which you possess today in testimony will not be yours tomorrow unless you do something about it. Your testimony is either going to increase or it is going to diminish, depending on you. Will you remember your responsibility, then? The Lord said, "If any man will do his will, he shall know of the doctrine, whether it be of God, or whether I speak of myself" (John 7:17).[18]

No truly converted Latter-day Saint can be immoral. No truly converted Latter-day Saint can be dishonest, nor lie, nor steal. That means that one may have a testimony as of today, but when he stoops to do things that contradict the laws of God, it is because he has lost his testimony and he has to fight to regain it again. Testimony isn't something that you have today and you keep always. Testimony is either going to grow and grow to the brightness of certainty, or it is going to diminish to nothingness, depending upon what we do about it. I say, the testimony that we recapture day by day is the thing that saves us from the pitfalls of the adversary.[19]

How is a testimony an anchor to the soul?

There was an occasion during [Christ's] ministry when His chief apostle, Peter, had fervently declared his faith and testimony of the divinity of the mission of the Master: "Thou art the Christ, the Son of the living God." The Lord had replied to Peter by declaring, ". . . flesh and blood hath not revealed it unto thee, but my Father which is in heaven" and that upon "this rock"—or in other words, the revealed testimony of the Holy Ghost, the revelation that Jesus is the Christ—His church is founded, and "the gates of hell shall not prevail against it." (Matthew 16:16–18.)[20]

The time is coming and facing you right now . . . when except you have that testimony of certainty that these things [the gospel, the Church, and so on] are true you will not be able to weather the storms that are going to beat upon you and try to tear you from your moorings today. But if you know with all your soul that these things are true . . . , you will know who Jesus your Savior is and who God your Father is; you will know what the influence of the Holy Ghost is. If you know those things you will stand as an anchor against all the storms that shall beat upon your house, as the Master's parable described. That one who hears His words and keeps His commandments shall be as the house that was built upon a rock, and when the storms came and the floods beat upon the house and the winds blew, it fell not, because it was founded upon a rock. "And every one that heareth these sayings of mine, and doeth them not, shall be likened unto a foolish man, which built his house upon the sand: And the rain descended, and the floods came, and the winds blew, and beat upon that house; and it fell: and great was the fall of it" (Matthew 7:26–27).

The Master was saying, and I am saying to you today, that the rains of disaster, the rains of difficulty, the floods and winds of severe trials are going to beat upon the house of every one of you. There will be temptation to sin, you will have hardship, you will have difficulty to face in your life. The only ones that will not fall when those tests come will be those who have their houses founded upon the rock of testimony. You will know no matter what comes; you will not be able to stand on borrowed light. You can only stand on the light that you have by the witness of the Spirit that all of you have the right to receive.[21]

It is not alone sufficient for us as Latter-day Saints to follow our leaders and to accept their counsel, but we have the greater obligation to gain for ourselves the unshakable testimony of the divine appointment of these men and the witness that what they have told us is the will of our Heavenly Father.[22]

I come to you today as a special witness charged with, above all else, the responsibility of bearing that witness. There have been intimate circumstances when I have known with a surety. When I was searching for the Spirit to deliver a talk on the Easter theme, the resurrection of the Lord, I closeted myself, read the four gospels, particularly down to the Crucifixion, the Resurrection, and I had something happen to me. As I read, it was as though I was reliving, almost, the very incident, not just a story. And then I delivered my message and bore testimony that now, as one of the least of my brethren, I, too, had a personal witness of the death and the resurrection of our Lord and Master. Why? Because I had had something burned into my soul that I could speak with a certainty that is beside all doubt. So can you. And the most satisfying thing in all the world, the greatest anchor to your soul, in time of trouble, in time of temptation, in times of sickness, in times of indecision, in times of your struggles and work, [is that] you can know with a certainty that defies all doubt that God lives.[23]

Suggestions for Study and Discussion

- Why is revelation from the Holy Spirit "the most powerful witness you can have" that the Savior lives?

- What counsel did President Lee give about how to receive a testimony of the gospel? What has helped you to receive your testimony?

- How can we come to know Heavenly Father and Jesus Christ?

- What do you think President Lee meant when he said, "Testimony is as elusive as a moonbeam; . . . you have to recapture it every morning of your life"?

- What might cause our testimonies to diminish or die? What must we do so that the light of our testimonies may "grow to the brightness of certainty"?

- Once we gain a testimony, how can we help others to strengthen their testimonies?

- In what ways is the knowledge that God lives an anchor to our souls in times of trouble? When has your testimony of the Savior been a source of strength to you?

Notes

1. " 'But Arise and Stand upon Thy Feet'— and I Will Speak with Thee," address given at Brigham Young University, 7 Feb. 1956, Historical Department Archives, The Church of Jesus Christ of Latter-day Saints, 2.
2. *Stand Ye in Holy Places* (1974), 92–93.
3. *Stand Ye in Holy Places,* 193, 196.
4. *The Teachings of Harold B. Lee,* ed. Clyde J. Williams (1996), 140–41.
5. Address given at Lausanne Switzerland conference, 26 Sept. 1972, Historical Department Archives, The Church of Jesus Christ of Latter-day Saints, 8.
6. Address given in Pocatello, Idaho, 9 Mar. 1973, Historical Department Archives, The Church of Jesus Christ of Latter-day Saints.
7. *The Teachings of Harold B. Lee,* 93.
8. "Church and Divine Revelation," 1954, Historical Department Archives, The Church of Jesus Christ of Latter-day Saints, 17, 23.
9. In Conference Report, Oct. 1953, 26–27.
10. *The Teachings of Harold B. Lee,* 133.
11. *The Teachings of Harold B. Lee,* 137.
12. In Conference Report, Apr. 1971, 92; or *Ensign,* June 1971, 8.
13. *The Teachings of Harold B. Lee,* 135–36.
14. *Decisions for Successful Living* (1973), 39–40; paragraphing added.
15. *The Teachings of Harold B. Lee,* 331.
16. *The Teachings of Harold B. Lee,* 138.
17. *The Teachings of Harold B. Lee,* 139.
18. *The Teachings of Harold B. Lee,* 135.
19. *The Teachings of Harold B. Lee,* 139.
20. *Stand Ye in Holy Places,* 40.
21. *The Teachings of Harold B. Lee,* 140.
22. *The Teachings of Harold B. Lee,* 133.
23. *Education for Eternity,* "The Last Message" lecture given at the Salt Lake Institute of Religion, 15 Jan. 1971, 11.

To Hear the Voice of the Lord

*How can we receive personal revelation
from the Lord?*

Introduction

President Harold B. Lee once said: "I have a believing heart that started with a simple testimony that came when I was a child—I think maybe I was around ten or eleven years of age. I was with my father out on a farm away from our home, trying to spend the day busying myself until my father was ready to go home. Over the fence from our place were some tumbledown sheds that would attract a curious boy, and I was adventurous. I started to climb through the fence, and I heard a voice as clearly as you are hearing mine, calling me by name and saying, 'Don't go over there!' I turned to look at my father to see if he were talking to me, but he was way up at the other end of the field. There was no person in sight. I realized then, as a child, that there were persons beyond my sight, for I had definitely heard a voice. Since then, when I hear or read stories of the Prophet Joseph Smith, I too have known what it means to hear a voice, because I've had the experience."[1]

Although the Lord might not speak to us audibly, as we learn to talk to Him and recognize how He communicates with us, we begin to know Him. President Lee said that "to know God and Jesus Christ whom he has sent (see John 17:3), as the Master told his disciples, is to begin on the sure course that leads to eternal life in the presence of these glorified beings."[2]

The prophet Enos sought the Lord in earnest prayer. We should also seek diligently to "communicate with . . . our Heavenly Father, and receive an answer to our inquiry and strength for our days."

Teachings of Harold B. Lee

In what ways does Heavenly Father communicate with His children?

I listened to an inspired sermon at Brigham Young University by President [J. Reuben] Clark. . . . He analyzed the various kinds of revelation that come. He talked first of a theophany, which he described as an experience where the Father or the Son or both put in a personal appearance, or speak directly to man. Moses talked with the Lord face to face [see Moses 1:1–4]; Daniel had a theophany, or personal appearance [see Daniel 10]. When the Master came to John the Baptist for baptism, you remember, a voice spoke out of the heavens and said, "This is my beloved Son, in whom I am well pleased." [Matthew 3:17.] At the conversion of Paul, . . . there was also a personal appearance, and an audible voice was heard [see Acts 9:1–6]. At the transfiguration, when Peter, James, and John went with the Master to a high mountain where Moses and Elias appeared before them, again a voice was heard speaking out of the heavens, saying, "This is my beloved Son, in whom I am well pleased. . . ." (Matthew 17:5.)

Perhaps the greatest of all theophanies of our time was the appearance of the Father and the Son to the Prophet Joseph Smith in the grove [see Joseph Smith—History 1:14–17]. Following that there were several appearances, one of which is recorded in the 110th section of the Doctrine and Covenants, when the Savior appeared to Joseph and Oliver. . . .

Another way by which we receive revelation was spoken of by the prophet Enos. He pens this very significant statement in his record in the Book of Mormon: "And while I was thus struggling in the spirit, behold, the voice of the Lord came into my mind. . . ." [Enos 1:10.]

In other words, sometimes we hear the voice of the Lord coming into our minds, and when it comes, the impressions are just as strong as though He were sounding a trumpet in our ear. . . .

In a story in the Book of Mormon, Nephi upbraids his brothers, calling them to repentance, and gives voice to the same thought when he says: ". . . and he hath spoken unto you in a still small voice, but ye were past feeling, that ye could not feel his words. . . ." (1 Nephi 17:45.)

Thus the Lord, by revelation, brings thoughts into our minds as though a voice were speaking. May I bear humble testimony to that fact? I was once in a situation where I needed help. The Lord knew I needed help, as I was on an important mission. I was awakened in the wee hours of the morning and was straightened out on something that I had planned to do in a contrary way, and the way was clearly mapped out before me as I lay there that morning, just as surely as though someone had sat on the edge of my bed and told me what to do. Yes, the voice of the Lord comes into our minds and we can be directed thereby.

We also receive revelation by the power of the Holy Ghost. The Lord said to the Prophet Joseph Smith in the early days of the Church, "Yea, behold, I will tell you in your mind and in your heart, by the Holy Ghost, which shall . . . dwell in your heart. Now, behold, this is the spirit of revelation. . . ." (D&C 8:2–3.) The Master comforted His disciples, you remember, just before His crucifixion when He said, ". . . if I go not away, the Comforter will not come unto you. . . . Howbeit when he, the Spirit of truth [or the Holy Ghost], is come, he will guide you into all truth: . . . he will shew you things to come" (John 16:7, 13), "and bring all things to your remembrance. . . ." (John 14:26.) Thus we see the power of the Holy Ghost. The Prophet Joseph Smith, speaking about this, said, "No man can receive the Holy Ghost without receiving revelations. The Holy Ghost is a revelator." (*Teachings of the Prophet Joseph Smith*, p. 328.)

May I change that about . . . and say, Any Latter-day Saint who has been baptized and who has had hands laid upon him from those officiating, commanding him to receive the Holy Ghost, and who has not received a revelation of the spirit of the Holy Ghost, has not received the gift of the Holy Ghost to which he is entitled. Therein lies a very important matter. Let me refer to what the Prophet Joseph Smith said about revelation:

"A person may profit by noticing the first intimation of the spirit of revelation; for instance, when you feel pure intelligence flowing into you, it may give you sudden strokes of ideas, so that by noticing it, you may find it fulfilled the same day or soon; (i.e.) those things that were presented unto your minds by the Spirit of God, will come to pass; and thus by learning the Spirit of God and understanding it, you may grow into the principle of revelation, until you become perfect in Christ Jesus." [*History of the Church,* 3:381.]

On what matters may you receive a revelation? Is it startling to you to hear that you—all members of the Church who have received the Holy Ghost—may receive revelation? Not for the president of the Church, not on how to look after the affairs pertaining to the ward, the stake, or the mission in which you live; but every individual within his own station has the right to receive revelation by the Holy Ghost. . . .

Every man has the privilege to exercise these gifts and these privileges in the conduct of his own affairs; in bringing up his children in the way they should go; in the management of his business, or whatever he does. It is his right to enjoy the spirit of revelation and of inspiration to do the right thing, to be wise and prudent, just and good, in everything that he does. I know that is a true principle, and that is the thing that I would like the Latter-day Saints to know. Now then, all of us should try to strive and give heed to the sudden ideas that come to us, and if we'll give heed to them and cultivate an ear to hear these promptings we too—each of us—can grow in the spirit of revelation.

Now there's one more way by which revelations may come, and that is by dreams. Oh, I'm not going to tell you that every dream you have is a direct revelation from the Lord. . . . But I fear that in this age of sophistication there are those of us who are prone to rule out all dreams as of no purpose, and of no moment. And yet all through the scriptures there were recorded incidents where the Lord, by dreams, has directed His people. . . .

The thing that all of us should strive for is to so live, keeping the commandments of the Lord, that He can answer our prayers, the prayers of our loved ones, the prayers of the General Authorities, for us. We always pray for the members of the Church, and we thank God when we know that they are praying for us. If we will live worthy, then the Lord will guide us—by a personal appearance, or by His actual voice, or by His voice coming into our mind, or by impressions upon our heart and our soul. And oh, how grateful we ought to be if the Lord sends us a dream in which are revealed to us the beauties of the eternity or a warning and direction for our special comfort. Yes, if we so live, the Lord will guide us for our salvation and for our benefit.

As one of the humblest among you, and occupying the station I do, I want to bear you my humble testimony that I have received by the voice and the power of revelation the knowledge and an understanding that God is. . . .

I bear you my solemn testimony that the Church today is guided by revelation. Every soul in it who has been blessed to receive the Holy Ghost has the power to receive revelation. God help you and me that we will always so live that the Lord can answer the prayers of the faithful through us.[3]

How can we pray to our Father in Heaven so that He can guide us?

There is a lot of difference between saying a prayer and talking with God. There are a few whom I have heard pray who did talk with God, one of whom was the late [Elder] Charles A. Callis. I never heard him pray at the holy altars in the temple, I never heard him when we knelt together in prayer when we were out on a difficult mission but what he seemed, as he talked, to be reaching right into the portals of our Father's holy dwelling place, and he talked with divine beings. Do not say prayers, do not read prayers, but learn to talk with God and that talking with God is the kind of prayer that I think was meant by Moroni when he wrote in the closing chapter of our Book of Mormon . . . :

"I would exhort you that ye would ask God, the Eternal Father, in the name of Christ, if these things are not true; and if ye shall ask with a sincere heart, with real intent, having faith in Christ, he will manifest the truth of it unto you, by the power of the Holy Ghost." [Moroni 10:4.]

. . . This is what I understand to be a prayer of faith, . . . faith in God and in His Son, Jesus Christ, without which no person can talk with God.[4]

52

I came across an experience that our beloved Richard Evans [of the Quorum of the Twelve] had on one of his trips. . . . He was sitting by a man at dinner some evenings ago, by the side of a distinguished industrialist, who told him simply in a few sentences how he faced the heavy problems of his life and how he met the decisions of each day. "When I get up in the morning," he said, "I often feel that I can't face it, but if I go down on my knees and say simply, 'God, help me to do what I have to do this day,' strength comes, and I feel that I'm equal to it. And I think of Him simply as my father and I talk to Him simply and directly as I used to talk to my father when he was here on earth." . . .

[Elder Evans reflected:] "I was mellowed and humbled by the direct and simple friend with whom I sat the other evening. He was not of my faith, but [it is] my own earnest belief he could not have talked to God with so much satisfaction and assurance if he had thought of Him as merely a force, or as an ineffable essence, the nature and purpose of which he knew nothing, or at least nothing that would bring him the assured feeling that he was in fact talking to his father." . . .

As Jacob said to his family . . . , "O how great the holiness of our God! For he knoweth all things, and there is not anything save he knows it." (2 Nephi 9:20.) Now, if you will just keep that in mind you have a beginning point, you have a relationship with Him. We are His son, His daughter. He knows us. He knows the very things and the times before appointed, and the place where we would live, and the times in which we would live. So in Him only can we place full trust.[5]

One of the most prized of all the possessions that we can have or the prized knowledge that we can possess is that the Lord hears and answers prayers—or, to put it in another way, that we learn how to talk with God. Praying is not just a matter of saying words, as some various churches would teach, but to recognize that God, our Heavenly Father, and His Son, Jesus Christ, are living, real personalities and that through the ministry of the other member of the Godhead, the Holy Ghost or Holy Spirit, we can communicate with Him, our Heavenly Father, and receive an answer to our inquiry and strength for our days.[6]

In humility be prepared to say with Paul, "Lord, what wilt thou have me to do?" (Acts 9:6). And with dauntless courage say with the boy Samuel, "Speak, Lord; for thy servant heareth" (1 Samuel 3:9). Be humble, be prayerful, and the Lord will take you by the hand, as it were, and give you answer to your prayers [see D&C 112:10].[7]

President [David O.] McKay taught us this in the temple one day. . . . "I want to tell you one thing: When the Lord tells you what to do, you've got to have the courage to do it or you had better not ask him again." I've learned that lesson, too. Sometimes in the middle of the night I've been awakened and am unable to sleep until I've gotten out of bed and put down on paper the thing that I have been wrestling with. But it takes a lot of courage to act when directed as an answer to prayers.[8]

Fast two meals on the first Sunday of the month and pay the full value of those two meals from which you have abstained. . . . The Lord said to Isaiah, that those who would thus fast and deal out their bread to the hungry, could call and the Lord would answer, could cry and the Lord would say, "Here I am." [See Isaiah

Like the boy Samuel, we should be willing to say, "Speak, Lord;
for thy servant heareth" (1 Samuel 3:9) and then act courageously
on the answer to our prayer.

58:6–9.] That's one way to get on speaking terms with the Lord. Try it this year. Live the law of fasting perfectly.⁹

When we stand at the crossroads of two alternative decisions, let us remember what the Lord said we should do: Study the whole matter out in our mind to a conclusion; before action, ask the Lord if it be right; and attune ourselves to the spiritual response—either to have our bosom burn within us to know that our conclusion is right, or to have a stupor of thought that will make us forget it if it is wrong [see D&C 9:7–9]. Then, as the Lord has promised, ". . . the Spirit shall be given unto [us] by the prayer of faith." (D&C 42:14.) . . .

If we seek earnestly, we can reach into that spiritual dimension for answers that will secure for us not only great blessings, but also the sublime witness in our hearts that our acts, our life, and our labors have the seal of approval of the Lord and Creator of us all.¹⁰

What can we do to receive personal revelation from the Lord?

The most important thing you can do is to learn to talk to God. Talk to Him as you would talk to your father, for He is your Father, and He wants you to talk to Him. He wants you to cultivate ears to listen, when He gives you the impressions of the Spirit to tell you what to do. If you learn to give heed to the sudden ideas which come to your minds, you will find those things coming through in the very hour of your need. If you will cultivate an ear to hear these promptings, you will have learned to walk by the spirit of revelation.¹¹

How do we develop the spiritual quality in our natures in order to serve our earthly missions more completely and thus become attuned with [God's] infinite power . . . ?

Ammon answered that question in part: "Yea, he that repenteth and exerciseth faith, and bringeth forth good works, and prayeth continually without ceasing—unto such it is given to know the mysteries of God. . . ." (Al. 26:22.) . . .

David, the psalmist, learned even as a young man the source of spiritual power. The spirit whispered, "Be still, and know that I am God. . . . The God of Jacob is our refuge." (Ps. 46:10–11.)

Prophets of old learned, as all must know, how to communicate with the Lord by prayer, to talk with and then receive answers in the Lord's own way. . . .

The Lord told Elijah, the prophet: "Go forth, and stand upon the mount before the Lord. And, behold, the Lord passed by, and a great and strong wind rent the mountains, and brake in pieces the rocks before the Lord; but the Lord was not in the wind: and after the wind an earthquake; but the Lord was not in the earthquake:

"And after the earthquake a fire; but the Lord was not in the fire: and after the fire a still small voice.

"And it was so, when Elijah heard it, that he wrapped his face in his mantle, and went out, and stood in the entering in of the cave. . . ." (1 Kings 19:11–13.)

All too often when God speaks in this still, small voice, as he did to Elijah in the cave, it may not be audible to our physical hearing because, like a faulty radio, we may be out of tune with the infinite.

. . . So often today, men and women are living so far apart from things spiritual that when the Lord is speaking to their physical hearing, to their minds with no audible sound, or to them through his authorized servants who, when directed by the Spirit, are as his own voice, they hear only a noise as did they at Jerusalem. Likewise, they receive no inspired wisdom, nor inward assurance, that the mind of the Lord has spoken through his prophet leaders.

. . . Enos, grandson of Lehi, gives us to understand why some can receive a knowledge of the things of God while others cannot. Enos recounts his struggle to obtain a forgiveness of his sins that he might be worthy of his high calling.

He then concludes: "And while I was thus struggling in the spirit, behold, the voice of the Lord came into my mind again, saying: I will visit thy brethren according to their diligence in keeping my commandments. . . ." [Enos 1:10.]

There you have, in simple language, a great principle: It isn't the Lord who withholds himself from us. It is we who withhold ourselves from him because of our failure to keep his commandments.[12]

When we approach the Lord for a blessing we want to make sure that we put ourselves in the state of worthiness to receive that for which we pray.[13]

Wouldn't you like to so live that when God spoke you would be able to hear it, or to be able to be worthy to have a visitation from an angelic visitor, or perhaps to be ready to go into the presence of the Lord? The Lord told us how we could be ready. Here he said in a great revelation these words: "Verily, thus saith the Lord: It shall come to pass that every soul who forsaketh his sins and cometh unto me, and calleth on my name, and obeyeth my voice, and keepeth my commandments, shall see my face and know that I am" (D&C 93:1).

When the voice came from the heavens to people in the land Bountiful they heard it not. It was just to them a confusion of noises, and when they tuned their hearts they could hear words but they couldn't understand; but when with all their hearts and minds they concentrated upon it, then the voice could be understood. (See 3 Nephi 11:3–5.)[14]

God grant that each of us may so live that we may enjoy that communion with Deity through the Holy Ghost, and know without doubt that he does live, and be prepared one day to enter into his presence.[15]

Suggestions for Study and Discussion

- On what matters may we receive revelation? How can we increase our ability to hear the voice of the Lord and "grow into the principle of revelation"?
- What are some of the ways we receive revelation through the still, small voice of the Spirit?

- What are the differences between saying a prayer and talking with God? What does it mean to pray "with real intent"? (Moroni 10:4).

- How does knowing that you are a son or daughter of God affect the way you approach Him in prayer? How does that knowledge enable you to trust Him?

- When you are faced with important decisions, what should you do to receive direction from the Lord? Why does it take courage to act on the promptings of the Spirit?

- How do we sometimes "withhold ourselves" from our Father in Heaven? How can we draw continually nearer to Him in our own lives and in our families?

Notes

1. *Stand Ye in Holy Places* (1974), 139.
2. In Conference Report, Oct. 1966, 115; or *Improvement Era,* Dec. 1966, 1142.
3. *Stand Ye in Holy Places,* 138–42, 144–45.
4. "How Primary Teachers Can Strengthen Their Testimonies," address to the 47th annual Primary conference, 3 Apr. 1953, Historical Department Archives, The Church of Jesus Christ of Latter-day Saints, 6–7.
5. "To Be on Speaking Terms with God," Salt Lake Institute of Religion devotional, 12 Oct. 1973, Historical Library files, The Church of Jesus Christ of Latter-day Saints, 4–5, 7.
6. Address to the Lausanne Switzerland conference, 26 Sept. 1972, Historical Department Archives, The Church of Jesus Christ of Latter-day Saints, 2.
7. *The Teachings of Harold B. Lee,* ed. Clyde J. Williams (1996), 126.
8. *Qualities of Leadership,* address to the Latter-day Saint Student Association convention, Aug. 1970, 5.
9. "Cram for Life's Final Examination," address given at Brigham Young University, 5 Jan. 1954, Historical Department Archives, The Church of Jesus Christ of Latter-day Saints, 9.
10. *Ye Are the Light of the World* (1974), 115, 120.
11. *The Teachings of Harold B. Lee,* 130.
12. In Conference Report, Oct. 1966, 115–17; or *Improvement Era,* Dec. 1966, 1142–43.
13. *The Teachings of Harold B. Lee,* 129.
14. *The Teachings of Harold B. Lee,* 429.
15. In Conference Report, Oct. 1966, 119; or *Improvement Era,* Dec. 1966, 1144.

The Scriptures, "Great Reservoirs of Spiritual Water"

How does diligent study of the scriptures increase our spirituality and lead us toward eternal life?

Introduction

President Harold B. Lee and his wife, Freda Joan Lee, journeyed through Europe and the Holy Land in 1972, teaching missionaries and members the doctrines of the gospel. Elder Gordon B. Hinckley and his wife, Marjorie Pay Hinckley, accompanied them. Sister Hinckley recalled: "It was interesting to see how President Lee moved into a situation. When we met with the missionaries, it was usually in the morning in a chapel filled with full-time and part-time local missionaries. As he stood to address them, he would seldom start with a word of greeting or preliminary remarks but would open the scriptures and begin a discourse. He moved through the scriptures with such ease that sometimes it was difficult to know when the words were his and when he was quoting. After one such meeting I asked him how he had gone about memorizing the scriptures. . . . He thought for a moment and then said, 'I don't think I ever consciously memorized a scripture. I guess I have just worked them through so much that they have become a part of me and my vocabulary.' "[1]

Teachings of Harold B. Lee

Why should we study the scriptures?

Just as water was and is today essential to the physical life . . . , just so is the gospel of the Lord Jesus Christ essential to the spiritual life of God's children. That analogy is suggested by the words of the Savior to the woman at the well in Samaria, when He said:

President Harold B. Lee loved the scriptures and used them to teach
the Saints. He said, "If we're not reading the scriptures daily, our testimonies
are growing thinner, our spirituality isn't increasing in depth."

". . . whosoever drinketh of the water that I shall give him shall never thirst; but the water that I shall give him shall be in him a well of water springing up into everlasting life." (John 4:14.)

Great reservoirs of spiritual water, called scriptures, have been provided in this day and have been safeguarded that all might partake and be spiritually fed, and that they thirst not. That these scriptures have been considered of great importance, is indicated by the words of the Savior, "Search the scriptures; for in them ye think ye have eternal life: and they are they which testify of me" (John 5:39); and the experience of the Nephites being sent back to procure the brass plates which contained the scriptures so vital to the welfare of the people. The use of those scriptures was suggested in the statement of Nephi when he said, ". . . for I did liken all scriptures unto us, that it might be for our profit and learning." (I Nephi 19:23.) . . . Through these generations the messages from our Father have been safeguarded and carefully protected, and mark you likewise that in this day the scriptures are the purest at their source, just as the waters were purest at the mountain source; the purest word of God, and that least apt to be polluted, is that which comes from the lips of the living prophets who are set up to guide Israel in our own day and time.[2]

Our Father has in every dispensation given to us, His children, the holy scriptures by His inspiration to make us wise in overcoming temptation through faith in Him. These scriptures are "profitable for doctrine, for reproof, for correction, for instruction in righteousness: That the man of God may be perfect, throughly furnished unto all good works." (2 Timothy 3:16–17.) So important in the Father's plan of salvation are the scriptures that incidents are recorded wherein God commanded the taking of life to obtain possession of precious writings without which His children would stumble and be blinded by the darkness of the world [see 1 Nephi 4:13].[3]

We have been prone in the last while to be more concerned about reading commentaries about the scriptures. But there is nothing quite so vital as taking those scriptures in our hands and reading them. . . . [T]here is something that's more electric, more spiritual, something that is more deeply meaningful when

I read from the scriptures themselves. . . . There is nothing so vital, so necessary today, as to ingrain in your children a love for the scriptures themselves.[4]

The Master counseled us to search the scriptures, for in them we would find the way to eternal life, for they testify of the way men must travel to gain eternal life with Him and with "the Father which hath sent [Him]" (John 5:30).[5]

How does study of the Book of Mormon help us develop and maintain our spirituality?

It has always seemed to me that the words of the Prophet Joseph Smith in counsel to the brethren, impressing the value of the Book of Mormon, have greater significance than many of us attach to them. His statement was: "I told the brethren that the Book of Mormon was the most correct of any book on earth, and the keystone of our religion, and a man would get nearer to God by abiding by its precepts, than by any other book" (*History of the Church,* 4:461).

To me this means that not only in this volume of scriptures do we have portrayed the accurate truths of the gospel, but also that by this second witness we may know more certainly the meaning of the teachings of the ancient prophets and, indeed, of the Master and His disciples as they lived and taught among men.[6]

If one wants to get close to God, he can do it by reading the Book of Mormon.[7]

You . . . can do nothing better to whet your spiritual appetites and to maintain your spiritual tone than to read and reread year by year the precious things as taught in the Book of Mormon. It was given to us, the fulness of the gospel through the angel Moroni to commit to man. We had, for instance, a story told us by President German E. Ellsworth, who bore his testimony in the temple before all the other mission presidents. He said that years ago while he was presiding over the Northern States Mission he had a dream or a vision in which he had been visiting the Hill Cumorah and was filled with the thoughts of the events that transpired round about that sacred place. There came to him the unmistakable challenge: "Preach to the world the Book of Mormon. It will lead the world to Christ."[8]

If you want to fortify students against . . . the apostate teachings, the so-called higher critics that are going to challenge their faith in the Bible, give them a fundamental understanding of the teachings of the Book of Mormon. Review it again and again.

How long has it been since you have read the Book of Mormon? I was startled a little while ago by interviews with two men who were years ago in our seminary system and both of whom have gone into other teaching positions, who have obtained their graduate degrees. They have slipped away from gospel truths and now have been challenging and quarreling with and trying to destroy and criticize the teachings of the Church.

I have talked with both of them, and when I inquired about their reading the Book of Mormon, one of them said to me: "It has been fourteen years since I have read anything in the Book of Mormon."

Another said, "I can't remember when I last read anything from the Book of Mormon." So it will be with any of us, if we do not continue to saturate ourselves with the teachings of this most precious book which the Lord has given us for a purpose— that is, to correct all of these errors and dissensions in our day just as He promised He would in other days.[9]

I talked with a man who is prominent at our state university. . . . While a member of the Church, he had been insidiously inciting and magnifying the doubts that were intended to destroy the faith of these youngsters. He said, "I haven't been doing it this last quarter, though, Brother Lee."

When I asked, "What has changed you?" he made an interesting confession:

"For twenty years I had never looked at the Book of Mormon, but I was given an assignment in the Church to do something. That assignment took me into the study of the Book of Mormon and the gospel, and I have joined the Church all over again in the last few months. Now when my students come to me, disturbed because of the teachings of philosophy, I say to them in private, 'Now, don't get disturbed. You and I know that the gospel is true and the Church is right.' "[10]

In what ways do the scriptures provide a standard of truth?

Recent years have ushered in educational theories and philosophies that have questioned all the old standards of religion, morality and family relationships. Modern iconoclasts have been at work . . . to destroy faith in the old and trusted authoritative teachings of the scriptures and to [replace them with] the uninspired, man-made ethical doctrines that change with time and place.[11]

I say that we need to teach our people to find their answers in the scriptures. If only each of us would be wise enough to say that we aren't able to answer any question unless we can find a doctrinal answer in the scriptures! And if we hear someone teaching something that is contrary to what is in the scriptures, each of us may know whether the things spoken are false—it is as simple as that. But the unfortunate thing is that so many of us are not reading the scriptures. We do not know what is in them, and therefore we speculate about the things that we ought to have found in the scriptures themselves. I think that therein is one of our biggest dangers of today.

When I meet with our missionaries and they ask questions about things pertaining to the temple, I say to them, as I close the discussion, "I don't dare answer any of your questions unless I can find an answer in the standard works or in the authentic declarations of Presidents of the Church."

The Lord has given us in the standard works the means by which we should measure truth and untruth. May we all heed his word: "Thou shalt take the things which thou hast received, which have been given unto thee in my scriptures for a law, to be my law to govern my church" (D&C 42:59).[12]

Always there is a temptation to go beyond what the Lord has revealed and attempt to use imagination in some cases or to speculate as to these teachings. I wish you would remember that. Don't dare to go beyond what the Lord has revealed. If you don't know, say you don't know; but don't say you don't know when you ought to know, because you ought to be students of the scriptures. Inquiries about the teachings of the gospel of Jesus Christ should be answered, whenever possible, from the scriptures.[13]

We have what no other church has: four great books, the truth of which, if we would read them all, is so clear that we need not be in error. For instance, when we want to know about the interpretation of the parable of the tares as the Lord meant it, all we have to do is read the revelation known as the 86th section of the Doctrine and Covenants and we have the Lord's interpretation. If we want to know something as contained in the teachings of the Beatitudes or the Lord's Prayer, we can read the more correct version in Third Nephi. Many concepts that otherwise would be obscure are made clear and sure in our minds.[14]

Why should we use the scriptures when we teach the gospel?

It is the business of those who are to teach His children to teach the principles of the gospel. We are not set apart to teach notions or guesses at truth. We are not set apart to teach philosophies or sciences of the world. We are set apart to teach the principles of the gospel as found in the four standard works—the Bible, the Book of Mormon, the Doctrine and Covenants, and the Pearl of Great Price.

As we think of that as our limitation, it is our privilege to know those truths and to have the most complete canon of scriptures known to the world. Only members of the Church have that great privilege.[15]

We are convinced that our members are hungry for the gospel, undiluted, with its abundant truths and insights. . . . [L]et us not make the mistake of boring [our members] . . . in our homes or in Church classes by giving them diluted sips of the gospel when they would drink thirstily from the well of living waters! . . . There are those who have seemed to forget that the most powerful weapons the Lord has given us against all that is evil are, by His own declarations, the plain, simple doctrines of salvation as found in the scriptures. We are shocked when we hear that some of our brethren in so-called sophisticated communities . . . have chosen to discard the outlined courses of study in favor of varied dissertations on subjects which have but remote resemblance to fundamental gospel truths.[16]

All that we teach in this Church ought to be couched in the scriptures. . . . We ought to choose our texts from the scriptures, and wherever you have an illustration in the scriptures or a revelation in the Book of Mormon, use it, and do not draw from other sources where you can find it here in these books. We call these the standard Church works because they are standard. If you want to measure truth, measure it by the four standard Church works. . . . If it is not in the standard works, you may well assume that it is speculation. It is man's own personal opinion, to put it another way; and if it contradicts what is in the scriptures, you may know by that same token that it is not true. This is the standard by which you measure all truth. But if you do not know the standards, you have no adequate measure of truth.[17]

I am thinking back . . . about how I was taught the scriptures when I was a Primary child. . . . Remember, faith comes by hearing the word of God, as Paul said [see Romans 10:17]. . . . In my Primary class, I had a great teacher—not great in the sense that she had gone to school and had received degrees for perfection in the science of teaching, pedagogy, but she had a way of believing . . . that in order for her to build faith in us she had to teach us the scriptures.[18]

Are we growing in testimony and spirituality by diligent study of the scriptures?

Are you . . . continually increasing your testimony by diligent study of the scriptures? Do you have a daily habit of reading the scriptures? If we're not reading the scriptures daily, our testimonies are growing thinner, our spirituality isn't increasing in depth. We, ourselves, must be studying the scriptures and have a daily habit.[19]

The way you build spirituality [is] by study of the gospel.[20]

Strive in your homes, and teach others, to take some time of each day to have a quiet hour, meditation. Let there be study of the scriptures at least thirty minutes of each day. At an early morning hour, or at late night, as best suits your schedule, allow yourself an hour of prayerful meditation where you can tune in with God and discuss with Him problems that are too much for human understanding, too great for human strength.[21]

Let no day pass without reading from these sacred books. But it is not enough merely to learn of His life and works by study. It was the Master who replied in answer to the question as to how one might know of Him and His doctrine: "If any man will do his will, he shall know" (John 7:17). Would you think an authority on science to be one who had never experimented in a laboratory? Would you give much heed to the comments of a music critic who did not know music . . . ? Just so, one like yourself who would "know God" must be one who does His will and keeps His commandments and practices the virtues Jesus lived.[22]

We are in the service of the Lord. We have the right to spiritual direction, if we live worthily. God grant that we may so live and study the scriptures, and let this be a reading habit that we indulge in daily, that we not fail of the high appointments for which we have been called in our Father's kingdom.[23]

Suggestions for Study and Discussion

- In what ways are the scriptures as essential to our spiritual life as water is to our physical life? How does study of the scriptures help us overcome temptation?

- In what ways does the Book of Mormon lead us to Jesus Christ? How does the Book of Mormon help us detect truth from error? How has your study of the Book of Mormon influenced your life?

- What experiences have you had with finding answers to your questions in the scriptures?

- When we teach, why is it important to rely on the scriptures and the teachings of the prophets?

- How have you been able to make scripture study a priority in your life? How have you been able to encourage your children or other family members to study the scriptures?

- How does our study of the scriptures increase our ability to fulfill the "high appointments for which we have been called in our Father's kingdom"?

Notes

1. *Glimpses into the Life and Heart of Marjorie Pay Hinckley,* ed. Virginia H. Pearce (1999), 21.
2. In Conference Report, Oct. 1943, 101.
3. *Stand Ye in Holy Places* (1974), 370.
4. *The Teachings of Harold B. Lee,* ed. Clyde J. Williams (1996), 152–53.
5. *The Teachings of Harold B. Lee,* 150.
6. *The Teachings of Harold B. Lee,* 154.
7. *The Teachings of Harold B. Lee,* 155.
8. "Restoration of the Gospel," 1954, Historical Department Archives, The Church of Jesus Christ of Latter-day Saints, 19–20.
9. *The Teachings of Harold B. Lee,* 157.
10. *Ye Are the Light of the World* (1974), 105.
11. *Decisions for Successful Living* (1973), 11.
12. *The Teachings of Harold B. Lee,* 153.
13. *The Teachings of Harold B. Lee,* 154.
14. *Ye Are the Light of the World,* 109.
15. *Ye Are the Light of the World,* 96.
16. *The Teachings of Harold B. Lee,* 450–51.
17. *The Teachings of Harold B. Lee,* 148–49.
18. "How Primary Teachers Can Strengthen Their Testimonies," 47th annual Primary conference, 3 Apr. 1953, Historical Department Archives, The Church of Jesus Christ of Latter-day Saints, 9.
19. Regional representatives' seminar, 12 Dec. 1970, Historical Department Archives, The Church of Jesus Christ of Latter-day Saints, 10.
20. Dedication of the Southern California Region welfare ranch, 6 July 1950, Historical Department Archives, The Church of Jesus Christ of Latter-day Saints.
21. *The Teachings of Harold B. Lee,* 152.
22. *The Teachings of Harold B. Lee,* 150.
23. *The Teachings of Harold B. Lee,* 152.

Joseph Smith, Prophet of the Living God

Why is a testimony of the prophetic mission of Joseph Smith crucial to our testimony of the gospel of Jesus Christ?

Introduction

President Harold B. Lee had a strong testimony of the Prophet Joseph Smith and often used the Prophet's words as he taught gospel principles. He knew that a testimony of the Prophet Joseph Smith's mission is essential to a testimony of the gospel of Jesus Christ. He encountered many people who did not share this testimony of the Prophet. One was a friend who had read the Book of Mormon and spoken of his "reverence for its teachings." President Lee asked him, "Why don't you do something about it? . . . Why don't you join the Church?" The man responded thoughtfully: "I suppose the whole reason is because Joseph Smith is too close to me. If he had lived two thousand years ago, I suppose I would believe. But because he is so close, I guess, is the reason I can't accept." Said President Lee of his friend's response, "Here was a man saying, 'I believe in the dead prophets that lived a thousand-plus years ago, but I have great difficulty believing in a living prophet.' "[1]

In another instance, a woman said, "You know, I could always accept everything in the Church except one thing. . . . I never could accept the fact that Joseph Smith was a Prophet of God." Observed President Lee, "How one could accept the Gospel without accepting him who was the instrument in its restoration, I will never know."[2]

President Lee stated: "We must know for certainty in our hearts and minds that Jesus is the Christ, the Savior of the world.

President Harold B. Lee testified: "I . . . know that Joseph Smith
was a prophet of the living God. I know that he lived and died to bring to
this generation the means by which salvation could be gained."

We must know that this is indeed the Church of Jesus Christ, the kingdom of God on earth in these last days; and finally we must have a testimony that Joseph Smith was a prophet of God."3

Teachings of Harold B. Lee

Why must we have a testimony of Joseph Smith as a prophet of God?

What is it that characterizes a true Prophet of God? First he is God's mouthpiece of that day and to his group. Second, he re-states the ancient truths and seeks to hold the people to unchanging laws of the gospel. Third, he receives additional revelations from the Lord to meet the problems of the progressive unfolding plan. Such new truths emanating from Deity come only through the Prophet of the day. Such a man was Joseph Smith, in every sense a Prophet of God. Yes, truly as [the] Prophet Amos has said, "Surely the Lord God will do nothing, but he revealeth his secret unto his servants the prophets." [Amos 3:7.]4

From the depths of my soul, I . . . know that Joseph Smith was a prophet of the living God. I know that he lived and died to bring to this generation the means by which salvation could be gained. I know that he sits in a high place and holds the keys of this last dispensation. I know that for those who follow him and listen to his teachings and accept him as a true prophet of God and his revelations and teachings as the word of God, the gates of hell will not prevail against them. [See D&C 21:4–6.]5

We must accept the divine mission of the Prophet Joseph Smith as the instrumentality through which the restoration of the gospel and the organization of the Church of Jesus Christ was accomplished. Each member of the Church, to be prepared for the millennial reign, must receive a testimony, each for himself, of the divinity of the work established by Joseph Smith. It was this that was taught plainly by the Saints after the advent of the Savior upon the earth, and one of the leaders in our day has said it again, when he declared, I suppose with reference to the parable of the five foolish and five wise virgins in the Master's parable [see Matthew 25:1–13], "The time will come when no man nor woman will be able to endure on borrowed light. Each will have to be guided by the light within himself." [Orson F. Whitney, *Life of Heber C. Kimball* (1945), 450.][6]

You who have searched deeply into the scriptures, you who have sought to gain a testimony of the divine witness of the Spirit that every one of you has a right to receive by the witness of the Holy Ghost, there can be within you . . . one of the most thrilling of all the experiences that can ever come to you when you can say in your heart, "I know with all my soul now as I have never known to the extent that I know it now that Jesus is the Lord, the Savior of the world, and that Joseph Smith, the martyr, was the prophet whom the Lord used to bring His Church into existence in this day."[7]

How was Joseph Smith prepared for his calling as the Prophet of the Restoration?

Joseph Smith was the one whom the Lord raised up from boyhood and endowed with divine authority and taught the things necessary for him to know and to obtain the priesthood and to lay the foundation for God's kingdom in these latter days.[8]

Historically, prophet leaders were chosen from humble walks of life, not theologically trained in theological seminaries. Call the roll of many of the prophets. I took occasion to go back over history: Elisha was a prosperous farmer; Amos was a shepherd in Judea; the prophet Isaiah was a citizen in Jerusalem; Micah was a Judean villager; Jeremiah was a youth of an ancient priest family; Ezekiel was a priest in the temple; Peter, Andrew, James, and John were fishermen; Jesus and his father Joseph were carpenters. Probably this explains why the Lord chose [the Prophet Joseph Smith as] the prophet leader of this dispensation. . . . He chose one who could be made wise as to the things of God—things which in all likelihood would have been foolishness to those who had been schooled only in the things of the world.[9]

In the life of the boy prophet Joseph Smith, before he was given the outbursting of two of the greatest revelations that have ever been given to man, both of those revelations were preceded by a demonstration of the power of evil—in the Sacred Grove, and on the Hill Cumorah. It seemed to have been necessary that the Prophet was to understand the nature and power of that force in order that he could be prepared to contend successfully against it.[10]

A prophet does not become a spiritual leader by studying books about religion, nor does he become one by attending a theological seminary. . . . One becomes a prophet or a religious leader by actual spiritual contacts. The true spiritual expert thus gets his diploma directly from God.[11]

What great things has the Lord established through the Prophet Joseph Smith?

The mission of the Prophet Joseph Smith was known . . . at least 2,400 years before he was born. The prophecies . . . concerning Moses and Joseph were recorded on the brass plates and obtained from Laban by the sons of Lehi as you will remember. There was found this prophecy which could have made reference to no one other than the Prophet Joseph Smith:

"Yea, Joseph [undoubtedly referring to that Joseph who was sold into Egypt] truly said: Thus saith the Lord unto me: A choice seer will I raise up out of the fruit of thy loins; . . . and unto him will I give power to bring forth my word unto the seed of thy loins—and not to the bringing forth my word only, saith the Lord, but to the convincing them of my word, which shall have already gone forth among them. . . . Behold, that seer will the Lord bless; and they that seek to destroy him shall be confounded. . . . And his name shall be called after me; and it shall be after the name of his father. And he shall be like unto me; for the thing, which the Lord shall bring forth by his hand, by the power of the Lord shall bring my people unto salvation." [See 2 Nephi 3:7, 11, 14–15.][12]

In this dispensation, as has been the case in all previous dispensations of the gospel upon the earth, there was given through the modern prophet, Joseph Smith, the true knowledge of God

With the First Vision, the dispensation of the fulness of times
was ushered in by "a revelation of the personality of God the Father
and the Son" to the Lord's chosen prophet.

and his Son, our Savior, when, as glorified personal beings who
could talk with and be seen of men, they conversed with him, as
though to demonstrate their tangible reality, as the dispensation
of the fulness of times was ushered in, in preparation for the
second coming of the Lord to reign as Lord of lords and King of
kings at the commencement of the millennium.[13]

Whenever we have declined in faith and knowledge the Lord,
in His mercy, has brought back the more complete knowledge of
God and His Son, and whenever we have an outpouring of divine knowledge regarding the Father and the Son we say that we
have had a new dispensation. So it was in the time of Adam; so
it was in the time of Abraham; in the time of Moses; when He
came to the Nephites; to the people of Enoch; and so it was that

the Savior came among men to teach them the relationship of God and the Son of God. . . .

Significant, then, in order to commence the dispensation of the fulness of times, it was ushered in by what? A revelation of the personality of God the Father and the Son to the boy prophet Joseph Smith.[14]

"Joseph Smith, the Prophet and Seer of the Lord, has done more, save Jesus only, for the salvation of men in this world, than any other man that ever lived" (D&C 135:3). Now, some may think that to be an exaggerated statement, but [it is not] when we think of what He gave to us through this marvelous young man who, in a short space of two years, brought forth the great volume of scripture which was a second witness to the mission of the Lord, the Book of Mormon. . . . This young man, without the gift of an educated man, but moved by the power of Almighty God, translated that record from an unknown language into the language we have it today, in the which was to be found the fulness of the everlasting gospel.[15]

Joseph Smith, the young man not schooled in the theologies of the day, not schooled in the high schools of learning of his day . . . [was] one who could be submissive to the teachings and whisperings of the Spirit. Joseph Smith could not have established this church. He could not have brought forth the work of the Lord, the Book of Mormon. They may scoff at the Prophet Joseph Smith as a man. They may question how this church began, but here the thing stands as a monument—the Book of Mormon itself. Joseph, the man, could not have done this, but Joseph, actuated by the power of Almighty God, could and did perform the miraculous service of bringing forth the kingdom out of obscurity in the restored gospel of Jesus Christ.[16]

[Moroni] announced to the Prophet . . . that the time was at hand for the gospel in all its fulness to be preached in power unto all the nations. This was in fulfillment of that which had been promised to John when the angel would fly in the midst of heaven, "having the [fulness of the] everlasting gospel to preach to them that dwell on the earth" (Revelation 14:6). The restoration of that fulness of the gospel was accomplished when the Book of Mormon, which was declared to be a record in which the fulness of the gospel was contained, was restored to the world through the Prophet Joseph Smith.[17]

On the 21st of September 1823 [Moroni appeared to Joseph Smith and declared, in part,] "that the preparatory work for the second coming of the Messiah was speedily to commence; that the time was at hand for the Gospel in all its fullness to be preached in power, unto all nations . . . that a people might be prepared for the Millennial reign," which means for the coming of the Lord (*History of the Church,* 4:537). In other words, the prime purpose for the restoration of the gospel is to prepare a people who will be ready to stand in the presence of the Lord when He comes; otherwise, . . . we could not endure His presence.[18]

Today the work of the kingdom of God in the earth is a monument to the name of the Prophet Joseph Smith. Millions have been caught up by the glory of his mission, as he has proclaimed it and directed it throughout the whole earth. We are the inheritors of that priceless pearl of great price, the gospel of Jesus Christ, which was restored through him as God's instrument, to help us to live, and die if necessary, that we may in due season be prepared for that Millennial reign. This we should never forget. This is the time for us, while there is yet time, to be prepared to meet our God.[19]

Suggestions for Study and Discussion

- How can we each strengthen our testimony of the mission of the Prophet Joseph Smith? What has strengthened your testimony of the Prophet?

- How can we follow the example of the Prophet Joseph to increase our own wisdom and spirituality? What Christlike qualities are evident in the life of the Prophet Joseph Smith?

- What are some of the essential truths of the gospel that were revealed through the Prophet Joseph Smith?

- What has Joseph Smith done for the salvation of all God's children? In what ways is your life different because of the revelations received by the Prophet Joseph Smith?

- How can you share your testimony of the Prophet Joseph Smith with others?

Notes

1. "The Place of the Living Prophet, Seer, and Revelator," address to seminary and institute of religion faculty, Brigham Young University, 8 July 1964, Historical Department Archives, The Church of Jesus Christ of Latter-day Saints, 2–3.

2. "He Lived Great, Died Great in Eyes of God and His People," *Church News,* 10 Dec. 1955, 4.

3. *The Teachings of Harold B. Lee,* ed. Clyde J. Williams (1996), 371.

4. "He Lived Great," 13.

5. *The Teachings of Harold B. Lee,* 371.

6. In Conference Report, Oct. 1956, 62.

7. "Two Great Commemorations," Christmas message to Church Office Building employees, 14 Dec. 1972, Historical Department Archives, The Church of Jesus Christ of Latter-day Saints, 6.

8. In Conference Report, Oct. 1972, 18; or *Ensign,* Jan. 1973, 23.

9. "A Man among Men—A Man of Inspiration," address given on the Fourth Annual David O. McKay Honor Day, 29 Sept. 1968, Historical Department Archives, The Church of Jesus Christ of Latter-day Saints, 12.

10. *The Teachings of Harold B. Lee,* 372.

11. "He Lived Great," 5.

12. "He Lived Great," 5.

13. In Conference Report, Apr. 1969, 132–33; or *Improvement Era,* June 1969, 105.

14. *The Teachings of Harold B. Lee,* 373–74.

15. *The Teachings of Harold B. Lee,* 372.

16. *The Teachings of Harold B. Lee,* 372.

17. *The Teachings of Harold B. Lee,* 374.

18. *The Teachings of Harold B. Lee,* 375.

19. In Conference Report, Munich Germany Area Conference 1973, 7.

This photograph shows the First Presidency sustaining
President Harold B. Lee as the President of the Church at a solemn assembly on
6 October 1972. President N. Eldon Tanner is at the podium, and President
Marion G. Romney is to President Lee's right.

Heeding the True Messenger of Jesus Christ

How can we more faithfully follow the living prophet?

Introduction

Harold B. Lee became the eleventh President of the Church at the passing of President Joseph Fielding Smith in July 1972. Soon thereafter, President Lee visited a room in the Salt Lake Temple where portraits of his ten predecessors were hung. "There, in prayerful meditation," he recalled, "I looked upon the paintings of those men of God—true, pure men, God's noblemen—who had preceded me in a similar calling." He contemplated the character and achievements of each of the prophets of this last dispensation and finally came to the last portrait. "President Joseph Fielding Smith was there with his smiling face, my beloved prophet-leader who made no compromise with truth. . . . He seemed in that brief moment to be passing to me, as it were, a sceptre of righteousness as though to say to me, 'Go thou and do likewise.' . . .

"I know, with a testimony more powerful than sight, that as the Lord declared, 'The keys of the kingdom of God are committed unto man on the earth [from the Prophet Joseph Smith through his successors down to the present], and from thence shall the gospel roll forth unto the ends of the earth.' " [D&C 65:2.][1]

The President of the Church is the only man upon the earth who alone is authorized to exercise all of the keys of the priesthood. A latter-day prophet has taught: "When a President of the Church is ill or not able to function fully in all of the duties of his office, his two Counselors, who with him comprise a Quorum of the First Presidency, carry on the work of the Presidency. Any major questions, policies, programs, or doctrines are prayerfully considered in council by the Counselors in the First Presidency and the Quorum of the Twelve Apostles. No decision emanates from the First Presidency and the Quorum of the Twelve without total unanimity among all concerned. Following this inspired pattern, the Church will move forward without interruption."[2]

As members of the Lord's Church, we can have complete confidence in the guidance of the living prophet, whom President Lee called the "true messenger" of the Lord. President Lee taught that "if the children of the Lord, which includes all who are upon this earth, regardless of nationality, color, or creed, will heed the call of the true messenger of the gospel of Jesus Christ, . . . each may in time see the Lord and know that He is."[3]

By following the Prophet of the Lord, we may arrive safely at our ultimate destination—the presence of our Father in Heaven.

Teachings of Harold B. Lee

In what ways is the President of the Church the keeper of the Lord's kingdom?

Keep in mind that the head of this church is not the President of the Church. The head of this church is the Lord and Master, Jesus Christ, who reigns and rules. . . . In all this turmoil we can be sure that He is guiding, lest we forget.[4]

"[Jesus] is the head of the body, the Church: who is the beginning, the firstborn from the dead; that in all things he might have the preeminence." (Colossians 1:18.) It is true, however, that in each dispensation when his gospel has been upon the earth and his Church has been established, the Lord has appointed and has vested authority in one man at a time in each such dispensation who has borne the title of president of the Church, or prophet, seer and revelator to the Church. Such titles, or the conferring of such authority, does not make of one "the Head of the Church," which title belongs to Jesus Christ. It does make of him, however, God's mouthpiece and the one who acts in God's stead and through whom he speaks to his people by way of instruction, to give or to withhold principles and ordinances, or to warn of judgments. . . .

. . . The president of the Church is the keeper of the Lord's House or Kingdom. Into his hands are committed the keys to every part. At the Lord's direction he gives keys of authority to other members of the Church to baptize, to preach the gospel, to lay hands on the sick, to preside or to teach in various offices. To a few only he gives the authority to officiate in the ordinances of the temples or to perform marriages therein "to bind on earth and in heaven."[5]

A prophet is an inspired and divinely appointed revealer and interpreter of God's mind and will. He has held the keys to the kingdom of God in our day, such as were given to Peter as the earthly head of the Church in his day.[6]

May I read to you something that has been written [by President J. Reuben Clark Jr.] for another occasion: "We must have in mind . . . that only the President of the Church, the Presiding High Priest, . . . has the right to receive revelations for the Church, either new or amendatory, or to give authoritative interpretations of scriptures that shall be binding on the Church. . . . He is God's sole mouthpiece on earth for the Church of Jesus Christ of Latter-day Saints, the only true Church. He alone may declare the mind and will of God to his people. No officer of any other Church in the world has this high right and lofty prerogative." [*Church News,* 31 July 1954, 10.][7]

The only one authorized to bring forth any new doctrine is the President of the Church, who, when he does, will declare it as a revelation from God, and it will be so accepted by the Council of the Twelve and sustained by the body of the Church.[8]

How is the President of the Church chosen?

To those who ask the question: How is the President of the Church chosen or elected? the correct and simple answer should be a quotation of the fifth article of faith: "We believe that a man must be called of God, by prophecy, and by the laying on of hands by those who are in authority, to preach the Gospel and administer in the ordinances thereof."

The beginning of the call of one to be President of the Church actually begins when he is called, ordained, and set apart to become a member of the Quorum of the Twelve Apostles. Such a call by prophecy, or in other words, by the inspiration of the Lord to the one holding the keys of presidency, and the subsequent ordination and setting apart by the laying on of hands by that same authority, places each Apostle in a priesthood quorum of twelve men holding the apostleship.

Each Apostle so ordained under the hands of the President of the Church, who holds the keys of the kingdom of God in concert with all other ordained Apostles, has given to him the priesthood authority necessary to hold every position in the Church, even to a position of presidency over the Church if he were called by the presiding authority and sustained by a vote of a constituent assembly of the membership of the Church.

. . . Immediately following the death of a President, the next ranking body, the Quorum of the Twelve Apostles, becomes the presiding authority, with the President of the Twelve automatically becoming the acting President of the Church until a President of the Church is officially ordained and sustained in his office. . . .

All members of the First Presidency and the Twelve are regularly sustained as "prophets, seers, and revelators." . . . This means that any one of the Apostles, so chosen and ordained, could preside over the Church if he were "chosen by the body [which has been interpreted to mean the entire Quorum of the Twelve], appointed and ordained to that office, and upheld by the confidence, faith, and prayer of the church," to quote from a revelation on this subject, on one condition, and that being that he was the senior member, or the President, of that body (see D&C 107:22).[9]

When I sat in as a younger member of the Council of the Twelve, the first Church reorganization I was permitted to participate in was when President [Heber J.] Grant passed away. . . . As the [new] President named his counselors and they took their places at the head of the room, down inside me I had a witness that these were the men that the Lord wanted to be the Presidency of the Church. It came to me with a conviction that was as though that truth was being trumpeted in my ears.

. . . Until the members of this church have that conviction that they are being led in the right way, and they have a conviction that these men of God are men who are inspired and have been properly appointed by the hand of God, they are not truly converted.[10]

[The Lord] reveals the law and He elects, chooses, or appoints the officers and holds the right to reprove, correct, or even to remove them at His pleasure. Hence the necessity of a constant [communication] by direct revelation between Him and His Church. As a precedent for the foregoing facts, we refer to the examples of all ages as recorded in the scriptures. This order of government began in Eden. God appointed Adam to govern the earth and gave him law. It was perpetuated in a regular succession from Adam to Noah and from Noah to Melchizedek, Abraham, Isaac, Jacob, Joseph, Moses, Samuel the prophet, John, Jesus, and His Apostles, all and each of which were chosen by the Lord and not by the people.

It is true the people have a voice in the government of the kingdom of God, but they do not confer the authority in the first place, nor can they take it away. For instance: The people did not elect the twelve Apostles of Jesus Christ, nor could they by popular vote deprive them of their apostleship. As the government of the kingdom anciently existed, so is it now restored. The people did not choose the great modern Prophet and Apostle Joseph Smith, but God chose him, in the usual way that He has chosen others before him—namely by open vision and by His own voice from the heavens.[11]

I have a consciousness as I have thought through this responsibility [as prophet] and have been close enough to the Brethren over the years, that one in this position is under the constant surveillance of Him in whose service we are. Never would He permit one in this position to lead this church astray. You can be sure of that. When I think of the process by which a man comes to leadership position in the Church, I think of my own experience for thirty-one and a half years, and all the circumstances which have come in my own life—what an overwhelming training program! When the change in the First Presidency came, I contrasted it with the way political parties bring a president of the United States to office, or the inauguration of a king, to see how, by the Lord's plan, these changes are made without rancor, without bickering. The plan is set and the Lord makes no mistakes, so He has told us.[12]

Why must we follow the prophet?

Now, may this be the day for us to reflect seriously, to remember what the Lord has already told us. His prophet is upon the earth today, and if you want to know the last revelation that has come to this people, you get down the last conference report and read carefully especially what the First Presidency said. . . . You will have the best and the last word that has been given from our Heavenly Father. We don't have to depend solely upon what is in the standard Church works. In addition to what the scriptures have told us, we have what the prophets today are telling us here and now, and it is for us if we want to be saved on Zion's hill, when these perils come, to hear and obey.[13]

So often today when our brethren do speak authoritatively, we have some who rise up to challenge and say, "Now, just where can I find some authority that you can cite for what you are saying?" We are tempted to say, "You go back and read the speech of the present leader of the Church on this subject, and you have all the authority that you should look for, because this is the Lord's way. His prophet is here, and revelation is just as needed and is just as much in evidence as it has been in any time in any dispensation of the gospel upon the earth."[14]

Now the only safety we have as members of this church is to do exactly what the Lord said to the Church in that day when the Church was organized. We must learn to give heed to the words and commandments that the Lord shall give through His prophet, "as he receiveth them, walking in all holiness before me; . . . as if from mine own mouth, in all patience and faith" (D&C 21:4–5). There will be some things that take patience and faith. You may not like what comes from the authority of the Church. It may contradict your political views. It may contradict your social views. It may interfere with some of your social life. But if you listen to these things, as if from the mouth of the Lord Himself, with patience and faith, the promise is that "the gates of hell shall not prevail against you; yea, and the Lord God will disperse the powers of darkness from before you, and cause the heavens to shake for your good, and his name's glory" (D&C 21:6).[15]

To you Latter-day Saints everywhere, that promise [in D&C 21:4–6] will be yours if you will follow the leadership the Lord has placed within the Church, giving heed to their counsel in patience and faith.[16]

Look to the President of the Church for your instructions. If ever there is a conflict, you keep your eyes on the President if you want to walk in the light.[17]

If our people want to be safely guided during these [troubled] times of deceit and false rumors, they must follow their leaders and seek for the guidance of the Spirit of the Lord in order to avoid falling prey to clever manipulators who, with cunning sophistry, seek to draw attention and gain a following to serve their own notions and sometimes sinister motives.[18]

Now there were a lot of people in the days of the Master who did not accept Him as the Son of God. There were some who said, "Oh, He is just the son of Joseph, the carpenter." Others said, "He is a Prince of Beelzebub," which means the son of the devil. When He performed some of these miraculous things they said, "He is a winebibber," meaning he had just been drinking strong wine. There were only a very few who could say, "Thou art the Christ, the Son of the living God." (Matthew 16:16.) Why couldn't everybody see Him as the Son of God?

We sing, "I wish I could have been with Him then, when He took little babes in His arms." [See "I Think When I Read That Sweet Story," *Children's Songbook,* 56.] A lot of our people would not have accepted Him any more then than they can accept the doctrines that come from the teachers of righteousness inspired by that same Savior. When we cannot accept those who represent Him here, it would not be a bit easier to accept the Master Himself, were He to appear. . . .

When I was on my mission, a group of us missionaries went with our mission president once to Carthage Jail. Impressed by the atmosphere of the place where the Prophet and his brother

Hyrum met their martyrdom, we asked him to recount the incidents that led up to the martyrdom. I was deeply impressed when the mission president said this: "When the Prophet Joseph Smith died, there were many who died spiritually with him. So has it been with every change of administration in the kingdom of God. When Brigham Young died, there were many who died with him spiritually, and so with John Taylor, and the passing of every President of the Church." . . .

Sometimes we die spiritually and cut ourselves off from pure spiritual light and forget that today, here and now, we have a prophet.[19]

The place of these heaven-endowed messengers who represent the Lord in every dispensation of the gospel upon the earth may be illustrated by an incident related by a traveler in northern Europe. Our traveler was leaving by boat from Stockholm, Sweden, traveling out into the Baltic Sea. To do so, the boat had to pass through a thousand or more islands. Standing on the forward deck, the traveler found himself becoming impatient because of what seemed to him to be a careless course. Why not a course near to this island or another and more interesting than the one the pilot had chosen? Almost in exasperation he was saying to himself, "What's wrong with the old pilot? Has he lost his sense of direction?" Suddenly he was aware of markers along the charted course which appeared as mere broom handles sticking up in the water. Someone had carefully explored these channels and had charted the safest course for ships to take. So it is in life's course on the way to immortality and eternal life: "God's engineers," by following a blueprint made in heaven, have charted the course for safest and happiest passage and have forewarned us of the danger areas.[20]

The Lord will prompt His servants to lead His church aright. His prophets will receive the inspiration of the Lord to say to the membership of the Church, "This is the way, walk ye in it" (Isaiah 30:21). Even in times of the crises which come in the days in which we live, as have been depicted in modern revelation, the picture the Lord would have us see is one of stability and solidarity. You remember He said to His disciples, "But my disciples shall stand in holy places, and shall not be moved" (D&C 45:32).[21]

Suggestions for Study and Discussion

- Who is the true Head of the Church? Through whom does the Lord give direction and instruction to His Church?

- How is new doctrine brought forth to the Church?

- How is the President of the Church prepared for his great responsibilities? How does the Lord direct the choosing of the Presidents of His Church?

- What counsel given by the living prophet has particularly blessed your life?

- Why do you think that some people honor prophets of the past but fail to honor the living prophet? What are the consequences of failing to heed the words of the living prophet or of challenging his authority?

- What promises are made to those who heed the words and commandments of the living prophet?

Notes

1. In Conference Report, Oct. 1972, 18–20; or *Ensign*, Jan. 1973, 23–25.

2. Howard W. Hunter, in Conference Report, Oct. 1994, 6–7; or *Ensign*, Nov. 1994, 7.

3. *The Teachings of Harold B. Lee*, ed. Clyde J. Williams (1996), 522.

4. *The Teachings of Harold B. Lee*, 527.

5. *Decisions for Successful Living* (1973), 103, 105.

6. *The Teachings of Harold B. Lee*, 531.

7. Conference talk with Cambridge Institute, 10 May 1970, Historical Library files, The Church of Jesus Christ of Latter-day Saints, 8.

8. *The Teachings of Harold B. Lee*, 543–44.

9. *The Teachings of Harold B. Lee*, 534–35.

10. *The Teachings of Harold B. Lee*, 542–43.

11. *The Teachings of Harold B. Lee*, 547–48; paragraphing added.

12. *The Teachings of Harold B. Lee*, 535–36.

13. *The Teachings of Harold B. Lee*, 471.

14. *The Teachings of Harold B. Lee*, 428–29.

15. *The Teachings of Harold B. Lee*, 525–26.

16. *The Teachings of Harold B. Lee*, 529.

17. *The Teachings of Harold B. Lee*, 532.

18. *The Teachings of Harold B. Lee*, 437.

19. *Ye Are the Light of the World* (1974), 31, 34–35.

20. *The Teachings of Harold B. Lee*, 534.

21. *The Teachings of Harold B. Lee*, 545.

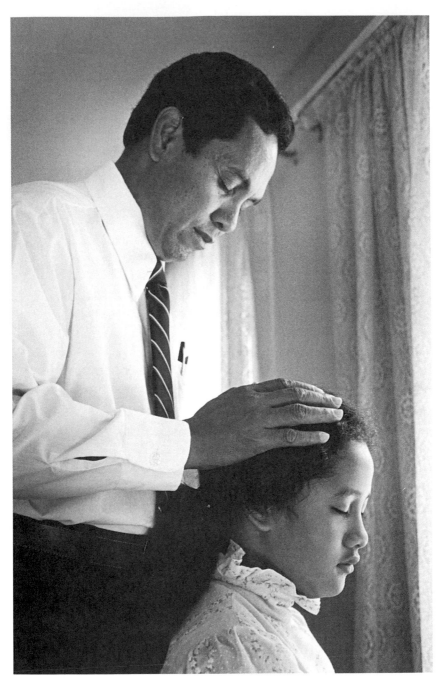

President Harold B. Lee counseled priesthood holders, "Prepare yourselves as clean and pure vessels so that the power of Almighty God may be manifested through you as you officiate in the sacred ordinances of the priesthood."

○○○

Loving, Faithful Priesthood Service

How can loving, faithful priesthood service bless all Church members?

Introduction

President Harold B. Lee told the following story about the Salt Lake Temple: "When the great Salt Lake Temple was being planned, Truman O. Angell, the architect, was asked to write an article . . . and give the people of the Church something of an idea what the temple, when completed, would look like. . . . Among other things, he referred to something that you will find on the west end of the temple. . . . Underneath the center spire on the west end, near the tabernacle, you will find what is referred to in the star constellations as the Dipper. You will note that the pointers of the Dipper are looking up towards a bright star which we usually call the North Star. When Truman O. Angell described what would be found in that place, he said, 'This was to signify that through the priesthood the lost may find their way.' "

President Lee then emphasized, "Through the priesthood and only the priesthood may we, as the sons and daughters of God, find our way back home."[1]

Teachings of Harold B. Lee

What is the priesthood?

There are two concepts that over the years have been expressed in defining the meaning of priesthood. One is that priesthood is the authority given by our Heavenly Father to man to authorize him to officiate in all matters pertaining to the salvation of mankind upon the earth. The other concept is expressed by another meaningful thought that priesthood is the power by which God works through man.[2]

The priesthood of God is here and has been handed down since the restoration of the Church through messengers who were sent to restore that authority that the ordinances of salvation might be administered to all the faithful of the earth. The priesthood of God holds the keys of salvation.[3]

The Master told Peter and the other apostles of a power beyond that of man which he called the "keys of the kingdom of heaven," and by this power he said, "Whatsoever thou shalt bind on earth shall be bound in heaven." (Matt. 16:19.) That power and authority, by which holy ordinances are administered, is known as the holy priesthood and is always to be found in the Church of Jesus Christ in every dispensation of the gospel upon the earth.[4]

[The priesthood] is the authority to administer in the ordinances according to the pattern which [the Lord] had revealed. This power . . . is the right delegated to man by the Lord to act in His name for the salvation of the souls of men. . . .

One of the purposes of [the] higher priesthood was to administer in the ordinances, to give to mankind that knowledge of God which the Master declared was necessary and which the Apostle Paul, in speaking of the organization of the Church, said was necessary to come to "the knowledge of the Son of God, unto a perfect man." [Ephesians 4:13.] And again there is that power of the lesser priesthood to officiate in other ordinances, such as these young men so beautifully administering to and passing the sacrament this evening. The Aaronic Priesthood, the Lord said, is the priesthood "which holds the keys of the ministering of angels, and of the gospel of repentance, and of baptism by immersion for the remission of sins," [D&C 13:1] and the law of carnal commandments. And so . . . the priesthood [is] necessary for the express purpose of giving power to those called to administer in the ordinances necessary to achieve the salvation the Lord has designed for His purpose.[5]

The Lord does reign in the midst of his Saints through his priesthood, which he delegates to man.[6]

How should the priesthood be used?

In a great revelation we know as the 121st section of the Doctrine and Covenants, given through the inspiration of the Lord to the Prophet Joseph Smith, the Lord said some very significant things. He said the priesthood could only be controlled upon the principles of righteousness, and that if we were to use our priesthood office improperly "to cover our sins, or to gratify our pride, our vain ambition, or to exercise control or dominion or compulsion . . . the Spirit of the Lord is grieved." (See D&C 121:37.) . . .

The penalty if we do use our priesthood unrighteously is that the heavens withdraw themselves and the Spirit of the Lord is grieved. When we lose the Spirit, our priesthood authority is taken from us and we are left to ourselves "to kick against the pricks," when we are being irritated by the admonitions and instructions of our leaders. Then we begin to persecute the saints, which means criticize, and finally to fight against God, and the powers of darkness overtake us if we do not repent and turn from that evil course. [See D&C 121:37–38.]

The qualities of acceptable priesthood leadership are also carefully defined in this revelation. One is to preside over the Church with patience and long-suffering, with gentleness and meekness, with love unfeigned. If one must discipline and reprove with sharpness, he must do it when moved upon by the Holy Ghost and then show forth afterwards an increase of love, lest the one whom he has reproved would think him to be an enemy. [See D&C 121:41–43.] In all our priesthood callings we must never forget that the business of the church and kingdom of God is to save souls, and that all over whom we preside are our Father's children, and He will aid us in our endeavors to save every one.

There is a classic example of how our Lord would have us minister to those who need our aid. When Peter and John, as recorded in the book of the Acts of the Apostles, approached a man who had never walked and who was at the gates of the temple begging alms, instead of giving him money, the apostle Peter, you will remember, said to him, "Silver and gold have I none; but such as I have give I thee: In the name of Jesus Christ of Nazareth rise up and walk." (Acts 3:6.)

Then followed a significant statement in the record of that incident. Peter took him by the right hand and lifted him up. [See Acts 3:7.] Remember that it wasn't enough for Peter to command him to walk; he then took him by the hand and lifted him up.

So must we, in dealing with our faltering saints, not be merely priesthood holders who criticize, scold, and condemn. We must, like the apostle Peter, take them by the arm, encourage them, and give them a sense of security and respect for themselves until they can rise above their difficulties and can stand on their own feet.

That is the way the priesthood of God can bring salvation and fellowship to those who are weak, that they may become strong.[7]

Our success . . . will be measured in part by our capacity to love those whom we seek to lead and to serve. When we truly love others it can eliminate the bad motives that often prevail in human relationships. When we truly love others we will act in their eternal interests and not to meet our own ego needs.[8]

How can priesthood holders "be about [their] Father's business"?

As a young boy of twelve years, Jesus, after having been found in the temple by Joseph and Mary, in response to their inquiry asked a significant question: "Wist ye not that I must be about my Father's business?" (Luke 2:49.) What did he mean by His Father's business?

In another revelation the Lord gave meaning to that young boy's question. To the elders of the Church assembled in Kirtland, Ohio, He impressed upon them their great responsibilities as holders of the sacred priesthood office of elder. "Wherefore," said he, "as ye are agents, ye are on the Lord's errand; and what-

Each priesthood holder should "think of his calling
as though he were on the Lord's errand. That is what it means
to magnify the priesthood."

ever ye do according to the will of the Lord is the Lord's business." (D&C 64:29.)

When one becomes a holder of the priesthood, he becomes an agent of the Lord. He should think of his calling as though he were on the Lord's errand. That is what it means to magnify the priesthood. Think of the Master asking each of you, as this young boy did of Joseph and Mary, Wist ye not that I must be about my Father's business? Whatever you do according to the will of the Lord is the Lord's business.[9]

When we officiate in the name of the Lord, as holders of the priesthood, we are doing it in the name and in behalf of our Heavenly Father. Priesthood is the power by which our Heavenly Father works through men. . . .

. . . I am afraid that some of our elders do not understand this, that when they are officiating as elders of the Church . . . or as high priests, it is as though when they perform the ordinance, the Lord through them is acting upon the heads of those for whom they minister. I have often thought one of the reasons why we are not magnifying our priesthood is because we don't understand that as holders of the priesthood, He is working through us by the power of the holy priesthood, and I would wish that we could all have that feeling, and so teach our young people what it means to hold the priesthood and to magnify it.[10]

What does it mean to have hands laid upon your head? Let me take you to the thirty-sixth section of the Doctrine and Covenants and read to you a verse that you may have skimmed over and haven't seen the significance of. This is a revelation given through Joseph Smith the Prophet to Edward Partridge, the first Presiding Bishop. This is what the Lord said: "And I will lay my hand upon you [Edward Partridge] by the hand of my servant Sidney Rigdon, and you shall receive my Spirit, the Holy Ghost, even the Comforter, which shall teach you the peaceable things of the kingdom" (D&C 36:2).

Do you see what He is saying—that whenever you perform a service by the authority of your priesthood it is as though the Lord were placing His hand on that person by your hand in order for you to bestow the blessings of life, of health, of priesthood, or whatever it may be. And whenever we exercise our priesthood, we are doing it as though the Lord were there with us, and through us, helping us to perform that ordinance.[11]

Now, to you who are male members of the Church: You have a right to hold what is called the priesthood of God. . . . Some have hands laid upon their head to receive this power and this authority, but never receive it. And why can't they receive it? The Lord has told us two things: because their hearts are set so much upon the things of this world, and second, they aspire so much to the honors of men (see D&C 121:35). Will you think back to those of your acquaintance and see why it is that some fall by the wayside in spiritual matters, and you will find the answer in one of those two things. Either their hearts were set so much upon the things of this world—was it money? was it social position? was it things in the educational world?—or were they aspiring so much to the honors of men that they couldn't be bothered with things in the Church. Yes, if you would be leaders in the Church and hold these . . . privileges, you must pay the price.[12]

Brethren, in your hands is given a sacred trust not only to have the authority to act in the name of the Lord, but to so prepare yourselves as clean and pure vessels so that the power of Almighty God may be manifested through you as you officiate in the sacred ordinances of the priesthood. Never take your priesthood into places where you would be ashamed to have the President of the Church see you.[13]

We must say, "Because I am a holder of the priesthood of the living God, I am a representative of our Heavenly Father and hold the priesthood by which He can work through me; I can't stoop to do some of the things that I might have done otherwise because of my fellowship with the priesthood of God." . . .

Brethren, we look to you to carry the banner of the holy priesthood of God. . . . Let us have our eyes fixed on the eternal value of things, with an eye single to the glory of God, and say each to himself, that "from now on, God being my helper, I am not going to engage in any activity unless it helps me to move myself further toward that goal of eternal life, eventually to return back to the presence of my Heavenly Father."[14]

Brethren of the priesthood, when you are called to a position, you fathers in the home, you have a right to have the blessings of the priesthood, and you have a right to have the revelations of the Spirit to guide and direct you if you are living so that the Lord can open the windows of heaven to you and give you direction in the specific callings to which you are called. Brethren, in order to receive that, you have to live for it. You have to qualify.[15]

Remember those marvelous promises of the Lord to you if you would be full of charity to all men and "let virtue garnish thy thoughts unceasingly; then shall thy confidence wax strong in the presence of God; and the doctrine of the priesthood shall distil upon thy soul as the dews from heaven.

"The Holy Ghost shall be thy constant companion, and thy scepter an unchanging scepter of righteousness and truth; and thy dominion shall be an everlasting dominion, and without compulsory means it shall flow unto thee forever and ever." (D&C 121:45–46.)

Those inspired words were from the Lord, and I repeat them as a reminder to each of you of your responsibilities as holders of the priesthood and the great blessings which will be yours if you magnify your callings as servants of the Most High God.[16]

How are all Church members blessed as priesthood holders serve in righteousness?

The priesthood holders are in truth the watchmen upon the towers of Zion. You are they who are set to preside over any branch of the Church and to be alert to the dangers that beset the world, both the seen and the unseen. You are a few of the priesthood holders as the shepherds of the flocks, flocks of Church members everywhere. Your responsibilities are many. You must fellowship new members as they come into the Church; search out the honest seekers after truth and bring them in contact with the missionaries; be continually mindful of the needs of the fatherless and the widows. Particularly, to do that and to keep yourselves unspotted from the world, as the apostle James said, is "pure religion and undefiled." (James 1:27.) You are to see that iniquity does not abound and to see that all members are motivated to become active in the Church. You are to teach correct principles in order that members, leaders, and teachers know how to govern themselves. . . .

You who are presiding authorities are charged with the responsibility to the flock, or the branches, districts, wards, or stakes over which you preside. You should be as fathers, carefully and constantly teaching fathers the responsibility of looking over their own families and extending themselves as called to the various responsibilities in the Church, to be defenders of the faith.[17]

The real strength of this church lies in the power and authority of the holy priesthood which our Heavenly Father has given to us in this day. If we exercise properly that power and magnify our callings in the priesthood, we will see to it that the missionary work shall go forward, that the tithing shall be paid, that the welfare plan shall prosper, that our homes shall be safe, and that morality among the youth of Israel shall be safeguarded.[18]

Some years ago I went to a stake conference where the Manti Temple is located down in southern Utah. It was a dark, stormy night and it was snowing. As we left our meetings and went to the home of the stake president, we stopped there in the car and looked up at the temple situated high on a hill. As we sat impressed by the sight of that beautifully lighted temple shining through the snowy and dark night, the stake president said something to me that was very meaningful. He said, "That temple, lighted as it is, is never more beautiful than in a storm or when there is a dense fog." To understand the importance of that, may I say to you that never is the gospel of Jesus Christ more important to you than in a storm or when you are having great difficulty. Never is the power of the priesthood, which you hold, more wonderful than when there is a crisis in your home, a serious illness, or some great decision that has to be made, or there is a great threat of flood, or fire, or famine of some kind. Vested in the power of the priesthood, which is the power of Almighty God, is the power to perform miracles if the Lord wills it so, but in order for us to use that priesthood, we must be worthy to exercise it. A failure to understand this principle is a failure to receive the blessings of holding that great priesthood.[19]

Suggestions for Study and Discussion

- How does the priesthood help us "find our way back home" to our Heavenly Father?

- Why is it important for priesthood holders to remember that the priesthood should be used to save souls and minister to those in need? In the account found in Acts 3:1–9, how did Peter and John set an example of righteous use of priesthood power?

- What can we learn from Doctrine and Covenants 121:41–44 about how priesthood holders should exercise the priesthood?

- Why must priesthood holders be righteous if they are to give faithful priesthood service? According to President Lee, what is the penalty for failing to use the priesthood righteously?
- As a priesthood holder, how can the knowledge that you are on the Lord's errand help you magnify your priesthood callings?
- How can sisters help priesthood holders to magnify their priesthood callings?
- What are some particular ways in which your life has been blessed by priesthood power?

Notes

1. *Be Loyal to the Royal within You,* Brigham Young University Speeches of the Year (20 Oct. 1957), 1–2.
2. *Stand Ye in Holy Places* (1974), 251–52.
3. In Conference Report, Munich Germany Area Conference 1973, 8.
4. *Decisions for Successful Living* (1973), 123.
5. Address to Mutual Improvement Association, 1948, Historical Department Archives, The Church of Jesus Christ of Latter-day Saints, 2.
6. In Conference Report, Oct. 1972, 64; or *Ensign,* Jan. 1973, 63.
7. *Stand Ye in Holy Places,* 253–55.
8. *The Teachings of Harold B. Lee,* ed. Clyde J. Williams (1996), 481.
9. *Stand Ye in Holy Places,* 255.
10. In Conference Report, Apr. 1973, 129; or *Ensign,* July 1973, 98.
11. *The Teachings of Harold B. Lee,* 487–88.
12. *The Teachings of Harold B. Lee,* 487.
13. *The Teachings of Harold B. Lee,* 501.
14. In Conference Report, Oct. 1973, 115, 120; or *Ensign,* Jan. 1974, 97, 100–101.
15. *The Teachings of Harold B. Lee,* 488.
16. *Stand Ye in Holy Places,* 256–57.
17. In Conference Report, Munich Germany Area Conference 1973, 68.
18. *The Teachings of Harold B. Lee,* 486–87.
19. *The Teachings of Harold B. Lee,* 488.

Priceless Riches of the Holy Temple

How can we better prepare ourselves to receive the blessings of the temple and provide these blessings to others?

Introduction

In March 1956, at the dedication of the Los Angeles California Temple, President Harold B. Lee repeated a father's story about his son who had been assigned to fly dangerous missions during a war.

"[The] father said to him, 'Son, how were you able to get back safely to your home base . . . ?' The boy said, 'Oh, that is easy, Dad, I just fly the beam.' But the father pursued the question by asking, 'Suppose you have lost the beam and something has gone wrong with that radio equipment by which the flyer learns to fly his course.' 'Oh,' he said, 'I would use my compass.' 'Well, suppose a shot has destroyed the compass; then what?'

"The boy [pondered] thoughtfully and then he said, 'Dad, I would begin to fly my plane higher and higher above the smoke and fog and dust of the earth until I got up where I could see the stars, and when I had flown that high, I would chart my course by the stars. That never failed and I could always find my way back home.' "

President Lee continued: "Down here on the earth outside of His sacred presence there are the things that money can buy, there are the things that we call the honors of men and the things that we strive for and seem to think are most important. But [the temple] is where we climb high above the smoke and the fog of these earthly things and we learn to read by God's eternal stars a course that will lead us safely back home."[1]

Teachings of Harold B. Lee

What blessings can we receive in the house of the Lord?

We come [to the temple], as I think of it, to receive the fullness of the blessings of the Priesthood. . . .

We come here to this Holy House to learn, to know God as he really is, and just how each of us, for ourselves, might obtain an exaltation in his presence. . . .

It is here we begin to lay the foundation stones of an eternal heavenly home, for here in this Church is the power to bind on earth that the same might be bound in Heaven.[2]

Somehow we must get across the fact to all our people, young and old, that in our holy temples the temple endowment is the sure guide to happiness here and eternal life in the world to come.[3]

When you enter a holy temple, you are by that course gaining fellowship with the Saints in God's eternal kingdom, where time is no more. In the temples of your God you are endowed not with a rich legacy of worldly treasure, but with a wealth of eternal riches that are above price.

The temple ceremonies are designed by a wise Heavenly Father who has revealed them to us in these last days as a guide and a protection throughout our lives, that you and I might not fail to merit exaltation in the celestial kingdom, where God and Christ dwell.

May you strive diligently and be guided to prepare yourselves to gain these priceless riches in the house of the Lord.[4]

We have two classes of revelation: There are revelations which might be said to be open revelations, like those written in the Doctrine and Covenants and elsewhere, which may be given to the world. And then we have what we might speak of as closed revelations. These are to be divulged and given only in sacred places which are prepared for the revealing of the highest ordinances which belong to the Aaronic and to the Melchizedek Priesthoods, and those ordinances are in the house of the Lord.[5]

As early as 1841, the Lord revealed to Joseph Smith that "there is not a place found on earth that he may come to and restore

As we prepare to attend the temple, we should remember
President Harold B. Lee's counsel: "May you who come here come with
sanctified hearts, with eyes and minds and hearts single to God so
that you will feel His presence."

again that which was lost unto you, or which he hath taken away, even the fulness of the priesthood. . . .

"For I deign to reveal unto my church things which have been kept hid from before the foundation of the world, things that pertain to the dispensation of the fulness of times." (D&C 124:28, 41.)

These revelations, which are reserved for and taught only to the faithful Church members in sacred temples, constitute what are called the "mysteries of Godliness." The Lord said He had given to Joseph "the keys of the mysteries, and the revelations which are sealed. . . ." (D&C 28:7.) As a reward to the faithful, the Lord promised: "And to them will I reveal all mysteries, yea, all the hidden mysteries of my kingdom from days of old. . . ." (D&C 76:7.) . . .

In the writings of the Prophet Joseph Smith there is found an explanation of these so-called mysteries that are embodied in what the Prophet speaks of as the holy endowment. He said in part:

"I spent the day in the upper part of the store, that is in my private office . . . in council with [then he names several of the early leaders], instructing them in the principles and order of the Priesthood, attending to washings, anointings, endowments and the communication of keys pertaining to the Aaronic Priesthood, and so on to the highest order of the Melchizedek Priesthood, setting forth the order pertaining to the Ancient of Days, and all those plans and principles by which any one is enabled to secure the fullness of those blessings which have been prepared for the Church of the Firstborn, and come up and abide in the presence of the Eloheim in the eternal worlds." (*Teachings of the Prophet Joseph Smith,* p. 237.)

President Brigham Young, at the laying of the cornerstone for the Salt Lake Temple, added this further enlightenment as to the meaning of the endowment and the purpose of temple building with relation thereto:

". . . Your endowment is, to receive all those ordinances in the house of the Lord, which are necessary for you, after you have departed this life, to enable you to walk back to the presence of the Father, passing the angels who stand as sentinels, . . . and gain your eternal exaltation in spite of earth and hell." [*Discourses of Brigham Young,* sel. John A. Widtsoe (1954), 416.][6]

How can we serve as "saviors on Mount Zion" for those who have died?

If the acceptance of the gospel is so essential to the welfare of man's eternal soul, you may well ask what is to become of the millions who have died without a knowledge of the gospel or the Lord's plan, by which the full effect of his atonement might be realized. If missionary work were to have been limited only to mortality, many souls would have been condemned without a hearing. Every one, good or bad, because of the atonement, will be resurrected, for "As in Adam all die, even so in Christ shall all be made alive." (I Cor. 15:22.) But only those who repent and are baptized for the remission of their sins will lay full claim to the redeeming blood of his atonement. . . . Baptism by immersion for the remission of sins, the only means by which man can accept the gospel, is an earthly ordinance, and so in the Plan of Salvation, our Father, with equal consideration for all his children, has provided a way for all members of his Church and Kingdom on the earth to be "saviors on Mt. Zion" by performing a vicarious work in behalf of those in the world of spirits, "the prison house," that they could not perform for themselves.

This work for the dead performed in holy temples by members of the Church does in reality make of them who do this work "saviors" to those who have died without a knowledge of the gospel, for thereby they may claim the complete gift of the Savior promised to all mankind through his atonement. Reference to that service that may be rendered for those in the spirit world, as it was undoubtedly being performed by the saints in the days of the Apostle Paul and which we can now perform for our own dead, was given by him as an argument in proof of the resurrection. Said he: "Else what shall they do which are baptized for the dead, if the dead rise not at all? why are they then baptized for the dead?" (I Corinthians 15:29.) Temples in this day have been built in which this work so essential to the work of salvation might again be performed.[7]

[The Lord] said that the gates of hell should not prevail against Christ's church (Matthew 16:18). Now, the gates of hell would have prevailed against the Lord's work if there hadn't been given the ordinances pertaining to the salvation of those who are dead. During those periods when the priesthood to perform the saving ordinances of the gospel was not upon the earth, there were millions who lived, many of whom were faithful souls. If there hadn't been a way by which the saving ordinances of the gospel could be performed for those who thus died without the knowledge of the gospel, the gates of hell would have prevailed against our Father's plan of salvation.[8]

[In our genealogical research] the Lord is not going to open any doors until we get as far as we can on our own. We have to go toward that blank wall and then we have to have enough faith to ask the Lord to help to make an opening so that we can take the next step. And there can be information given to you from sources that reveal the fact that heaven and earth are not far away.

Many of you have lived to a time in life where you have had loved ones who have gone on. You have had certainty of the nearness, sometimes, of those who have drawn very near to you. And sometimes they have brought to you information that you could not have otherwise had.[9]

I have a conviction born of a little experience to which I bear testimony that there are forces beyond this life that are working with us. . . .

I have the simple faith that when you do everything you can, researching to the last of your opportunity, the Lord will help you to open doors to go further with your genealogies, and heaven will cooperate, I am sure.[10]

If we were united in our temple work and in our genealogical research work, we would not be satisfied with the present temples only, but we would have sufficient work for temples yet to come, to the unlocking of the doors of opportunity to those beyond who are our own kin, and thus would ourselves become saviors on Mount Zion. Our failure to be united will be our failure to perpetuate our family homes in the eternity.[11]

How can we better prepare ourselves to participate in temple blessings?

In doing this vicarious work for the dead by those of us who are saviors on Mount Zion, the Lord wants it to be done as nearly as possible by those who are without blemish. Just as he wanted the animal sacrifice to be of animals without blemish, he wants us to come here pure and clean and worthy to do the work, the vicarious work, as saviors on Mount Zion.

And so we have counseled our bishops and our stake presidents to take meticulous care in preparing their people to be ready to receive a recommend and not to allow those to come here who have not repented of their sins, who have made mistakes, to come here unrepentant, and in so doing defile this holy house. I think there could be no worse hell on earth than for one to come here into this near presence to our Father with a sense of guilt and uncleanness still upon that person. It would be a devastating and a shattering experience.[12]

Perhaps the most sacred place nearest to heaven on earth is our temple, to the extent that we go there undefiled and to the extent that our bishops and stake presidents make careful examination of all who apply for recommends to see that, so far as is possible, they are living certain standards [so they do not come] there with any uncleanness that would defile the spirit that we wish to be there.

Remember that now. Remember our sacred responsibilities and our hope that we ourselves might begin to make sure that every time we go, we go with clean hands and with pure hearts and we teach this to others. [See Psalm 24:3–4.][13]

We have a number of those who want to go to the temple soon after they have been baptized. It has been a long-standing rule . . . which says it should be *at least* a year. . . . The reason why we say at least a year is to hope that the bishops and stake presidents will interview carefully enough to make sure that they have been in the Church long enough to have their feet on the ground and that they know the basic doctrines of the Church before we expect them to understand the higher ordinances, the temple ordinances. The questions then for those going to the temple should not be only for worthiness but also for readiness to receive the ordinances of the temple.[14]

The receiving of the endowment requires the assuming of obligations by covenants which in reality are but an embodiment or an unfolding of the covenants each person should have assumed at baptism, as explained by the prophet Alma to the effect that "ye are desirous to come into the fold of God, and to be called his people, and are willing to bear one another's burdens, that they may be light; Yea, and are willing to mourn with those that mourn; yea, and comfort those that stand in need of comfort, and to stand as witnesses of God at all times and in all things, and in all places that ye may be in, even until death" (Mosiah 18:8–9). Any [people] who [are] prepared to assume those obligations declared by Alma and "who humble themselves before God . . . and come forth with broken hearts and contrite spirits . . . and are willing to take upon them the name of Jesus Christ, having a determination to serve him to the end" (D&C 20:37), need have no hesitancy in going to a holy temple and receiving, in connection with the covenants taken, promises of great blessings predicated upon compliance therewith.[15]

How must we prepare [to come to the temple]? A sculptor has written at the portals of the Cardston Alberta Temple that confession and thought by the late Elder Orson F. Whitney that we all should have in mind. He wrote:

"Hearts must be pure to come within these walls,
Where spreads a feast unknown to festive halls.
Freely partake, for freely God hath given
And taste the holy joys that tell of heaven.
Here learn of Him who triumphed o'er the grave,
And unto men the keys, the Kingdom gave;
Joined here by powers that past and present bind
The living and the dead perfection find."

President Joseph F. Smith caught the secret of that perfection when he said: "It is not easy for men to give up their vanities, to overcome their preconceived notions, and surrender themselves heart and soul to the will of God which is always higher than their own. . . . When men and women realize they are getting into deep water where their footing is insecure, they should retreat, for they may be sure that the course they have been taking will lead them more and more away from their bearings which are not always easy to regain. The religion of the heart, the unaffected and simple communion which we should hold with God, is the highest safeguard of the Latter-day Saints." (*Gospel Doctrine,* p. 9.) . . .

Well, with that contemplation . . . , I feel I would like to bear my testimony to you through an experience I had. Only four weeks ago along in the early morning hours I was given a glorious dream. In that dream it seemed that I was in the company of brethren being instructed by the President of the Church, and while there were others there, it seemed that everything he was saying was just for me. . . . That dream came back to me, today—came back to me with a vividness that was overwhelming, for this was the message: "If you want to learn to love God, you must learn to love His children and to love serving His children. No person loves God unless he loves service and unless he loves our Heavenly Father's children."

And then it seemed that after the President had taught that lesson, which impressed itself so forcibly upon my mind, he said, "Brethren, let us kneel in prayer." And I awoke after he had prayed, with the most heavenly feeling that I think I have ever had, wondering if I could continue until I could reach the high standard of love for service and love for the children of the Lord that had [been] impressed [upon me] in that dream.[16]

Thank God for the revelations by the power of the Holy Ghost, which bears witness to my soul that I know with all my soul that [the Lord] lives, that He is the Savior of the world. I know that [the temple] is a sanctified, holy place where He can lay His head because of the holiness herein. May you who come here come with sanctified hearts, with eyes and minds and hearts single to God so that you will feel His presence.[17]

Suggestions for Study and Discussion

- In what ways has the temple been "a guide and a protection" to you?

- How would you contrast worldly treasures with the wealth of eternal riches that are obtained in the temple?

- Why is it essential that we participate as often as we can in temple worship?

- What blessings have come to you as a result of doing temple and family history work?

- Why must we come to the house of the Lord with clean hands and pure hearts? Besides being worthy, what are some other ways we can prepare to attend the temple?

- Why is learning to love and serve others an important preparation for participating in temple blessings?

Notes

1. *The Teachings of Harold B. Lee*, ed. Clyde J. Williams (1996), 573.
2. Los Angeles California Temple dedicatory service, Mar. 1956, Historical Department Archives, The Church of Jesus Christ of Latter-day Saints, 159–61.
3. *The Teachings of Harold B. Lee*, 578.
4. *The Teachings of Harold B. Lee*, 582.
5. *The Teachings of Harold B. Lee*, 577–78.
6. *Ye Are the Light of the World* (1974), 210–11.
7. *Decisions for Successful Living* (1973), 118–19; paragraphing added.
8. *The Teachings of Harold B. Lee*, 570.
9. *The Teachings of Harold B. Lee*, 584.
10. *The Teachings of Harold B. Lee*, 585.
11. *The Teachings of Harold B. Lee*, 584.
12. *The Teachings of Harold B. Lee*, 581.
13. *The Teachings of Harold B. Lee*, 581.
14. *The Teachings of Harold B. Lee*, 578–79.
15. *The Teachings of Harold B. Lee*, 574.
16. Los Angeles California Temple dedicatory service, 161–63.
17. *The Teachings of Harold B. Lee*, 580.

The Divine Purpose
of Marriage

*What can we do to strengthen eternal marriages and
prepare young people to marry in the temple?*

Introduction

President Harold B. Lee taught the great importance of marrying in the temple and of husbands and wives working together throughout their lives to strengthen their marriage:

"Marriage is a partnership. Someone has observed that in the Bible account of the creation woman was not formed from a part of man's head, suggesting that she might rule over him, nor from a part of a man's foot that she was to be trampled under his feet. Woman was taken from man's side as though to emphasize the fact that she was always to be by his side as a partner and companion. At the marriage altar you are pledged to each other from that day to pull the load together in double harness. The Apostle Paul with reference to marriage counseled: 'Be ye not unequally yoked.' (II Cor. 6:14.) While his counsel has to do more particularly with matters that pertain to an equality of religious interests and spiritual desires, yet the figure his statement suggests should not be overlooked. Like a yoke of oxen pulling a load along the highway, if one falters, becomes lazy and indolent or mean and stubborn, the load is wrecked and destruction follows. For similar reasons, some marriages fail when either or both who are parties thereto fail in carrying their responsibilities with each other. . . .

"But even more important than that you be 'yoked equally' in physical matters, is that you be yoked equally in spiritual matters. . . . Certain it is that any home and family established with the object of building them even into eternity and where children are welcomed as 'a heritage from the Lord' [see Psalm 127:3] have a much greater chance of survival because of the sacredness that thus attaches to the home and the family."[1]

Teachings of Harold B. Lee

Why is eternal marriage essential for our exaltation?

Let us consider the first marriage that was performed after the earth was organized. Adam, the first man, had been created as well as the beasts and fowls and every living thing upon the earth. We then find this recorded: "And the Lord God said, It is not good that the man should be alone; I will make him an help meet for him." After the Lord had formed Eve, he "brought her unto the man. And Adam said, This is now bone of my bones, and flesh of my flesh: she shall be called Woman, because she was taken out of Man. Therefore shall a man leave his father and his mother, and shall cleave unto his wife: and they shall be one flesh." (Genesis 2:18, 22–24.) . . . With the completion of that marriage the Lord commanded them to "be fruitful, and multiply, and replenish the earth, and subdue it." (Genesis 1:28.)

Here was a marriage performed by the Lord between two immortal beings, for until sin entered the world their bodies were not subject to death. He made them one, not merely for time, nor for any definite period; they were to be one throughout the eternal ages. . . . Death to them was not a divorce; it was only a temporary separation. Resurrection to immortality meant for them a reunion and an eternal bond never again to be severed. "For as in Adam all die, even so in Christ shall all be made alive." (I Corinthians 15:22.)

If you have carefully followed an explanation of this first marriage, you are prepared to understand the revelation given to the Church in our generation in these words:

"If a man marry a wife by my word, which is my law, and by the new and everlasting covenant, and it is sealed unto them by the Holy Spirit of promise, by him who is anointed, unto whom I have appointed this power and the keys of this priesthood . . . , it shall be done unto them in all things whatsoever my servant hath put upon them, in time, and through all eternity; and shall be of full force when they are out of the world; and they shall pass by the angels, and the gods, which are set there, to their exaltation and glory in all things, as hath been sealed upon their heads." (Doc. and Cov. 132:19.) . . .

Marriage for time and for eternity is the strait gate and the narrow way (spoken of in the scriptures) "that leadeth unto the exaltation and continuation of the lives, and few there be that find it," but "broad is the gate, and wide the way that leadeth to the deaths; and many there are that go in thereat." (Doc. and Cov. 132:22, 25.) If Satan and his hosts can persuade you to take the broad highway of worldly marriage that ends with death, he has defeated you in your opportunity for the highest degree of eternal happiness through marriage and increase throughout eternity. It should now be clear to your reasoning why the Lord declared that in order to obtain the highest degree in the Celestial glory, a person must enter into the new and everlasting covenant of marriage. If he does not, he cannot obtain it. (Doc. and Cov. 131:1–3.)[2]

Those who make themselves worthy and enter into the new and everlasting covenant of marriage in the temple for time and all eternity will be laying the first cornerstone for an eternal family home in the celestial kingdom that will last forever. Their reward is to have "glory added upon their heads forever and forever" (see Abraham 3:26).[3]

What can husbands and wives do to strengthen their temple marriage throughout their lives?

If [young people] would resolve from the moment of their marriage, that from that time forth they would resolve and do everything in their power to please each other in things that are right, even to the sacrifice of their own pleasures, their own appetites, their own desires, the problem of adjustment in married life would take care of itself, and their home would indeed be a happy home. Great love is built on great sacrifice, and that home where the principle of sacrifice for the welfare of each other is daily expressed is that home where there abides a great love.[4]

There lie yet ahead greater joys and, yes, greater anxieties than you have yet known, for remember that great love is built on great sacrifice and that a daily determination in each other to please in things that are right will build a sure foundation for a happy home. That determination for the welfare of each other must be mutual and not one-sided or selfish. Husband and wife must feel equal responsibilities and obligations to teach each other. Two of the things that today strike at the security of modern homes is that young husbands have never sensed their full obligation in supporting a family, and young wives have sidestepped the responsibility of settling down to the serious business of raising a family and of making a home.[5]

Marriage is fraught with the highest bliss and yet attended by the weightiest responsibilities that can devolve upon man and woman here in mortality. The divine impulse within every true man and woman that impels companionship with the opposite sex is intended by our Maker as a holy impulse for a holy purpose—not to be satisfied as a mere biological urge or as a lust of the flesh in promiscuous associations, but to be reserved as an expression of true love in holy wedlock.[6]

I have said many times to young couples at the marriage altar: Never let the tender intimacies of your married life become unrestrained. Let your thoughts be as radiant as the sunshine. Let your words be wholesome and your association together be inspiring and uplifting, if you would keep alive the spirit of romance throughout your marriage together.[7]

Sometimes, as we travel throughout the Church, a husband and wife will come to us and ask if, because they are not compatible in their marriage—they having had a temple marriage— it wouldn't be better if they were to free themselves from each other and then seek more congenial partners. To all such we say, whenever a couple who have been married in the temple say they are tiring of each other, it is an evidence that either one or both are not true to their temple covenants. Any couple married in the temple who are true to their covenants will grow dearer to each other, and love will find a deeper meaning on their golden wedding anniversary than on the day they were married in the house of the Lord. Don't you mistake that.[8]

President Harold B. Lee taught that "great love is built on great sacrifice, and that home where the principle of sacrifice for the welfare of each other is daily expressed is that home where there abides a great love."

Those who go to the marriage altar with love in their hearts, we might say to them in truth, if they will be true to the covenants that they take in the temple, fifty years after their marriage they can say to each other: "We must have not known what true love was when we were married, because we think so much more of each other today!" And so it will be if they will follow the counsel of their leaders and obey the holy, sacred instructions given in the temple ceremony; they will grow more perfectly in love even to a fulness of love in the presence of the Lord Himself.[9]

Faults and failings and the superficiality of mere physical attractions are as nothing compared with the genuineness of good character that endures and grows more beautiful with the years. You, too, may live in the enchantment of your happy homes long after the bloom of youth has faded if you but seek to find the pure diamond quality in each other that needs but the polishing of success and failure, adversity and happiness to bring luster and sparkle that will shine with brilliance even through the darkest night.[10]

What counsel is given to those who do not now have an eternal marriage?

Some of you do not now have a companion in your home. Some of you have lost your wife or husband or you may not yet have found a companion. In your ranks are some of the noblest members of the Church—faithful, valiant, striving to live the Lord's commandments, to help build the kingdom on earth, and to serve your fellow men.

Life holds so much for you. Take strength in meeting your challenges. There are so many ways to find fulfillment, in serving those who are dear to you, in doing well the tasks that are before you in your employment or in the home. The Church offers so much opportunity for you to help souls, beginning with your own, to find the joy of eternal life.

Do not let self pity or despair beckon you from the course you know is right. Turn your thoughts to helping others. To you the words of the Master have special meaning: "He that findeth his life shall lose it: and he that loseth his life for my sake shall find it." (Matthew 10:39.)[11]

The Lord judges us not alone by our actions but by the intent of our hearts. . . . Thus, [women] who have been denied the blessings of wifehood or motherhood in this life—who say in their heart, if I could have done, I would have done, or I would give if I had, but I cannot for I have not—the Lord will bless you as though you had done, and the world to come will compensate for those who desire in their hearts the righteous blessings that they were not able to have because of no fault of their own.[12]

You wives who are longing to have your husbands active in the Church, wishing that they were here today instead of the bitterness that's in their hearts, wondering what can be done that one day . . . you can have them with you in the temple of our God. And you husbands who wish that you had your wives with you. We're saying to you that if you'll be faithful to your trust, you'll love your husbands and love your wives, and you'll offer a constant prayer night and morning, day and night, there will come a power into you members of the Church by the power of the Holy Ghost, which you who have been baptized and are faithful have a right to enjoy. That power so wielded may bring to you the ability to break down opposition in your companions and lead them closer to the faith.[13]

Some of you may decide to marry out of the Church with the secret hope of converting your companion to your religious views. Your chances for happiness in your married life are far greater if you make that conversion before marriage.[14]

What can we do to help young people understand the blessings of temple marriage and prepare for it?

The effectiveness of the Latter-day Saint home rests, of course, on the manner of marriage contracted for that home. A marriage for just the here and now will, naturally, be concerned primarily with this world. A marriage for eternity will have an entirely different perspective and foundation. . . .

. . . Of course, we realize that simply going to the temple without proper preparation in every way does not bring the blessings we seek. Eternal marriage rests on a maturity and commitment that—with the endowment and ordinances—can open the gates of heaven for many blessings to flow to us.

. . . Temple marriage is more than just a place where the ceremony occurs; it is a whole orientation to life and marriage and home. It is a culmination of building attitudes toward the Church, chastity, and our personal relationship with God—and many other things. Thus, simply preaching temple marriage is not enough. Our family home evenings, seminaries, institutes and auxiliaries must build toward this goal—not by exhortation alone—but by showing that the beliefs and attitudes involved in temple marriage are those which can bring the kind of life here and in eternity that most humans really want for themselves. Properly done, we can show the difference between the "holy and the profane" [see Ezekiel 44:23] so that the powerful natural instincts of motherhood are decisive in the young woman who wavers between those holy instincts and the path of pleasure seeking. With real judgment and combined curricular effort, we can show the young man that the way of the world—however much it gets glamorized and regardless of how clever its Casanovas appear—is the way of sadness; it is the way which will finally frustrate those deep inner yearnings he has for hearth and home and the joys of fatherhood.[15]

While all the problems of life are not solved by a temple marriage, yet, certainly, for all who enter worthily, it becomes a haven of safety and an anchor to that soul when the storms of life beat fiercely. . . .

Mine has been the rich experience, for nearly twenty years, of being entertained each week end in some of the most successful homes of the Church, and, by contrast, almost weekly I am permitted a glimpse into some of the unhappy homes. From these experiences I have reached in my own mind some definite conclusions: First, our happiest homes are those where parents have been married in the temple. Second, a temple marriage is most successful if husband and wife entered into the sacred ordinances of the temple clean and pure in body, mind, and heart. Third, a temple marriage is most sacred when each in the partnership has been wisely schooled in the purpose of the holy endowment and the obligations thereafter of husband and wife in compliance with instructions received in the temple. Fourth, parents who themselves have lightly regarded their temple covenants, can expect little better from their children because of their bad example.

In this day, the fashions, the sham, the pretenses, and the glamour of the world have badly distorted the holy concepts of home and marriage, and, even the marriage ceremony itself. Blessed is the wise mother who paints a living picture to her daughter of a sacred scene in an exquisite, heavenly sealing room where, shut out from all that is worldly, and in the presence of parents and intimate family friends, a beautiful youthful bride and groom clasp hands across a holy altar. Thank God for that mother who shows her daughter that here, nearest to heaven on earth, heart communes with heart, in a mutuality of love that begins a oneness which defies the ravages of hardship, heartaches, or disappointments to destroy, and supplies the greatest stimulus for life's highest attainments![16]

God grant that the homes of the Latter-day Saints may be blessed and that there shall come into them happiness here and the foundation for exaltation in the celestial kingdom in the world to come.[17]

Suggestions for Study and Discussion

- What can married couples do to keep their eternal marriage covenants a high priority in their daily lives? How should being married for eternity affect the way spouses treat one another and their children?

- How can we teach the importance of eternal marriage to our children?

- Why is "great love . . . built on great sacrifice"? How does unselfishness strengthen a marriage?

- What can those whose companions are not active in the Church do to strengthen their marriages? How can those who are not currently married fill their lives with expressions of godly love and sacrifice?
- What does it mean to you to be "yoked equally" in marriage?
- How can marriage partners "grow more perfectly in love even to a fulness of love in the presence of the Lord"?

Notes

1. *Decisions for Successful Living* (1973), 174–75.
2. *Decisions for Successful Living,* 125–27; paragraphing added.
3. *The Teachings of Harold B. Lee,* ed. Clyde J. Williams (1996), 169.
4. *The Teachings of Harold B. Lee,* 239–40.
5. *Ye Are the Light of the World* (1974), 339.
6. *The Teachings of Harold B. Lee,* 236.
7. *The Teachings of Harold B. Lee,* 254.
8. *The Teachings of Harold B. Lee,* 249.
9. *The Teachings of Harold B. Lee,* 243.
10. *Decisions for Successful Living,* 177–78.
11. *Decisions for Successful Living,* 249.
12. *Ye Are the Light of the World,* 291–92.
13. Address to Virginia Stake conference, 30 June 1957, Historical Department Archives, The Church of Jesus Christ of Latter-day Saints.
14. *Decisions for Successful Living,* 129.
15. "Special Challenges Facing the Church in Our Time," regional representatives' seminar, 3 Oct. 1968, 13–14.
16. "My Daughter Prepares for Marriage," *Relief Society Magazine,* June 1955, 349–51.
17. In Conference Report, Oct. 1948, 56.

CHAPTER 13

Teaching the Gospel in the Home

How can parents make their home a sanctuary and a place of preparation for eternal life?

Introduction

President Harold B. Lee said of the importance of teaching the gospel in the home:

"As we read from the writings of the early prophets, we discover what seems to have been the underlying evil which brought about the wickedness which caused God, who had created mankind, to weep. In a revelation to his faithful prophet Enoch, God declared that the remnant of his children were without natural affection, even hating their own blood, which in all likelihood meant their children.

"In his answer to Enoch's question as to why he wept, God replied that '. . . among all the workmanship of mine hands there has not been so great wickedness as among thy brethren.'

"Then he added: '. . . behold, their sins shall be upon the heads of their fathers. . . .' (Moses 7:36–37.) Evidently the parents of that generation had committed the great sin of failing to comply with the command given to all parents from Adam's day down to our own day. They had failed to teach the doctrines of salvation to their children.

"The Lord has warned us that, as it was in the days of Noah, so shall it be at the coming of the Son of Man. God grant that this people will heed the call of our prophet-leaders and teach their children as the Lord has commanded and escape the chastening hand of Almighty God."[1]

This chapter will discuss the great responsibilities given to parents to teach the gospel to their children and prepare them to live righteous lives.

Teachings of Harold B. Lee

Why is the home the most important place to teach the gospel?

Our homes must not only be sanctuaries but also places of preparation from which our youth can go forth confidently to lead and to face a turbulent world. We all know that what is learned at home has an amazing persistence; what is seen and experienced at home either helps or haunts our youth for years to come. Our homes could be models for all of mankind, but we will have to take much more seriously the counsel of Church leaders on this topic than we have done heretofore. This has always been a special challenge, but is made more so now because of the general decay in the homes of our time. Children can "feel and see" the gospel in action at home. They can see its rightness and power firsthand; they can see how it meets the needs of the individual.[2]

Again and again has been repeated the statement that the home is the basis of a righteous life. . . . Both the revelations of God and the learning of men tell us how crucial the home is in shaping the individual's total life experience.[3]

It is becoming increasingly clear that the home and family are the key to the future of the Church. An unloved child, a child who has not known discipline, work, or responsibility, will often yield to satanic substitutes for happiness—drugs, sexual experimentation, and rebellion, whether it is intellectual or behavioral. . . .

There is no better place than in the home to teach and learn about marriage, love, and sex as these can properly combine in a sanctified temple marriage. There is no better place to deal with the doubts of our young than where there is love—at home. Love can free our youth to listen to those whom they know they can trust. . . .

Can a child come to love his neighbor unless he has known love himself? Can a young person who has never been trusted learn to trust? Can a boy who has never known work or responsibility see how those vital traits are needed to hold our whole society together? Can a girl who has not been a part of honest,

President Harold B. Lee admonished, "Teach your families in your
family home evening; teach them to keep the commandments of God,
for therein is our only safety in these days."

candid discussions of gospel principles in her home cope with
the criticisms of the world and the intellectual assaults on her
religion? . . . Without experiencing a gospel principle in action, it
is much more difficult to believe in that principle. . . .

In a time that we have been told would be much as in the days
of Noah, we must help our young to learn how to make right
choices, to grow in justified self-esteem, especially when they
can be under the direct influence of the home, where family love
can make repentance both possible and significant. The environment of our young outside the home and Church will often
be either empty, so far as values are concerned, or it will contain
ideas that contradict the principles of the gospel.[4]

Upon the parents in the home and upon the Church there is
placed a great responsibility to so teach the truths of the gospel
that an anchor will be provided for each soul. Without such an
anchor, man would be as the "waves of the sea driven by the
winds and tossed," driven by every wind of doctrine of uncertain
origin that would muddle his thinking as to that which is wrong
in the sight of God [see Ephesians 4:14; James 1:6]. We should
be the best-educated people on the face of the earth if we heed
the injunctions of the Lord.

If our youth are thus fortified, they will not be disturbed in their religious faith when they come in contact with false educational ideas that contradict the truths of the gospel. They are armed against the poison darts of slander and hypocrisy.

Young men . . . , if guided in their thinking by "rock bottom" truth, will not yield in an unguarded moment of weakness to a temptation that would be a moral blight throughout their lives. . . .

Young sweethearts approaching marriage, if guided by thoughts conveyed by gospel truth, would sanctify themselves by keeping the law of celestial marriage to gain eternal happiness.[5]

The Lord said that the power was not given to Satan to tempt little children, "until they begin to become accountable before me" (D&C 29:47). This very significant statement follows: "That great things may be required at the hand of their fathers" (D&C 29:48). Now, that means parents. Why is it that the Lord doesn't permit Satan to tempt a little child until he comes to the age of accountability? It's in order to give parents their golden opportunity to plant in the hearts of little children those vital things except for which, when that time of accountability comes, they may have waited too long.[6]

We, the fathers, the teachers, the mothers, we have [a] great [task] in building human souls. True, Satan cannot tempt little children before they come to the age of accountability; but Satan gets in his licks by trying to make those of us who are entrusted with their care and their training to be negligent and careless and allow them to develop those little tendencies that will lead them away, and will [make them] unfit for the great responsibilities in meeting the contest with Satan, and fail to put on that armor by the time they come to the age of accountability.[7]

We must impress upon every father that he will be held responsible for the eternal welfare of his family: that means coming into the Church with his family; that means going to sacrament meeting with his family; that means holding family home evenings to keep his family intact; it means preparing himself to take them to the temple, so that there can be prepared thereby the steps that will make for an eternal family home.[8]

Oh, you mothers, you fathers, I plead for the return to a sense of the complete responsibility for those treasured souls. Except you prepare them for this day that is coming, who is going to? That day when [the Lord] shall come as a thief in the night, are you preparing them to stand in His presence? When they are out there on the battlefield, when they are faced with danger, and faced with temptation, is your motherly love going to extend over those thousands of miles and hold that son or daughter steadfast?[9]

What gospel principles should we teach children?

The prophet Enos wrote about the teachings of his father. He said, "I, Enos, knowing my father that he was a just man—for he taught me . . . also in the nurture and admonition of the Lord— and blessed be the name of my God for it" (Enos 1:1). I have pondered that statement, "My father taught me in the nurture." What does that mean? Nurture means the process of moral training and discipline. "My father taught me and disciplined me in moral training." What does admonition mean? It means gentle or friendly reproof, warnings or reminders. Blessed be the name of God for the father and mother that teach in the nurture and admonition of the Lord![10]

The Lord himself has spoken plainly about this preparation for the safeguarding of youth from the dangerous pitfalls that would destroy them. He has placed a serious charge upon the homes of this land. Here are his words:

"And again, inasmuch as parents have children in Zion, or in any of her stakes which are organized, that teach them not to understand the doctrine of repentance, faith in Christ the Son of the living God, and of baptism and the gift of the Holy Ghost by the laying on of the hands, when eight years old, the sin be upon the heads of the parents. . . .

"And they shall also teach their children to pray, and to walk uprightly before the Lord." [D&C 68:25, 28.][11]

The most powerful weapon we have against the evils in the world today, regardless of what they are, is an unshakable testimony of the Lord and Savior, Jesus Christ. Teach your little children while they are at your knee and they will grow up to be stalwart. They may stray away, but your love and your faith will bring them back.[12]

Parents should remember their labors in all faithfulness, to see that there are no idlers, that children do not grow up in wickedness, but are to be taught to seek earnestly the riches of eternity, that their eyes are not full of greediness (see D&C 68:30–31). Now that is the responsibility of a father and a mother. The Lord gives the prime responsibility in the teaching of families to parents.[13]

Every child must be taught that he is an offspring of divine parentage and that it is the business of every child to learn to act like a son or daughter of God so that in time of need he might pray and be entitled to receive favors due a faithful child.

Every child must be taught that his body is a temple of God and whoso defileth a temple of God, him will God destroy [see 1 Corinthians 3:16–17].

Every child must learn that faith sufficient to perfection can only be developed by sacrifice and except he learns to sacrifice of his appetites and fleshly desires in obedience to the laws of the Gospel he cannot be sanctified and made holy before the Lord.

Every child must be taught to be reverent towards the symbols of sacred things and respectful of authority in the home, in the Church, and in the community.

Every child must be properly schooled in the use of his hands and head and made to understand that all passions are God-given and serve a godly purpose if kept under control.

Every child must be taught to use profitably his leisure time and that play is not an end in itself. It is but the rehearsal for the part he is to play in his mature life.

Every child must be given sufficient experience to learn that unselfish service brings joy and that the work one does for which he is not paid is that which produces the greatest happiness.[14]

Our children should hear, in the privacy of the home, the testimonies of their parents. How wise is the father or grandfather who takes occasion to bear his personal testimony to each of his children, individually![15]

How can family home evenings help parents fulfill their gospel teaching responsibilities?

Greater emphasis on the teaching of the children in the home by the parents was brought forth in what we call the family home evening program. This was not new. . . . In the last epistle written to the Church by President Brigham Young and his Counselors, it was urged that parents bring their children together and teach them the gospel in the home frequently. So family home evening has been urged ever since the Church was established in this dispensation.[16]

If we neglect our families here in having family home night and we fail in our responsibility here, how would heaven look if we lost some of those through our own neglect? Heaven would not be heaven until we have done everything we can to save those whom the Lord has sent through our lineage. So, the hearts of you fathers and mothers must be turned to your children right now, if you have the true Spirit of Elijah, and not think that it applies merely to those who are beyond the veil. Let your hearts be turned to your children, and teach your children; but you must do it when they are young enough to be schooled. And if you are neglecting your family home evening, you are neglecting the beginning of the mission of Elijah just as certainly as if you were neglecting your research work of genealogy.[17]

Are we constantly working within our own home circle with children and grandchildren? Are we searching out our own sheep who are in danger of straying away from the shepherd or the sheepfold? Are we teaching our families [in] family home evening? Are we having home evenings ourselves, or are we saying, "Well, these lessons don't apply to us, and Mother and I are all alone, and this is just for those with little children"?[18]

Now let me ask you a question. If you knew that you were suffering from an incurable disease and that your time on earth was to be limited and you had a family of little children dependent upon you for counsel, for direction, for leadership, what would you do in order to prepare them for your passing? Have you ever stopped to ask yourself that kind of a sobering question?

Let me read you . . . from [a mother's] letter: "When I first joined the Church, I used to contemplate the kind of a home I hoped to have someday. I projected my thinking to picture what to me was the most beautiful, satisfying situation I could envision. My husband and I formalize that mental picture when we gather our children together and teach them the gospel. . . . One thing that has both surprised and delighted us is the fact that our children have, without exception, learned to love our family home evenings. . . . I have begun to realize more and more how quickly our children grow up and how short a time we have as parents to teach them. . . .

"I had a serious illness last fall. I hope this doesn't seem vain, but for the first time I realized how important I was to my own children. . . . As I lay helpless to care for any of their needs, knowing that except for my Heavenly Father's intervention my influence upon them was ending in this life, how desirable and precious seemed the hours in the weeks and months and years ahead.

"I determined many things then concerning how to use that time, were it granted to me. One was to make a little bit of heaven on earth, to spend the time nightly reading and talking to the children. . . . Besides the other things they have been interested in, I have read most of the Book of Mormon to them from the children's volume. . . . I have no doubt that it is meaningful to them when I hear my eight-year-old offer thanks in his prayers for the prophets who kept the records, or when my five-year-old son is thankful that Nephi got away safely into the wilderness with the faithful when Laman and Lemuel sought to kill him. Our experience has been that any time we have an opportunity to help our children expand in their love and understanding of the gospel and the Father who created them, our love for one another also increases and our family solidarity is influenced in the most significant way. For this reason, the weekly family home evening is of paramount importance to us."[19]

In your homes, I pray you, say as Joshua did of old: "As for me and my house, we will serve the Lord" (Joshua 24:15). Teach your families in your family home evening; teach them to keep the commandments of God, for therein is our only safety in these days. If they will do that, the powers of the Almighty will descend upon them as the dews from heaven, and the Holy Ghost will be theirs.[20]

Suggestions for Study and Discussion

- Why is the home crucial in shaping our children's "total life experience"? Why must parents make teaching the gospel to their children a high priority from the time their children are young?

- How can we make our homes sanctuaries from the unrighteousness and trouble of the world?

- How can parents teach the principles in Doctrine and Covenants 68:25–28 to their children? How can parents help their children "learn that unselfish service brings joy"?

- Why is it important for children to hear their parents' testimonies of gospel principles?

- In what ways does the mission of Elijah apply to parents rearing their children?

- Why is it important to hold regular family home evenings? How have you been able to make your family home evenings successful?

Notes

1. In Conference Report, Apr. 1965, 13; or *Improvement Era*, June 1965, 496.
2. *The Teachings of Harold B. Lee,* ed. Clyde J. Williams (1996), 297–98.
3. *The Teachings of Harold B. Lee,* 267.
4. *Ye Are the Light of the World* (1974), 64–66.
5. *Stand Ye in Holy Places* (1974), 370–71.
6. *The Teachings of Harold B. Lee,* 269.
7. *The Teachings of Harold B. Lee,* 268.
8. *The Teachings of Harold B. Lee,* 293.
9. *The Teachings of Harold B. Lee,* 276.
10. Address to third annual Primary conference, 3 Apr. 1959, Historical Department Archives, The Church of Jesus Christ of Latter-day Saints, 1–2.
11. *Decisions for Successful Living* (1973), 24–25.
12. *The Teachings of Harold B. Lee,* 273.
13. *The Teachings of Harold B. Lee,* 277.
14. "For Every Child, His Spiritual and Cultural Heritage," *Children's Friend,* Aug. 1943, 373.
15. *The Teachings of Harold B. Lee,* 279.
16. *The Teachings of Harold B. Lee,* 266–67.
17. *The Teachings of Harold B. Lee,* 280–81.
18. *The Teachings of Harold B. Lee,* 268.
19. Address to general conference home teaching meeting, 8 Apr. 1966, Historical Department Archives, The Church of Jesus Christ of Latter-day Saints, 4.
20. *The Teachings of Harold B. Lee,* 273.

President Harold B. Lee is well known for his counsel to parents:
"The most important of the Lord's work you will ever do will be within the
walls of your own homes."

Love at Home

*How can parents strengthen the bonds of love
between themselves and their children?*

Introduction

"The family is most important in our quest for exaltation in our Heavenly Father's kingdom," taught President Harold B. Lee.[1] With this high purpose in mind, he spoke often about the importance of love in strengthening family ties. He encouraged parents and children to apply the spirit of the mission of Elijah to their living family members and turn their hearts toward one another in love. He said:

"You've had recalled to you something that you've applied only to temple work—the mission of the prophet Elijah where Malachi said, and it has been repeated in a modern revelation: 'Behold, I will reveal unto you the Priesthood, by the hand of Elijah the prophet, before the coming of the great and dreadful day of the Lord. And he shall plant in the hearts of the children the promises made to the fathers, and the hearts of the children shall turn to their fathers. If it were not so, the whole earth would be utterly wasted at his coming.' (D&C 2:1–3.)

"Today that scripture undoubtedly has a more significant meaning. Unless the hearts of the children are turned to their parents and the hearts of the parents are turned to their children in this day, in mortality, the earth will be utterly wasted at His coming. There was never a time when so much was needed as today in the homes of the Latter-day Saints and the world generally. Most of the ills that afflict youth today are because of the breakdown in the homes. The hearts of the fathers must be turned to their children, and the children to their fathers, if this world is going to be saved and the people prepared for the coming of the Lord."[2]

Teachings of Harold B. Lee

How can we encourage greater love and happiness in our homes?

It has been my privilege to visit, with the others of the General Authorities, regularly in the finest homes of our people, and it is from those visits that I have gleaned some . . . of the elements that build for strength and happiness in the home. . . .

I see these families showing respect towards each other; father to mother, and affection for her, and mother to father; no quarrelings, no bickerings before the children at least, misunderstandings talked out sensibly—I saw one such home with nine lovely children where the children bear testimony to the fact that they have never heard their father and mother quarrel. The result is now that in the nine homes of these children, following this period of instruction, and the good example of parents, there are nine more lovely and secure families living happily together. . . .

The maintenance of spiritual contacts, the exercise of family prayers, the constant attention to Church duties have all been some of the things that have helped these homes to be successful.[3]

I had a father who came to me a few years ago agonizing over the fact that all members of his family—all of his children—were having trouble in their own families, now they were married. He said to me with great sorrow, "What in the world is the matter in my family that they're all having difficulty? None of them have happy, congenial homes." Well, I didn't say it, but I saw into that man's home when those children were yet unmarried around the table. I saw selfishness, unwillingness to sacrifice for each other's welfare. I saw grabbing, hollering, scolding, fighting, and jangling. I knew what they'd been feeding on in their youth. I wasn't surprised that they didn't have happy homes.[4]

Happiness comes from unselfish service. And happy homes are only those where there is a daily striving to make sacrifices for each other's happiness.[5]

The love of God is not something that you get just for the asking. It was John who said, "If a man say, I love God, and hateth his brother, he is a liar: for he that loveth not his brother whom he hath seen, how can he love God whom he hath not seen?" (1 John 4:20.) You cannot love God and then despise your brother with whom you are associated. Any man who thinks he is a spiritual giant and his home is in disorder because of neglect and his failure to care for his wife and his own children, that man is not on his way to cultivating a love for God.[6]

Let us not forget Paul's wise urging when he said "confirm" our love to those around us, especially to those who may be swallowed up in sadness (see 2 Corinthians 2:7–8). Peter said much the same thing in 1 Peter, the first chapter, in urging members to not only exhibit "unfeigned love" but to "see that ye love one another with a pure heart fervently" (1 Peter 1:22). In the kingdom our capacity to love is crucial because we live in a time when "the love of men shall wax cold" (D&C 45:27).[7]

Strengthen your family ties and be mindful of your children. . . . Be sure that the home is made the strong place to which children can come for the anchor they need in this day of trouble and turmoil. Then love will abound and your joy will be increased.[8]

How can fathers and mothers show greater love to their children?

I had an experience that taught me something as a grandfather. It was the night of [a Church] dance festival up at the stadium, and my daughter's two oldest . . . were giving her a lot of bad time, as she called it. So I said, "How would you like it if I take your two boys up to the stadium to the dance festival?"

She said, "Oh, Daddy, if you'd do it, I'd be so happy."

I didn't know what I was getting into. . . . As that spectacle began, I didn't know there was so much difference between a seven-year-old and a five-year-old. The seven-year-old was entranced by that spectacle down on the football field. But that five-year-old, his attention span was pretty short. He'd squirm and then he'd want to go and get a hot dog and he'd want to go get a drink and he'd want to go to the toilet, and he was just on the move all the time. And here I was sitting in the front with the General Authorities, and they were smiling as they saw this little show going on and as I tried to pull my grandson here and there, trying to make him behave. Finally, that little five-year-old turned on me and with his little doubled-up fist he smacked me to the side of the face and he said, "Grandfather, don't shove me!" And you know, that hurt. In that twilight, I thought I could see my brethren chuckling a bit as they saw this going on, and my first impulse was to take him and give him a good spanking; that's what he deserved. But, I'd seen his little mother do something. I'd seen her when he was having a temper tantrum and she had a saying, "You have to love your children when they're the least lovable." And so I thought I'd try that out. I had failed in the other process.

So I took him in my arms and I said to him, "My boy, Grandfather loves you. I so much want you to grow up to be a fine big boy. I just want you to know that I love you, my boy." His little angry body began to [relax], and he threw his arms around my neck and he kissed my cheek, and he loved me. I had conquered him by love. And incidentally, he had conquered me by love.[9]

A successful mother of sons and daughters will tell you that teenagers need to be loved and be loved the most when they are the least lovable. Think about it, you fathers and mothers.[10]

I recall an incident in my own family where one of my young granddaughters was being criticized by her father for not properly taking care of her room, making her bed, etc., etc. And then with considerable feeling she said, "Well, Daddy, why do you only see the thing to criticize and never see the good things that I do?" This brought the father to some serious reflections, and that night he placed under her pillow a letter of love and understanding telling her of all the things that he admired in her, and thus began to bridge over the hurt that had been implied by his constant criticism with no approval for the good things.[11]

I remember a little boyhood experience. We had pigs that were tearing up the garden, causing great mischief on the farm. Father sent me two miles to the store to get an instrument so we could ring the noses of the pigs. We had great difficulty rounding them up and getting them in the pen, and as I was fooling around with this instrument that I had been sent to purchase, I pressed down too hard and it broke. Father would have been justified in giving me a scolding right there, after all the effort and money wasted, but he just looked at me, smiled, and said, "Well, son, I guess we won't ring the pigs today. Turn them out and we'll go back tomorrow and try it over again." How I loved that father, that he didn't scold me for an innocent little mistake that could have made a breach between us.[12]

A father may have to discipline his child, but he should never do it in anger. He must show forth an increase of love thereafter, lest that one so reproved were to esteem him to be an enemy (see D&C 121:43). The Lord forbid the feeling of a child that his father or mother is an enemy.[13]

Parents, remember that now is your opportunity; you may feel yourself harassed as you struggle through the days with an unruly child, but you are living the happiest and the most golden years of your life. As you tuck them into their beds at night, please be kind to them. Let them hear a kind voice amid all the angry, vile voices that they will hear throughout life. Let there be an anchor to which these little ones can turn when all else fails. The Lord help you so to do.[14]

I had a doctor come to me. He is a brain surgeon. . . . [His] little child had had a sled given to him for Christmas and there was no snow. The first snowfall came about thirty days after Christmas that year. [The doctor] said, as he rushed away to the hospital, "When I come home we'll go for a snow ride," and the little boy answered, "Oh no you won't, Daddy, you haven't time for me." All through the morning he had been disturbed by this childish remark because, all too true, he had spent so much time in his profession that he hadn't taken the time he ought to with his little children. So his troubled question was, "Will you discuss a little while how I can balance my life? With brain surgery advancing so rapidly today, I could bury myself and think of nothing else in order to keep pace with my profession." As we talked, we concluded that a man has responsibility to himself, he has responsibility to his family, he has responsibility to the Church, and he has responsibility to his profession; and in order for him to live a balanced life he must so try to find the avenues by which he gives service in each of these areas.[15]

If a father's love for his sons is strong, and from their infancy he has taken them into his arms in loving embrace and let them feel the warmth of his affection for them, I believe that such comradeship will ripen with maturity and keep them near when a crisis in the boy's life requires the steadying hand of a father who understands. The mother who awaits with anticipation the return of her daughter from a late dancing party to receive the goodnight kiss, together with treasured confidences expressed at the height of girlish bliss, will be richly rewarded with the daughter's undying love that will be an eternal bulwark against sin because mother trusts her.

Parents who are too busy or too tired to be troubled with the innocent disturbances of children and push them aside or out of the home for fear of their disturbing the orderliness of immaculate housekeeping may be driving them, because of loneliness, into a society where sin, crimes and infidelity are fostered. What will it profit a father, otherwise worthy of the Celestial Kingdom, if he has lost his son or daughter in sin because of his neglect? All the pleasurable uplift societies in the world, social or religious, will never compensate the mother for the souls lost in her own home while she is trying to save humanity or a cause, no matter how worthy, outside of her home.[16]

I have frequently counseled, and I repeat it to you again, to all of you here: *"The most important of the Lord's work you will ever do will be within the walls of your own homes."* We must never forget that.[17]

What influence can parental love and gospel teaching have on children who go astray?

I had a troubled couple that came in just the other day. They have a sixteen-year-old daughter who is the oldest in the family and she is causing a lot of trouble. They were about to give up. I quoted what Brother Marvin J. Ashton said, that home is not a failure so long as it doesn't give up (see Conference Report, April 1971, p. 15). Now, that's true. The home must continue to love and to work with [young people], till we get youth past that dangerous age. No home is a failure unless it quits trying to help.[18]

The greatest demonstration of the power of the Almighty we see today is the redemption of human souls from spiritual darkness into spiritual light. I saw and heard such a miracle recently when a man who had been incorrigible much of his life, now reaching up to his middle-age years, spoke by his own request at the funeral services of his elderly mother. His father and mother, obedient to the Lord's instruction, had persisted in teaching their children, including this son, who vigorously and rudely resisted their efforts. Despite this opposition, the father continued in his role as a faithful father should; he not only taught, but every Sunday he fasted and prayed, especially for this wayward son. The father was shown in a dream, as though to reassure him, his unruly son walking in a dense fog. In the dream he saw this son walk out of the fog into bright sunlight, cleansed by genuine repentance. We have seen that boy now a changed man and enjoying some of the Lord's choicest blessings in the Church because of his faithful parents who didn't fail him.[19]

Now this I would like to say to you mothers: Don't give up on that [wayward] boy or girl; one day he may, like the Prodigal Son, return to the home from which he came, as a ship in a storm returns to a safe harbor.[20]

As a youth one may become divorced from the influence of a good home and he may become careless and wayward, but if the good mother's teachings of his childhood have been impressed upon his heart, he will return to them for safety, as does a ship to safe anchorage in a storm.[21]

Don't give up on the boy or girl in that insufferable state of [egotism] through which some teenagers go. I plead with you for those boys and those girls. Don't give up on the boy or girl in that impossible stage of independence and disregard of family discipline. Don't give up on him or her when they show a shocking display of irresponsibility. The know-it-all, self-sufficient person wants nothing of counsel, which to him is just a preachment of an old-timer who has lost step with youth. . . .

We had a missionary grandson in the North British Mission. He hadn't been there very long until he wrote back an interesting letter in which he said the advice of his parents now comes back to him with great force. It is like a book on a shelf that has been there for nineteen years and he has just begun to take it down and start to read it for the first time. That is your son and your daughter. You may think they are not listening. They may think they are not listening, but one time yours may be the book that they will take down and read again when they need it most.

There are forces that come into play after parents have done all they can to teach their children. Such a force influenced the younger Alma, who, with the sons of Mosiah, set out to destroy the work of their great fathers. An angel, you remember, was sent, and he knocked Alma down. Alma lay as though he were dead for three days and nights, and the angel said:

"Behold, the Lord hath heard the prayers of his people, and also the prayers of his servant, Alma, who is thy father; for he has prayed with much faith concerning thee that thou mightest be brought to the knowledge of the truth; therefore, for this purpose have I come to convince thee of the power and authority of God, that the prayers of his servants might be answered according to their faith." (Mosiah 27:14.)[22]

Perhaps there is no mother or father who hasn't said, "May the Lord help me to live 'twenty-five' hours every day to dedicate my life to motherhood and fatherhood so that no child of mine can ever rightly say that I didn't do everything in my power to persuade him to desist." Some of our children remain firm and true, and yet others begin to stray away, and sometimes we don't understand why. But may we all resolve that as parents today we will live close to our children, we will counsel with them, we will give them the foundation of rock-bottom principles of divine truth.[23]

Suggestions for Study and Discussion

- As parents, what has helped you to strengthen the love between you and your children? How can parents pay attention to each child's special needs?
- Why should parents always show respect for one another in public and within their home?

- How can parents encourage unselfishness and sacrifice for the good of others in their home?

- Why is it important for parents to love their children even when they are the least lovable? In what ways can parents show approval for the good things their children do?

- How can parents balance the demands of family, church, and work?

- What do you think President Lee meant when he said, "The most important of the Lord's work you will ever do will be within the walls of your own homes"?

- How does the gospel help parents to keep their children from going astray? Why is it important to recognize that after all we can do, our children may still make some wrong choices? What assurances does the gospel provide to faithful parents who continue to love and work with their children?

Notes

1. Press release for Mexico and Central America Area Conference 1972, 2.
2. *The Teachings of Harold B. Lee*, ed. Clyde J. Williams (1996), 281.
3. In Conference Report, Oct. 1948, 52, 55.
4. *The Teachings of Harold B. Lee*, 271.
5. *The Teachings of Harold B. Lee*, 296.
6. *The Teachings of Harold B. Lee*, 296.
7. *The Teachings of Harold B. Lee*, 606.
8. In Conference Report, Munich Germany Area Conference 1973, 112.
9. Address to Sunday School general conference, 5 Oct. 1973, Historical Department Archives, The Church of Jesus Christ of Latter-day Saints, 7–8.
10. *The Teachings of Harold B. Lee*, 296.
11. *The Teachings of Harold B. Lee*, 199.
12. *The Teachings of Harold B. Lee*, 279–80.
13. *The Teachings of Harold B. Lee*, 279.
14. *The Teachings of Harold B. Lee*, 279.
15. *The Teachings of Harold B. Lee*, 613–14.
16. *Decisions for Successful Living* (1973), 24.
17. *The Teachings of Harold B. Lee*, 280.
18. *The Teachings of Harold B. Lee*, 278.
19. *The Teachings of Harold B. Lee*, 278.
20. *The Teachings of Harold B. Lee*, 279.
21. *The Teachings of Harold B. Lee*, 287.
22. *Ye Are the Light of the World* (1974), 275–76.
23. *The Teachings of Harold B. Lee*, 276.

The Righteous Influence of Mothers

How can mothers fulfill their sacred role of teaching and nurturing their children?

Introduction

President Harold B. Lee once told of a mother who was polishing pieces of silver in preparation for a reception in the evening. "Right in the midst of all her preparations, her little eight year old boy came in with his piggy bank and he said to his mother, 'Mother, how do you pay your tithing?'

"And now of all times that she did not want to be interrupted, this was that time, but she wiped her hands and she sat down and they shook the pennies and the nickels and dimes out of the piggy bank and then she explained how he paid tithing. When she had finished, he threw his arms around her neck and said, 'Oh, thank you, Mother, for helping me; now I know how to pay my tithing.' "

Commenting about the experience, the mother said something that is "very, very important for all . . . mothers to remember, 'Well, all my life I will have time to polish silver, but this may be the only time I will ever have to teach my boy the principle of tithing.' "[1]

President Lee taught that "successful motherhood today spans the years and the eternities."[2] He emphasized that a mother's glorious purpose "is the building of a home here and laying a foundation for a home in eternity."[3]

Teachings of Harold B. Lee

How can mothers have a righteous influence over their children?

Woman has within her the power of creation in company with her legal and lawful husband here, and if sealed in celestial wedlock, she may have eternal increase in the world to come. Woman is the homemaker in her own home and an exemplar to her posterity in the generations that succeed her. Woman is a helpmeet to her husband and may render him more perfect than he otherwise would be. Woman's influence can bless a community or a nation to that extent to which she develops her spiritual powers in harmony with the heaven-sent gifts with which she has been endowed by nature. . . . Year in and year out, she may cast the aura of her calming and refining influence to make certain that her posterity will enjoy the opportunities to develop to their fullest potential their spiritual and physical natures.[4]

Mothers are the creators of the atmosphere in the home and do much to provide the strong foundation for their sons and daughters, to provide them with strength when they leave the influence of their homes.[5]

Mothers, stay at the crossroads of the home. Some time ago, I was attending a quarterly stake conference. . . . I said to the president of the stake, . . . "Have you some mother here, an older mother, who had a large family and had the joy of seeing every one of her family married in the temple?"

He looked out over the audience and he said, "Well, there is Sister (I shall call her Sister Jones), she has had a family of eleven, and they all have been married in the temple." . . .

And as this lovely white-haired mother stood beside me at the microphone, I said, "Would you take a lesson out of your book and tell us, what have you done to reach this most marvelous achievement?"

And she replied, . . . "I might give you two suggestions. In the first place, when our family was growing up, I always was there at the crossroads of the home, when my children were coming to or going from the home. And second: whatever we did we did

Through their loving and untiring efforts, faithful mothers
throughout the world do all they can to ensure that their posterity
"will enjoy the opportunities to develop to their fullest potential."

together as a family. We played together, we prayed together, we
worked together, we did everything together. I guess that's all I
can think of."

I said to her, "Now you have preached two great sermons."[6]

Keep the mother of your home at the "crossroads" of the
home. There is a great danger today of homes breaking down
because of allurements to entice mothers to neglect their being
at home as the family members are coming to or going from the
home. Now, I recognize the necessity of some mothers being
required to earn sustenance for their family. But even here, Relief
Society presidents and bishops should take care lest they fail to
lend all aid possible to the mother of small children and to help
her, if possible, in planning the nature of work or the schedule
of time. All this lies within the province of the Relief Society
working with the home.[7]

Today I feel that women are becoming victims of the speed of
modern living. It is in building their motherly intuition and that
marvelous closeness with their children that they are enabled to

tune in upon the wavelengths of their children and to pick up the first signs of difficulty, of danger and distress, which if caught in time would save them from disaster.[8]

I read the other day again the words of the sainted mother of the Prophet Joseph the night that he went to get the plates. I read her writing:

"On the night of [September 21] I sat up very late. . . . I did not retire until after twelve o'clock at night. About twelve o'clock Joseph came to me and asked me if I had a chest with a lock and key. I knew in an instant what he wanted it for, and not having one I was greatly alarmed, as I thought it might be a matter of considerable moment. But Joseph, discovering my anxiety, said, 'Never mind, I can do very well for the present without it—be calm—all is right.'

"Shortly after this Joseph's wife passed through the room with her bonnet and riding dress, and in a few minutes they left together, taking Mr. Knight's horse and wagon. *I spent the night in prayer and supplication to God, for the anxiety of my mind would not permit me to sleep. . . .*" [Lucy Mack Smith, *History of Joseph Smith*, ed. Preston Nibley (1958), 102.]

I say to you mothers, if you ever have sons and daughters who amount to what they should in the world, it will be in no small degree due to the fact that your children have a mother who spends many nights on her knees in prayer, praying God that her son, her daughter, will not fail. I remember at the foolish years of my teenage life, my mother came to me with an intuitive impression and warning which I brushed off as foolish teenagers do. "Oh, mother, that's silly," I said, then within only a month, to stand face to face with the temptation about which mother had warned. I never had the courage to go back and tell her how right she was, but I was on guard because someone warned—my mother.[9]

A family consisting of my grandmother, my mother, and two or three of the younger children were seated before an open door, watching the great display of nature's fireworks as a severe thunderstorm raged near the mountain where our home was located. A flash of chain lightning followed by an immediate loud clap of thunder indicated that the lightning had struck very close.

I was standing in the doorway when suddenly and without warning my mother gave me a vigorous push that sent me sprawling on my back out of the doorway. At that instant, a bolt of lightning came down the chimney of the kitchen stove, out through the open doorway, and split a huge gash from top to bottom in a large tree immediately in front of the house. If I had remained in the door opening, I wouldn't be writing this story today.

My mother could never explain her split-second decision. All I know is that my life was spared because of her impulsive, intuitive action.

Years later, when I saw the deep scar on that large tree at the old family home, I could only say from a grateful heart: Thank the Lord for that precious gift possessed in abundant measure by my own mother and by many other faithful mothers, through whom heaven can be very near in time of need.[10]

How can mothers fulfill their responsibility for teaching the gospel to their children?

A mother's heart is a child's schoolroom. The instructions received at the mother's knee, and the parental lessons together with the pious and sweet souvenirs of the fireside, are never effaced entirely from the soul.

Someone has said that the best school of discipline is the home, for family life is God's own method of training the young, and homes are largely what mothers make them.[11]

What is the mother's role, then, in the great service of the kingdom? Her first and most important role is to remember the teaching of the gospel in the family.[12]

[I wish to refer to] woman's place in training her family. . . . The Lord said:

"But behold, I say unto you, that little children are redeemed from the foundation of the world through mine Only Begotten;

"Wherefore, they cannot sin, for power is not given unto Satan to tempt little children, until they begin to become accountable before me;

"For it is given unto them even as I will, according to mine own pleasure, that great things may be required at the hand of their fathers." (D&C 29:46–48.)

. . . What are those great things that God requires of the fathers of children (which, by inference, means mothers as well) during this period before little children begin to become accountable before the Lord? . . . Parents are admonished to have their children baptized when they are eight years of age and to teach them the fundamental principles of the gospel. Their children shall be baptized for the remission of their sins and shall then receive the laying on of hands. They should be taught to pray and to walk uprightly before the Lord.

Great accomplishments are required of fathers and mothers before Satan has power to tempt little children. It is the responsibility of the parents to lay a solid foundation by teaching Church standards by example and by precept.

To the sisters, this means they must make a career of motherhood. They must let nothing supersede that career.[13]

Recently I came across a talk that had been given by one of my daughters to a group of mothers and daughters. She told an experience with her first born son who began to teach her the responsibilities that she must have as a mother. She said, "Many years ago when my oldest son was a very little boy, I found myself one warm summer night after supper frantically trying to finish bottling some fruit." I am sure you young mothers can picture that scene. Everything had happened that day to keep you from getting to that project and you wanted to finish it. Now with the baby settled for the night and your husband off to his meeting on time, your little three and four year olds are about finished getting their pajamas and are getting ready for bed. You think to yourself, "Well, now I will get to that fruit."

[My daughter continued:] "This is the situation I found myself in that night as I began to peel and pit that fruit, when my two little boys appeared in the kitchen and announced that they were ready to say their prayers." But not wanting to be interrupted, she said very quickly to her boys, " 'Now why don't you run in and say your prayers all alone and Mother will just keep on working at this fruit.' David, the oldest, planted his little feet firmly in front of me and asked, not unkindly, 'But, Mommy, which is the most important, the prayers or fruit?' Little did I realize then as a young mother and a busy wife that in my life ahead that there would be many such dilemmas as I carried out this role of wife and mother in my home."

That is the challenge that you as mothers have when your little children are pressing for you to stand by and help them grow. . . .

Mothers, when your children begin to ask you questions, even about the delicate things in life, don't turn them aside. Take time to explain to their childish minds, or as they grow up, to their older minds. A successful mother is one who is never too tired for her sons and daughters to come and share their joys and their sorrows with her.[14]

I pray that the blessings of the Lord will be on you [my beloved sisters]. You have a greater power over the welfare of this Church than you have any idea. How you will discharge your responsibility as mothers, will determine greatly how the Church will go. That the Lord may help you so to do and build on a solid foundation of the home, is my humble prayer, and I bear you my humble testimony that within the Church of Jesus Christ are to be found the teachings and plans by which our homes can be kept safe, and I bear that testimony in the name of the Lord Jesus Christ.[15]

Suggestions for Study and Discussion

- What sacrifices does a mother make for her children? What blessings flow from such sacrifices?

- In what ways does "successful motherhood today" bless future generations for eternity?

- What does it mean to be at the crossroads of the home? Why is it important for mothers to be at the crossroads in their children's lives?

- How are women sometimes diverted from their sacred purposes by the speed and distractions of modern living? How can these distractions be minimized?

- What do the stories about Joseph Smith's mother and President Lee's mother teach about how mothers can be a righteous influence on their children?

- How have the prayers of your mother blessed your life? How have your prayers as a mother blessed your children?

- In what ways can husbands and fathers help mothers fulfill their responsibilities in the home? How can priesthood and Relief Society leaders help?

- Why must mothers give high priority to their responsibility to teach the gospel in the family? How can mothers do this?

- In what ways can parents prepare their daughters to become good mothers?

Notes

1. In Conference Report, Mexico and Central America Area Conference 1972, 91.
2. *The Teachings of Harold B. Lee*, ed. Clyde J. Williams (1996), 288.
3. *Ye Are the Light of the World* (1974), 317–18.
4. *Ye Are the Light of the World*, 318–19.
5. *The Teachings of Harold B. Lee*, 289.
6. "Obligations of Membership in Relief Society," *Relief Society Magazine*, Jan. 1969, 10.
7. *Ye Are the Light of the World*, 279.
8. *The Teachings of Harold B. Lee*, 288.
9. "The Influence and Responsibility of Women," *Relief Society Magazine*, Feb. 1964, 85.
10. *The Teachings of Harold B. Lee*, 290–91.
11. *The Teachings of Harold B. Lee*, 289.
12. *The Teachings of Harold B. Lee*, 287.
13. *Ye Are the Light of the World*, 314–15.
14. In Conference Report, Mexico and Central America Area Conference 1972, 90–91; paragraphing added.
15. In Conference Report, Mexico and Central America Area Conference 1972, 91.

Uniting to Save Souls

How do the principles of Church correlation help the Church and the family work together to save souls?

Introduction

While serving as a member of the Quorum of the Twelve Apostles, Harold B. Lee was charged by the First Presidency to oversee an effort to focus all Church programs on the ultimate purpose of the gospel of Jesus Christ—"to bring to pass the immortality and eternal life of man" (Moses 1:39). This effort was called correlation. Correlation includes emphasizing the importance of the family and the home by ensuring that Church auxiliaries, programs, and activities strengthen and support the family. It also includes placing all the organizations and work of the Church under priesthood direction. In the 1960s, many steps were taken to accomplish these purposes, including reemphasizing family home evening and reviewing the curriculum of the Church to ensure that it strengthened the home and family. Correlation in the Church continues today under the direction of the First Presidency, following principles revealed by the Lord.

President Lee taught: "All that we do is to be done 'with an eye single to the glory of God.' [D&C 82:19.] And what was the glory of God? As the Lord explained it to Moses, it was to bring to pass the immortality and eternal life of man. . . . In all our efforts in the . . . correlation program we have kept these observations always in mind. Simply stated, our two sole objectives in correlation were to keep the priesthood functioning as the Lord has clearly defined it, with the auxiliary organizations properly related thereto, and secondly that the parents and the family magnify their callings as the Lord has commanded. And so we see that everything that is done should be done with that one question in mind: does this activity further the interest of the kingdom, are we keeping our eye single to that prime purpose of the Lord's organization—to save souls and to bring to pass the immortality and the eternal life of man?"[1]

Teachings of Harold B. Lee

How does the Church help to "bring to pass the immortality and eternal life of man"?

To prepare us for acceptability in the presence of the Lord, we've got a church. What was it the Apostle Paul said—they gave some apostles, prophets, pastors, teachers, evangelists—in other words, organized the Church—for what? "For the perfecting of the saints, for the work of the ministry, for the edifying of the body of Christ: Till we all come in the unity of the faith, and of the knowledge of the Son of God, unto a perfect man." [See Ephesians 4:11–13.] The Lord knew we were not perfect, and he gave us the Church to help us become so.[2]

The business of the Church is not just to set up a social organization or to have for its purpose any other thing than the saving of souls.[3]

The purpose [of the Church is] to perfect the lives of those who have membership in the Church. . . . It [is] to educate the membership of the body or members of the Church in the doctrines and teachings thereof, that the membership might come to a unity of the faith and unto a knowledge of the Son of God unto a perfect man, which knowledge is, according to the Master Himself, as He declared in that [memorable] prayer in the New Testament, "And this is life eternal, that they might know thee the only true God, and Jesus Christ, whom thou hast sent" (John 17:3).[4]

Why be concerned about organization? . . . We organize to do the Lord's work better and easier by sharing the workload, by delegating responsibility. We organize and make the work of the Lord easier and better by acceptance and discharge of responsibility, which makes leaders of members. It is like the Master said when He gave His disciples only one injunction—"Follow me, and I will make you fishers of men"—which would be saying as we do today—"If you keep my commandments, I'll make you leaders of men and leaders among my people."[5]

The church and kingdom of God is a universal church and not confined to one nation nor to one people. Our constant endeavors are to give to all Saints of the Most High wherever they live every opportunity to grow and develop to the fullest extent possible, to develop in strength and in power for good in the earth, and to gain the reward of faithfulness.[6]

Why is it important to strengthen the family in everything we do in the Church?

Where is the first line of defense in this church? Is it the Primary? Is it the Sunday School? That is not the way our Heavenly Father has revealed it. You read again the sixty-eighth section of the Doctrine and Covenants. You will find that the Lord placed squarely on the forefront of the battlefields against the powers which would break down these defenses the home, the first line of defense (see D&C 68:25–32).[7]

The priesthood programs operate in support of the home; the auxiliary programs render valuable assistance. Wise [priesthood] leadership can help us to do our share in attaining God's overarching purpose, "to bring to pass the immortality and eternal life of man" (Moses 1:39). Both the revelations of God and the learning of men tell us how crucial the home is in shaping the individual's total life experience. . . . Much of what we do organizationally, then, is scaffolding, as we seek to build the individual, and we must not mistake the scaffolding for the soul.[8]

The home [is] the most basic and vital of all God's institutions. The key to our whole correlation program was given to us when the First Presidency declared one of the most fundamental principles on which we were to build: "The home is the basis of the righteous life, and no other instrumentality can take its place nor fulfill its essential functions. The utmost the auxiliaries can do is to aid the home in its problems, giving special aid and succor where it is necessary."

With that in mind, then, every activity in the Church should be so planned as to strengthen—not to subtract from—the functioning of a well-ordered home. If parental leadership is weak, the priesthood home teachers and auxiliaries must give the necessary guidance. This means in essence that every event sponsored by the Church must be planned with this in mind, with particular emphasis on the importance of urging every family to observe faithfully the weekly home evening, and urging and aiding fathers who hold the holy priesthood in assuming their proper role as the heads of their households.[9]

God will never ask any man to sacrifice his family in order to carry out his other duties in the kingdom. How many times have we tried to stress that the most important of the Lord's work we will ever do as fathers and husbands will be within the walls of our own home? Fathers are on the one assignment from which they cannot be released.[10]

As I thought of what we are doing now and its possible impact, the words of the Prophet Micah came, "But in the last days it shall come to pass, that the mountain of the house of the Lord shall be established in the top of the mountains, and it shall be exalted above the hills; and people shall flow unto it.

"And many nations shall come, and say, Come, and let us go up to the mountain of the Lord, and to the house of the God of Jacob; and he will teach us of his ways, and we will walk in his paths: for the law shall go forth of Zion, and the word of the Lord from Jerusalem." (Mic. 4:1–2.)

I say to you Latter-day Saint mothers and fathers, if you will rise to the responsibility of teaching your children in the home— priesthood quorums preparing the fathers, the Relief Society the mothers—the day will soon be dawning when the whole world will come to our doors and will say, "Show us your way that we may walk in your path."[11]

How can the auxiliary organizations work together under priesthood direction to strengthen the family?

Said in a very generalized way, correlation means . . . to place the priesthood of God where the Lord said it was to be—as the center and core of the Church and kingdom of God—and to see that the Latter-day Saint homes also have their place in the divine plan of saving souls.[12]

Now there have been established in the Church besides the priesthood organizations auxiliary organizations, or as referred to in the New Testament, "helps and governments" as added to the priesthood [see 1 Corinthians 12:28]. In regard to these organizations President Joseph F. Smith made this statement: "I have in mind our auxiliary organizations; what are they? Helps to the standard organizations of the Church. They are not independent. I want to say to the Young Men's and Young Ladies' Mutual Improvement Associations, and to the Relief Society, and to the Primaries, and to the Sunday Schools, and Religion classes, and all the rest of the organizations in the Church, that not one of them is independent of the Priesthood of the Son of God, not any of them can exist a moment in the acceptance of the Lord when they withdraw from the voice and from the counsel of those who hold the Priesthood and preside over them. They are subject to the powers and authority of the Church, and they are not independent of them; nor can they exercise any rights in their organizations independently of the Priesthood and of the Church." [*Gospel Doctrine,* 5th ed. (1939), 383.][13]

In the great, modern-day revelation on Church government, the Lord concludes with this statement:

"Behold, this is the way that mine apostles, in ancient days, built up my church unto me.

"Therefore, let every man stand in his own office, and labor in his own calling; and let not the head say unto the feet it hath no need of the feet; for without the feet how shall the body be able to stand?

"Also the body hath need of every member, that all may be edified together, that the system may be kept perfect." (D&C 84:108–110.)

Obviously, as you think about those scriptures, they were given to impress the need for the constant and continued consultations and correlations of the various subdivisions, the priesthood quorums and the auxiliaries and all other units within the kingdom of God for at least four reasons:

First, that each organization was to have its specific function, and it was not to usurp the field of the other, which would be like the eye saying to the hand, "I have no need of thee."

Second, that each subdivision is of equal importance in the work of salvation, just as each part of the physical body is essential to a complete human being.

Third, that all may be edified or educated together; and

Fourth, that the system may be kept perfect, or in other words, that within the framework of the Lord's plan of organization for the salvation of his children, the Church will perform as a perfectly organized human body, with every member functioning as it was intended.[14]

Sometimes, in the past, we have lapsed into patterns which seem to stress our accountability for programs rather than for the flock. We urge all involved . . . to follow that fundamental injunction as to the purpose of it all: "to bring to pass the immortality and eternal life of man" (Moses 1:39). Always, if we want a measure by which this program or that program is worthy: does this lend itself to the progress of the individual toward that goal of eternal life in the presence of the Father? If it does not, and it has no relationship thereto, then it has no place in being urged in the Church.[15]

Suggestions for Study and Discussion

- Why is it essential that in everything we do in the Church, we remember the Church's ultimate purpose—"to bring to pass the immortality and eternal life of man"? (Moses 1:39).

- How does the Church help us to perfect our lives? How does it help us to "grow and develop to the fullest extent possible"?

- Why is the home the most basic and vital of all God's institutions? What can we do in our Church responsibilities to strengthen the family?

- What do you think President Lee meant when he said that the priesthood is the "center and core of the Church"? How does the counsel given in D&C 84:108–10 help us understand how the priesthood and auxiliary organizations of the Church should work together?

- How do priesthood and auxiliary programs "operate in support of the home"? How have these programs supported your home?

- In our efforts to serve in the Church, why must we be careful that programs do not become more important than people? How can we accomplish this?

Notes

1. Address given at Sunday School general conference, 2 Oct. 1970, Historical Department Archives, The Church of Jesus Christ of Latter-day Saints, 7.

2. Address given at Brigham Young University, 3 Oct. 1950, Harold B. Lee Library Archives, Brigham Young University, 9–10.

3. Address given at organization of Virginia Stake, 30 June 1957, Historical Department Archives, The Church of Jesus Christ of Latter-day Saints.

4. *The Teachings of Harold B. Lee*, ed. Clyde J. Williams (1996), 587.

5. *The Teachings of Harold B. Lee*, 565.

6. *The Teachings of Harold B. Lee*, 385.

7. *The Teachings of Harold B. Lee*, 262.

8. *The Teachings of Harold B. Lee*, 267.

9. *The Teachings of Harold B. Lee*, 559.

10. *The Teachings of Harold B. Lee*, 292–93.

11. In Conference Report, Oct. 1964, 87; or *Improvement Era*, Dec. 1964, 1081.

12. *The Teachings of Harold B. Lee*, 563.

13. Address to Mutual Improvement Association, 1948, Historical Department Archives, The Church of Jesus Christ of Latter-day Saints, 3.

14. In Conference Report, Oct. 1961, 77–78.

15. Address given at regional representatives' seminar, 4–5 Apr. 1973, Historical Department Archives, The Church of Jesus Christ of Latter-day Saints, 10.

Sharing the Gospel

*How can we fulfill our God-given responsibility
to share the gospel with others?*

Introduction

Occasionally Elder Gordon B. Hinckley, of the Quorum of the Twelve, and his wife, Marjorie, would travel with President and Sister Harold B. Lee. "We went on two separate occasions with President and Sister Lee to England, Germany, Austria, Italy, Greece, and the Holy Land, where we met with missionaries, members, youth, and servicemen," said Sister Hinckley. "Never did anyone have more gracious, more courteous, more kind traveling companions."

"We were in England one Sunday. It had been a full day: two sessions of a conference and a fireside at night. When we got back to the hotel about 9:30, we were bone-weary and hungry. We went into the hotel dining room to get a little something to eat. The day was over—we could relax. At least, that is what I thought. The next thing I knew, the waitress had her pencil poised to write down our order. President Lee looked up at her and said, 'What church do you belong to?' The day was not over for him. He had embarked on a proselyting exercise. Before the meal was over he had learned all about this young woman. She had lost her husband and was lonely and afraid. She had promised to see the missionaries and learn more. It was a beautiful thing to see the president of the Church practice what he had been preaching all that day. When the waitress (a woman of perhaps thirty-five) learned that the man she was talking with was the president, the prophet, seer, and revelator of the Church of Jesus Christ, she could not believe that such a person would stoop to making conversation with such a one as she. She was greatly moved."[1]

Speaking of sharing the gospel, President Lee said, "May [we] realize that this is a responsibility which the Lord has given to his Church in every dispensation, . . . to teach the gospel to every creature in order that each be left without excuse in the day of judgment, and that all might be redeemed from the Fall and brought back into the presence of the Lord.[2]

Teachings of Harold B. Lee

Why is it important for us to share the gospel with others?

We keep our testimonies by living, praying and being active in the church and by keeping the commandments of God. It is then that the guiding Spirit will be with us, one of the most prized possessions a member of the church can have.

With this testimony, it is the responsibility of all of us to be aware of our obligation to bear witness of the divine mission of the Lord wherever we have the opportunity. If we apply ourselves there are many opportunities to teach the gospel, day by day and hour by hour, wherever we may be. If we have lived for it, if we have prepared for it and if we seek it, the guiding Spirit will give us the ability to teach. Remember, words are just words, in teaching the gospel, unless they are accompanied by the Spirit of the Lord. . . .

Our responsibility is to bring to the world the message of truth, to show the world that within the teachings of the gospel of Jesus Christ are to be found the solutions to every problem that afflicts mankind.[3]

We should accept every opportunity to bring the knowledge of the gospel to others—to our inactive Church member associates, to our nonmember friends in college, military service, and business, to our neighbors and friends.

The Lord gave this revelation to the Prophet: "For there are many yet on the earth among all sects, parties, and denominations, who are blinded by the subtle craftiness of men, whereby they lie in wait to deceive, and who are only kept from the truth because they know not where to find it." (D&C 123:12.)[4]

Elder Harold B. Lee as a missionary in the Western States Mission.
He served from November 1920 to December 1922.

There is no more welcome voice to the honest in heart than the voice of the true messenger preaching the gospel of Jesus Christ.[5]

You'll remember [Elder Charles A. Callis] told us about one time going up into Montana to visit a man who had filled a mission over in Ireland. After searching for this man, who was now an old, old man, he introduced himself and said, "Are you the missionary who labored in Ireland some years ago?" And the man said yes. "Well," he said, "are you the man who when giving your farewell address in the mission field declared that you guessed you had been a failure for the three years that you had been over there because you had only been able to baptize one dirty little Irish kid? Did you say that?" "Yes, I remember that I did say that." Brother Callis said, "Well, I would like to introduce myself. I'm Charles A. Callis of the Council of the Twelve Apostles of The Church of Jesus Christ of Latter-day Saints. I'm that dirty little Irish kid that you baptized while you were a missionary in Ireland." One soul who became an apostle of the Church and Kingdom of God.[6]

No man ever puts out his hand to help another without gaining for himself the right to a merited salvation because of his willingness to help others. Now, keep in mind that all of us are our Father's children, whether presently members of the Church or not. It is these others of our Father's children about whom we must be much concerned. They are just as dear to Him as those who are presently members of the Church. If any one of us sets himself to the task of bringing others into the fold, the Lord says he brings salvation to his own soul [see D&C 4:4].[7]

Why is willingness to sacrifice an important part of sharing the gospel?

The very core of that which we call Christianity is to be found in the record of the writer of the gospel of John in which he quoted the Master's testimony of his own divine mission as the Savior of the world. These were his words:

"For God so loved the world, that he gave his only begotten Son, that whosoever believeth in him should not perish, but have everlasting life." (John 3:16.)

Thus has been stated the highest service that we can render here in mortal life, the willingness to sacrifice of our own self for the welfare of others. The place of sacrifice and service in this sanctifying process of life was explained by the Prophet Joseph Smith:

"A religion that does not require the sacrifice of all things never has power sufficient to produce the faith necessary unto life and salvation. . . .

"It was through this sacrifice, and this only, that God has ordained that men should enjoy eternal life." [*Lectures on Faith* (1985), 69.]

If we could apply to ourselves and to our own lives that principle by which we might lay hold upon that precious gift, we would be indeed wise. It was King Benjamin who taught his people in his closing address:

". . . when ye are in the service of your fellow beings ye are only in the service of your God." (Mosiah 2:17.) . . .

Giving, then, is an expression of one's love, and when one truly gives himself, it is an evidence of an abiding love in that individual who thus is willing to give. . . .

The Prophet Joseph Smith so loved the truth that had been revealed to him that he was willing to sacrifice everything he possessed in the world, not withholding his life, all to the end that he might bear that testimony and that it might be heard by the nations of the earth. . . .

I was out visiting a stake some months ago and was asked to interview some young men as prospective missionaries. I had been told by the stake president that one of the young men had, after a long period of hospitalization, recovered from a severe shell shock that he had received while in military service. As I faced this young man for the interview, I asked him, "Why do you want to go on this mission?"

He sat thoughtfully for several moments, and then he replied, "When I went into the service, it was the first time I had ever been away from my home. I found conditions strange. I found temptation on every side and the invitation to sin. I needed strength to

Throughout the world, young men and women unselfishly
"stand as witnesses at all times and in all places of the divine responsibility
upon the Church to teach the gospel."

keep from sin, and I went before my Heavenly Father and prayed to him in faith to give me that strength to resist evil. God heard my prayer and gave me that strength. After the period of training was over and we neared the combat area, we heard the booming of the guns that foretold the message of death that was coming over constantly. I was afraid, and I was quaking all over. I prayed to God for courage, and he gave me courage, and there came over me a peace that I had never enjoyed before. . . . I was assigned to duty as an advance scout which meant I was ahead of the combat forces and sometimes was almost surrounded by the enemy. I knew that there was only one power in the earth that could save me, and I prayed to that power to protect me, to save my life, and God heard my prayer and returned me back to my company."

Then he said to me: "Brother Lee, I have all those things to be grateful for. It is little enough that I can do to go out now as an ambassador of Jesus Christ, to teach mankind these blessed things that I have received as a child in my home."

As I heard such an expression of faith from that young man, I contrasted it with those whom I had heard say that they thought by going into the mission field they would gain a training, they would see the world, they would gain valuable experience that would benefit them personally. . . .

A selfish grasping for personal advantage does not come from the teachings of truth but comes rather from the teachings of him who is an enemy of truth. . . .

That man who is ambitious for personal gain and personal advantage is never a happy man, for before him always are the receding horizons of life that will ever mock his attempts at acquisition and conquest. That man who serves unselfishly is the man who is the happy man.[8]

We witness in our missionary work the magnificent spectacle of young men and young women [going] . . . to all the ends of the earth, that by their unselfish services they stand as witnesses at all times and in all places of the divine responsibility upon the Church to teach the gospel.[9]

How can we teach the gospel with power and authority?

Alma . . . and the sons of Mosiah went out on missions and they performed a great missionary service. . . . Alma saw his brethren, the sons of Mosiah, journeying towards the land of Zarahemla.

"Now these sons of Mosiah were with Alma at the time the angel first appeared unto him; therefore Alma did rejoice exceedingly to see his brethren; and what added more to his joy, they were still his brethren in the Lord; yea, and they had waxed strong in the knowledge of the truth; for they were men of a sound understanding and they had searched the scriptures diligently, that they might know the word of God.

"But this is not all; they had given themselves to much prayer, and fasting; therefore they had the spirit of prophecy, and the spirit of revelation, and when they taught, they taught with power and authority of God." [Alma 17:2–3.]

Now, do you [understand] the formula by which you may teach with the power and authority of God? Wax strong in a knowledge of the truth, be men of sound understanding, search the scriptures diligently that we might know the word of God. But that is not all. We have to pray, and we have to fast, and we have to get the spirit of prophecy; and having done all those things, then we teach by power and authority of God.[10]

The Lord . . . said: "And I give unto you a commandment that you shall teach one another the doctrine of the kingdom," and then added, "Teach ye diligently and my grace shall attend you" (D&C 88:77–78). I have tried to define those words "diligently" and "grace." Diligently, the dictionary says, is "perseveringly attentive, prosecuted with careful attention," which is opposite laziness, or carelessness, or indifference. . . .

. . . I believe the definition of "grace" is implied in the fourth section of the Doctrine and Covenants where the Lord promised to those who would engage vigorously in missionary work: ". . . and lo, he that thrusteth in his sickle with his might, the same layeth up in store that he perisheth not, but bringeth salvation to his soul." [D&C 4:4.] The saving "grace" of the Lord's atoning power would extend to the giver as well as to those who would receive the saving ordinances of the gospel.[11]

Now, finally, this one thing that seems to me to be as important or more important than all others:

"And the Spirit shall be given unto you by the prayer of faith; and if ye receive not the Spirit ye shall not teach." [D&C 42:14.]

Now we can give you the tools in this missionary plan for presenting and studying the gospel; it is all there. But unless the missionary applies himself to diligent prayer, he will never get the Spirit, by which he can preach the gospel. That is what Nephi meant [when he] said:

"And now I, Nephi, cannot write all the things which were taught among my people; neither am I mighty in writing, like unto speaking; for when a man speaketh by the power of the Holy Ghost the power of the Holy Ghost carrieth it unto the hearts of the children of men." (2 Nephi 33:1.)

. . . When you have the Spirit and you are listening to and guided by and impressed with a spirit of discernment, which every one of you called into His service has the right to enjoy, then you can know and be guided by and your words accompanied with the power of the Holy Ghost, without which no one will ever be an effective teacher of the gospel of Jesus Christ.[12]

Why is living the gospel an essential part of sharing the gospel?

The best way in the world to make men interested in the gospel is to live the ideals and the standards which we expect of those who profess membership in the Church. That is the first thing that strikes home to a stranger. How do we, who profess to be members, deport ourselves as members of the Church? . . .

. . . No man or woman can teach the gospel if he doesn't live it. The first act to qualify yourself to be a missionary is to live the principles which you teach. Did you ever think that a sinner would be a very good teacher of repentance? Do you think that anyone would be very effective teaching others to keep the Sabbath day holy if he did not keep the Sabbath day holy himself? Do you think you could teach any of the other principles of the gospel if you do not believe it sufficiently to implant it in your own lives?[13]

Jesus [said]: "Therefore, hold up your light that it may shine unto the world. Behold I am the light which ye shall hold up— that which ye have seen me do. Behold ye see that I have prayed unto the Father, and ye all have witnessed." (3 Nephi 18:24.) Our task is to "hold up" to the world that which Jesus has done for man: the atonement, the example He set, and the teachings He has given us personally and through His prophets, ancient and modern. The Master also counseled us: "Let your light so shine before men, that they may see your good works, and glorify your Father which is in heaven." (Matt. 5:16.) . . .

In all leadership situations in which we seek to improve human behavior, it is difficult to overestimate the power of example— whether it consists of parents both showing and telling their children about the value of temple marriage or a returned missionary who shines forth as a result of the changes and maturation the gospel has wrought in him.[14]

"Ye are the light of the world; a city set upon a hill." [See Matthew 5:14.] What does that mean? . . .

. . . Any Latter-day Saint in Church circles, in military service, in social life, or in the business community is looked upon not just as an individual, but as the visible Church today. Someone has said: "Be careful how you act, because you may be the only Standard Church Works some people may ever read." The Lord here warns us that the standard of living in the Church must be visibly higher than the standard of living in the world.[15]

I was over in Seoul in Korea recently [1954], and one of the finest men we have over in that country is a man by the name of Dr. Ho Jik Kim. He is . . . an advisor to the Korean government. He is a leader of one of the educational institutions there, and around him he has gathered now thirty-four converts, many of them well-educated. We talked with him for some two hours, trying to lay a foundation that might establish itself into a beginning of missionary activities in the land of Korea. He told us about his conversion. "The thing that attracted me to the church," he explained, "was when I was invited into the homes of two Latter-day Saint men who were on the faculty of Cornell University. . . . The thing that I was most impressed by was the kind of home life they had. I never had been in homes where there was such a sweet relationship between husband and wife, and father and mother and children. I had seen them engage in family prayer. I was so impressed that I began to inquire about this religion of theirs. And one night after I had studied for a long time and had become convinced about the desirability of belonging to such a company, I knew first I must get a testimony. I went down on my knees and prayed nearly all night long and I received a testimony of the divinity of this work." But remember it all started because of the excellent example of a family that lived the kind of home life that the gospel expects of true Latter-day Saints.[16]

Suggestions for Study and Discussion

• What are some of the opportunities we have to teach the gospel "day by day . . . wherever we may be"? What are some qualities of those who successfully share the gospel with others?

- What lessons can we learn from President Lee's experience with sharing the gospel in the hotel restaurant?

- What blessings have come into your life because you have sought to share the gospel with others?

- What sacrifices are we asked to make in order to share the gospel? What should be our attitude toward making such sacrifices? What impresses you about the attitude of the young man who returned from war and went on a mission?

- What can we learn from Alma 17:2–3 about how to share the gospel with power and authority?

- Why is the companionship of the Holy Ghost essential if we are to be effective missionaries? What can we do to more fully have the guidance of the Spirit as we share the gospel?

- How can we overcome our hesitancy and fear in sharing the gospel?

- Why is our example of righteous living such a powerful teaching tool?

Notes

1. *Glimpses into the Life and Heart of Marjorie Pay Hinckley,* ed. Virginia H. Pearce (1999), 21–22.
2. In Conference Report, Apr. 1961, 35.
3. "Directs Church; Led by the Spirit," *Church News,* 15 July 1972, 4.
4. *Ye Are the Light of the World* (1974), 24–25.
5. In Conference Report, Apr. 1961, 34.
6. "'Wherefore, Now Let Every Man Learn His Duty, and to Act in the Office in Which He Is Appointed in All Diligence,'" address to General Priesthood Board meeting, 6 Nov. 1968, Historical Department Archives, The Church of Jesus Christ of Latter-day Saints, 10.
7. Address to Brigham Young University stake conference missionary session, 19 Oct. 1957, Historical Department Archives, The Church of Jesus Christ of Latter-day Saints, 3.
8. In Conference Report, Apr. 1947, 47–50.
9. In Conference Report, Apr. 1951, 33.
10. Address to institute of religion faculty, 3 Feb. 1962, Historical Department Archives, The Church of Jesus Christ of Latter-day Saints, 7–8.
11. In Conference Report, Apr. 1961, 34–35.
12. Address to Brigham Young University stake conference missionary session, 5–6.
13. Address to Brigham Young University stake conference missionary session, 2, 5.
14. "'Therefore Hold Up Your Light That It May Shine unto the World,'" address to regional representatives' seminar, 1 Oct. 1969, Historical Department Archives, The Church of Jesus Christ of Latter-day Saints, 3.
15. *Ye Are the Light of the World,* 12–13.
16. *By Their Fruits Shall Ye Know Them,* Brigham Young University Speeches of the Year (12 Oct. 1954), 5.

The bishops' storehouse for the Pioneer and Salt Lake Stakes,
Salt Lake City, Utah, 1933. Harold B. Lee was president of the
Pioneer Stake at that time.

Providing in the Lord's Way

*How can we be guided and blessed by the principles
revealed by the Lord for the temporal welfare
of His Saints?*

Introduction

While serving as a stake president during the Great Depression of the 1930s, Harold B. Lee organized efforts in his stake to relieve the destitute circumstances of many members. He later recalled: "We had been wrestling with this question of welfare. There were few government work programs; the finances of the Church were low. . . . And here we were with 4,800 of our 7,300 people [in the stake] who were wholly or partially dependent. We had only one place to go, and that was to apply the Lord's program as set forth in the revelations."

In 1935, President Lee was called into the office of the First Presidency and asked to lead an effort to help those in need throughout the Church, using the experience he had gained in his stake. President Lee said of this experience:

"It was from our humble efforts that the First Presidency, knowing that we had had some experience, called me one morning asking if I would come to their office. . . . They wished me now to head up the welfare movement to turn the tide from government relief, direct relief, and help to put the Church in a position where it could take care of its own needy.

"After that morning I rode in my car (spring was just breaking) up to the head of City Creek Canyon into what was then called Rotary Park; and there, all by myself, I offered one of the most humble prayers of my life.

"There I was, just a young man in my thirties. My experience had been limited. I was born in a little country town in Idaho. I had hardly been outside the boundaries of the states of Utah and Idaho. And now to put me in a position where I was to reach out to the entire membership of the Church, worldwide, was one of the most staggering contemplations that I could imagine. How could I do it with my limited understanding?

"As I kneeled down, my petition was, 'What kind of an organization should be set up in order to accomplish what the Presidency has assigned?' And there came to me on that glorious morning one of the most heavenly realizations of the power of the priesthood of God. It was as though something were saying to me, 'There is no new organization necessary to take care of the needs of this people. All that is necessary is to put the priesthood of God to work. There is nothing else that you need as a substitute.'

"With that understanding, then, and with the simple application of the power of the priesthood, the welfare program has gone forward now by leaps and bounds, overcoming obstacles that seemed impossible, until now it stands as a monument to the power of the priesthood, the like of which I could only glimpse in those days to which I have made reference."[1]

Teachings of Harold B. Lee

What are the foundation principles for the welfare work of the Church?

In the 104th Section of the Doctrine and Covenants, . . . we have as clearly defined in a few words the Welfare Program as anything I know. Now listen to what the Lord says:

"I, the Lord, stretched out the heavens, and built the earth, my very handiwork; and all things therein are mine. And it is my purpose to provide for my saints."

. . . Did you hear what the Lord said?

"It is my purpose to provide for my saints, for all things are mine. But it must needs be done in mine own way." . . .

"And behold this is the way that I, the Lord, have decreed to provide for my saints."

Now, get the significance of this one statement:

"That the poor shall be exalted, in that the rich are made low."

Now, that is the plan. . . . The Lord goes on to say:

"For the earth is full, and there is enough and to spare; yea, I prepared all things, and have given unto the children of men to be agents unto themselves. Therefore, if any man shall take of the abundance which I have made, and impart not his portion, according to the law of my gospel, unto the poor and the needy, he shall, with the wicked, lift up his eyes in hell, being in torment." [D&C 104:14–18.]

. . . Now, what does he mean by this phrase? His way is, "that the poor shall be exalted, in that the rich are made low." . . .

"Exalt," in the language of the dictionary, and the definition that I am sure the Lord is trying to convey means: "To lift up with pride and joy to success." That is how we should lift the poor up, "with pride and joy to success," and how are we to do it? By the rich being made low.

Now, do not mistake that word "rich." That does not always mean a man who has a lot of money. That man may be poor in money, but he may be rich in skill. He may be rich in judgement. He may be rich in good example. He may be rich in splendid optimism, and in a lot of other qualities that are necessary. And when individual Priesthood quorum members unite themselves together, we usually find all those rare qualities necessary to lift up the needy and distressed with pride and joy to success in the accomplishment. There could not be a more perfect working of the Lord's plan than that.

Now, keep in mind this further thought, that the Lord has told us time and again that the objective of all his work is spiritual. Do you remember what he said in the 29th section of the Doctrine and Covenants?

"Wherefore, verily I say unto you that all things unto me are spiritual, and not at any time have I given unto you a law which was temporal; neither any man, nor the children of men; neither Adam, your father, whom I created" (Doc. and Cov. 29:34).

. . . Do you let everything you do be with an eye single to the glory of that individual, the ultimate triumph of his spiritual over his physical? The whole purpose of the Lord in life is to so help us and direct us that at the end of our lives we are prepared for a celestial inheritance. Is not that it? Can you give every basket of food you give, can you give every service that you render with that great objective in mind? Is this the way to do it in order to help my brother or my sister to better attain and lay hold upon his celestial inheritance? That is the objective that the Lord sets.[2]

The welfare program has a great significance in the Lord's work. We must take care of [people's] material needs and give them a taste of the kind of salvation they do not have to die to get before we can lift their thinking to a higher plane. Therein is the purpose of the Lord's welfare program that He has had in His Church in every dispensation from the very beginning. It did not have its inception in 1936. It began when the Lord commenced to take care of His people on this earth.[3]

When a home is shattered because of the needs of food and shelter and clothing and fuel, . . . the first thing we have to do is to build a sense of security, a sense of material well-being, before we can begin to lift the family to the plane where we can instill in them faith. That is the beginning, but unless we have the objective of what we do as to the building of faith, the mere giving of material aid fails. Now, we must understand that, if we just try to build faith without first filling their stomachs and seeing that they are properly clothed and properly housed and properly warmed, perhaps we will fail in the building of faith.[4]

We have repeated often the statement that was given to us by President [Heber J.] Grant when this [welfare] program was launched. These were his words . . . :

"Our primary purpose was to set up, in so far as it might be possible, a system under which the curse of idleness would be done away with, the evils of a dole abolished, and independence, industry, thrift and self respect be once more established amongst our people. The aim of the Church is to help the people to help themselves. Work is to be re-enthroned as the ruling principle of the lives of our Church membership." [In Conference Report, Oct. 1936, 3.]

I traveled over the Church by request of the First Presidency with Elder Melvin J. Ballard in the early days of the welfare program to discuss with local Church leaders the details essential to its beginning. There were three favorite passages of scripture that he frequently quoted to the people. One statement that he often repeated was this: "We must take care of our own people, for the Lord has said that all this is to be done that: '. . . the church may stand independent above all other creatures beneath the celestial world.' (D. & C. 78:14.)"

. . . [He also quoted] from the one hundred fifteenth section of the Doctrine and Covenants: "Verily I say unto you all: Arise and shine forth, that thy light may be a standard for the nations," [and he taught that] this is the day of demonstration of the power of the Lord in behalf of his people. [D&C 115:5.] And again quoting the one hundred fourth section:

"Therefore, if any man shall take of the abundance which I have made, and impart not his portion, according to the law of my gospel, unto the poor and the needy, he shall, with the wicked, lift up his eyes in hell, being in torment." [D&C 104:18.]

I read these quotations to you today to remind you of the foundation stones on which the welfare work of the Church has been laid.[5]

What resources should be used to solve an individual welfare problem?

What are the resources that the Church has, or you might call them assets, in order to solve an individual welfare problem? How do you start to solve it? Suppose I should ask you this question at this time. Suppose that tonight a telephone call comes to the father of a family where he is at work, bringing him the distressing word that his little son has been hit with an automobile and has been rushed to the hospital, critically injured. This family is making only a very low income, just barely enough to keep the family together with food and the essentials. Now there faces the family immediately, a doctor bill, a hospital bill—how in the world are you going to handle it?

I fear if I should ask you that question and have you answer it here, most of you would say: "Well, we will call on the fast offering funds." And that is not the way the Welfare Program begins, and that is where we make our error. In the first place, we start out with the individual himself. We do not move from that point until we have helped the individual to do all he can to help his own problem. Now, sentiment and our emotional sympathy might push us to other conclusions, but that is the first, and then we reach out to the immediate relatives of that family. We are losing the family solidarity, we are losing the strength that comes from family unity, when we fail to give opportunity and to help to direct a way by which immediate relatives of that family, so distressed, can come to the aid of their own.

Then, the next point we move to is to call on the storehouse for the immediate necessities. In a home like that I have just described, I want you to see the advantage of giving to that family the clothing, the food, bedding, fuel that they need for a couple of months in order to relieve the cash that they otherwise would spend to pay for that emergency hospital bill, rather than merely taking fast offerings and passing it out to them in money. . . .

Now, beyond what you can do from the storehouse, then the next thing, of course, is to recommend to the bishop the use of the fast offering fund, which, he has been schooled, is to be used first from that which he provides from his own efforts and the efforts of his leaders. To that end, we must always put the gathering of fast offerings and the increasing of the fast offerings, and teaching the law of fasting, as one of the foremost parts of the Welfare Plan. . . .

Now then, following from that, we come to the rehabilitation aspects of our problems. There the Relief Society, and there the Priesthood quorums play their major part. Now what is the Relief Society's part in a rehabilitation program? Well, the first thing you do, as you visit the home of a distressed family, is to do as the bishop requires, make an analysis of the conditions of the home. . . .

You go there to make the analysis, find out conditions, and to make an order on the storehouse, if that be necessary, and report back to your bishop the needs of the family for his approval and withdrawal from the storehouse, or from funds that he has in his possession, if that be necessary. The second thing you do is to make certain that the home management problems of that home are studied, and that there be set in motion such direction that will help to cure the evils that are there. You must stand ready to meet home emergencies, sickness, death, and other conditions of that kind, that call upon a sisterly sympathy that ought to be expressed by the Relief Society. Then, too, you must be always morale builders in this part of the program. Yours must be the up-lifting hand, yours the one to steady the family situation through the emergency.[6]

Now is the time for priesthood members to know their quorum group. Each quorum should know their members and their needs and seek out those heavily in debt and in a kind way suggest how they can get out of debt. There never is a time when a man needs a friend quite so much as when he is plowed under by some such circumstances. Now is the time to give them strength of vision and power to go forward. Not only should we teach men to get out of debt but we should teach them likewise to stay out of debt.[7]

We expect the individual to do all he can to help himself, whether it be an emergency for a single family or for a whole community, that the relatives will do all they can to help, then the Church steps in with commodities from the storehouse, with fast offerings to meet their needs that commodities from the storehouse will not supply, and finally, the Relief Society and the priesthood quorums will assist with rehabilitation.[8]

How can we make our households more self-reliant?

In order for an individual or a community to be self-sustaining, the following five steps must be taken:

First: There must be no idleness in the Church.

Second: We must learn the lesson of self-sacrifice.

171

Third: We must master the art of living and working together.

Fourth: We must practice brotherhood in our priesthood quorums.

Fifth: We must acquire the courage to meet the challenge of each day's problems through our own initiative to the full limit of individual or local resources before requesting others to come and aid us in that solution.[9]

Keep in mind that the Church welfare program must begin with you personally and individually. It must begin with every member of the Church. We must be thrifty and provident. . . . You have to act for yourself and be a participant before the welfare program is active in your own household. . . .

Pursue the course . . . to see that food is in your homes; and counsel your neighbors and friends to do likewise, because someone had [the] vision to know that this was going to be necessary, and it will be necessary in the future, and has been the savior of our people in the past.

Now, let's not be foolish and suppose that because the sun is shining today that there won't be clouds tomorrow. The Lord has told us by revelation some of the things that are ahead of us, and we are living in the day when the fulfillment of those prophecies is now at hand. We are startled, and yet there is nothing happening today that the prophets didn't foresee. . . .

God help us to keep our own houses in order and to keep our eyes fixed upon those who preside in this Church and to follow their direction, and we won't be led astray.[10]

You show me a people who "have a mind to work," to keep out of the bondage of indebtedness, and to work unitedly together in an unselfish service to attain a great objective, and I'll show you a people who have achieved the greatest possible security in the world of men and material things.[11]

Disasters strike in every place. One of the worst of our disasters was [an earthquake] down in the San Fernando [California] Valley. We were concerned when days went by and we couldn't get communication because the telephones were jammed, and there was no way of getting word as to how our people were faring; so we got in touch with our [priesthood leader] just outside of the earthquake area and asked if he could get us word. And the word came back, "We are all right. We have drawn on the storage of foodstuffs that we have put aside. We had water stored." The regular water was contaminated, and people were distressed and in danger because of the contamination of the water; but the people who listened had stored water as well as foodstuffs and the other things to tide them through; and even though they didn't all have foodstuffs and didn't have water, those who listened and prepared didn't fear, and they set about together in a marvelous way to help each other.[12]

Suggestions for Study and Discussion

- As explained by President Lee, what is the Lord's way of caring for the poor and needy? (See D&C 104:14–18.)
- What are some of the resources we have that could be shared with the needy?
- Why should our efforts to serve the poor and needy be directed toward helping them prepare for eternal life? How can we do this?
- Why should individuals and families do all they can to help themselves? What blessings come to families who help their own in times of need? What part do the priesthood quorums and the Relief Society play in helping those in need?
- What does it mean to be self-reliant? What steps must we take to become more self-reliant?
- Why are the ability and willingness to work fundamentally important in becoming self-reliant? How can we teach our children to work?
- What blessings come to us when we heed our leaders' counsel to pay our debts and practice thrift in the management of our money?

173

Notes

1. In Conference Report, Oct. 1972, 123–24; or *Ensign,* Jan. 1973, 104.

2. "The Place of Relief Society in the Welfare Plan," *Relief Society Magazine,* Dec. 1946, 814–15.

3. "Let Others Assist You," address to welfare meeting, 4 Apr. 1959, Historical Library files, The Church of Jesus Christ of Latter-day Saints, 22.

4. "Place of Mothers in the Plan of Teaching the Gospel in the Home," *Relief Society Magazine,* Jan. 1965, 12.

5. In Conference Report, Apr. 1946, 69–70.

6. "The Place of Relief Society in the Welfare Plan," 812–13.

7. *The Teachings of Harold B. Lee,* ed. Clyde J. Williams (1996), 315.

8. *The Teachings of Harold B. Lee,* 306.

9. "What Is the Church Welfare Plan?" *Instructor,* July 1946, 316.

10. "Follow the Light," address to welfare agricultural meeting, Apr. 1969, Historical Department Archives, The Church of Jesus Christ of Latter-day Saints, 4–5.

11. *Decisions for Successful Living* (1974), 202.

12. "Listen and Obey," address to welfare agricultural meeting, 3 Apr. 1971, Historical Department Archives, The Church of Jesus Christ of Latter-day Saints, 4–5.

Take Time to Be Holy

How can we labor each day to feed ourselves spiritually?

Introduction

President Harold B. Lee often taught the importance of nourishing ourselves spiritually. He said that our bodies can be compared to fortresses that must constantly be kept well supplied in order to remain strong during times of attack by an enemy.

"The enemies of your own human 'fortress' are both physical and spiritual," he explained. They may include "an unexpected sorrow, a family disgrace, a shock in your finances, the [disloyalty] of a supposed friend, or a secret sin against the laws of God." When such things happen in our lives, we require "an additional supply from spiritual sources. . . . If you have lost contact with the Church by carelessness and your faith in God has dwindled, if you have not understood by study and learning the way to a forgiveness of your transgression, or if you have not obtained through prayerful understanding the assurance of a future reward for sacrifices and pain, then you have cut your spiritual supply lines and the strength that your soul needs is sapped. . . . Your fortress is doomed to certain capture by Satan's forces. You are then as the foolish man who built his house upon the sands, and when the storms come great will be the fall thereof [see Matthew 7:24–27].

"And so I beg of you . . . to live each day so that you might receive from the fountain of light [the] nourishment and strength sufficient to every day's need. Take time to be holy each day of your lives."[1]

Teachings of Harold B. Lee

How can we nourish our spiritual selves?

Within every one of you there dwells a spirit which is the exact counterpart of your full-grown physical body. To keep your physical body in vigor and health, food and drink must be provided at frequent intervals. Every germ cell of your bodies must have a nerve connection in order to maintain the vital life processes. Failure to maintain these nerve connections or to supply the required sustenance brings decay, stagnation, sickness and finally death to the physical body.

Your spiritual body needs nourishment at frequent intervals in order to assure its health and vigor. Earthly food does not satisfy this need. Food to satisfy your spiritual needs must come from spiritual sources. Principles of eternal truth, as contained in the gospel, and the proper exercise by engaging in spiritual activities are essential to the satisfying of your spiritual selves. Vital processes of the spirit are likewise maintained only by intelligent connection with spiritual fountains of truth. Spiritual sickness and death, which mean separation from the fountain of spiritual light, are sure to follow the severance of your connection with the spiritual nerve center, the Church of Jesus Christ.[2]

We develop our spiritual selves by practice. . . . We must train our spiritual selves with the same care, if we are to be fully developed, as we train our physical bodies. We must have daily exercise by our spirits by prayer, by doing daily good deeds, by sharing with others. We must feed our spirits daily by studying the scriptures every day, by [family home evening], by attendance at meetings, by the partaking of the sacrament. We must avoid harmful poisons which we have when we break one of God's commandments. It's just like poison to our spiritual bodies. . . .

Our spiritual checkups are when we are brought face to face with God's spiritual doctors—our bishops, our stake presidents, and occasionally with the General Authorities in interviews which are always done for the purpose of helping to prepare us for spiritual advancement. Sometimes there have to be, as a result of these interviews, some major operations on our spiritual selves.[3]

President Harold B. Lee taught, "Live each day so that you
might receive from the fountain of light [the] nourishment and strength sufficient to
every day's need. Take time to be holy each day of your lives."

All that is contrary to the will of God is as poison to your spiritual life and must be shunned as you would avoid labeled poisons in your medicine cabinets at home.[4]

The righteous man strives for self-improvement knowing that he has daily need of repentance for his misdeeds or his neglect. He is not so much concerned about what he can get but more about how much he can give to others, knowing that along that course only can he find true happiness. He endeavors to make each day his masterpiece so that at night's close he can witness in his soul and to his God that whatever has come to his hand that day, he has done to the best of his ability.[5]

How does keeping the Sabbath day holy nourish the spirit?

Sunday is more than a day of rest from the ordinary occupations of the week. It is not to be considered as merely a day of lazy indolence and idleness or for physical pleasures and indulgences. It is a feastday for your spirit bodies. The place of spiritual feasting is in the house of worship. Here you find fellowship with those who like yourselves are seeking spiritual nourishment. You are enjoined to sing and pray and pay your devotions to the Most High, and partake of the holy sacrament as a reminder of your obligations as a son or daughter of God here in mortality and in remembrance of the atonement of the Savior and to pledge again your loyalty to his name. . . .

Whether at home or in church, your thoughts and your conduct should be always in harmony with the spirit and purpose of the Sabbath. Places of amusement and recreation, while at proper times may serve a needed end, are not conducive of spiritual growth and such places will not keep you "unspotted from the world" but will rather deny you the "fulness of the earth" promised to those who comply with the law of the Sabbath. [See D&C 59:9, 16.] You who make the violation of the Sabbath a habit, by your failure to "keep it holy," are losing a soul full of joy in return for a thimble full of pleasure. You are giving too much attention to your physical desires at the expense of your spiritual health.

The Sabbath breaker shows early the signs of his weakening in the faith by neglecting his daily family prayers, by fault-finding, by failing to pay his tithes and his offerings; and such a one whose mind begins to be darkened because of spiritual starvation soon begins also to have doubts and fears that make him unfit for spiritual learning or advancement in righteousness. These are the signs of spiritual decay and spiritual sickness that may only be cured by proper spiritual feeding.

May we not hope that in addition to our worshipful activities on the Lord's Day we might also on that day reduce the drudgery of the home to a minimum, and that outside the home only essential chores will be performed. Make this a day of prayerful, thoughtful study of the scriptures and other good books. While filled with the joy of the Sabbath, write a letter to your sweetheart or an absent loved one or a friend who may need your spiritual strength. Make your homes the places for the singing and playing of beautiful music in harmony with the spirit of the day. At evening's close as you gather at your fireside with the family alone or with friends, discuss the precious truths of the gospel and close with the benediction of family prayer. My experience has taught me that the prompting of the conscience to a faithful Church member is the safest indicator as to that which is contrary to the spirit of worship on the Sabbath Day.

. . . But do not suppose that a strict observance of the law of the Sabbath is alone sufficient to keep your spiritual bodies in good health. Every day of the week must give nourishment to your spiritual selves. Family and secret prayers, the reading of the scriptures, love in your homes and unselfish daily service to others are manna from heaven to feed your souls. Observance of the weekly Family Home Evening is another strong force for righteousness in the home. . . .

And so I beg of you not to rob your spiritual bodies of that essential strength by breaking the Sabbath Day, but sincerely urge you to live each day so that you might receive from the fountain of light, nourishment and strength sufficient to every day's need.[6]

How do fasting and paying fast offerings benefit us spiritually?

I asked myself the question, "What is the law of fasting?" and I found President Joseph F. Smith defining it in these words in which I thought was given a rather excellent interpretation:

"It is, therefore, incumbent upon every Latter-day Saint to give to his bishop, on fast day, the food that he or his family would consume for the day, that it may be given to the poor for their benefit and blessing; or, in lieu of the food, that its equivalent amount, or, if the person is wealthy, a liberal donation, in money, be so reserved and dedicated to the poor." [*Gospel Doctrine,* 5th ed. (1939), 243.]

And then I asked myself, "What are the blessings the Lord promises us from fasting and paying fast offerings?" President [Heber J.] Grant in an expression which is on record, gave me these answers: first, the financial blessing and next, the spiritual. This is what he said, regarding the financial blessings:

"Let me promise you here today that if the Latter-day Saints will honestly and conscientiously from this day forth, as a people, keep the monthly fast and pay into the hands of their bishops the actual amount that they would have spent for food for the two meals from which they have refrained . . . we would have all the money necessary to take care of all the idle and all the poor." [*Gospel Standards,* comp. G. Homer Durham (1941), 123.]

Of the spiritual blessings he said this:

"Every living soul among the Latter-day Saints that fasts two meals once a month will be benefited spiritually and be built up in the faith of the gospel of the Lord Jesus Christ—benefited spiritually in a wonderful way." [*Gospel Standards,* 123.]

As I read that statement, I recalled what the Prophet Isaiah had declared as to the blessings that would come to him who would fast and deal out his bread to the hungry. . . . Here were four magnificent, spiritual promises that the Lord made to those who would fast and deal out their bread to the hungry; as written in Isaiah, the first promise:

"Then shall thy light break forth as the morning, and thine health shall spring forth speedily: and thy righteousness shall go before thee; the glory of the Lord shall be thy rereward."

Then the Lord promised:

"Then shalt thou call, and the Lord shall answer; thou shalt cry, and he shall say, Here I am."

And again the Lord promised:

"And if thou draw out thy soul to the hungry, and satisfy the afflicted soul; then shall thy light rise in obscurity, and thy darkness be as the noonday."

And, finally, this promise:

"And the Lord shall guide thee continually, and satisfy thy soul in drought, and make fat thy bones: and thou shalt be like a watered garden, and like a spring of water, whose waters fail not." [Isaiah 58:8–11.]

Those blessings translated into the incidents and the problems of life, are fairly well illustrated in an incident that was related by one of our mission presidents to the General Authorities a few years ago. While we were living through those days of suspense during wartime, this father related this incident:

It was fast day. He had risen early in the morning, the chores were done out on the farm, and he was now spending a few minutes, out in his fields before time to go to the early morning Priesthood meeting. . . .

This morning as he walked out in the fields, his mind was not particularly on his two sons who were over on the fighting front, but, suddenly, he was stopped as he walked through the fields, by a terrible impression which came upon him, that something was wrong with one of those sons. He turned to go back into the house. He said, "I didn't just walk, but I ran, and I called my family down into the front room, and said to them, 'Now, I don't want any of my family to eat a bite of food today, I want you to fast, and I want you to pray, and I want you to kneel down here with me and have family prayer, because I had an impression out there that something is wrong with our boy over in the war.' "

And so they gathered around and had their morning prayer. They fasted, and they did not stop their fast, but they continued to fast after that day. Ten days of anxiety went by, then there came, through the Red Cross, the word that on that morning (and when they corrected the difference in time, it was the exact moment when that father had that impression), his boy with his buddy had fallen on a "booby-trap" and his buddy had been literally blown to pieces, and this boy had been horribly mangled and had lain at the point of death.

Fasting and prayer—"Then shalt thou call, and the Lord shall answer; thou shalt cry, and he shall say, Here am I."[7]

How does meditation bring us closer to the Lord?

President [David O.] McKay said, "We don't take sufficient time to meditate." I get up early in the morning . . . , five o'clock, when my mind and spirit are clear and rested. Then I meditate. You can come closer to the Lord than you imagine when you learn to meditate. Let your spirits be taught by the Spirit.[8]

The Twelve will not soon forget President David O. McKay's admonition in our council meeting one morning when he impressed the vital importance of taking time to meditate in order to keep spiritually attuned. . . . "It's a great thing to be responsive to the whisperings of the Spirit and we know that when these whisperings come it is a gift and our privilege to have them. They come when we are relaxed and not under pressure of appointments."

The President then took occasion to relate an experience in the life of Bishop John Wells, formerly a member of the Presiding Bishopric. A son of Bishop Wells was killed in Emigration Canyon on a railroad track. . . . His boy was run over by a freight train. Sister Wells was inconsolable. She mourned during the three days prior to the funeral, received no comfort at the funeral, and was in a rather serious state of mind. One day soon after the funeral services, while she was lying on her bed relaxed, still mourning, she claims that her son appeared to her and said, "Mother, do not mourn. Do not cry. I am all right." He told her that she did not understand how the accident happened. He explained that he had given a signal to the engineer to move on and then made the usual effort to catch the railings on the freight train, but as he attempted to do so his foot caught in a root and he failed to catch the hand rail and his body fell under the train. It was clearly an accident. He said that as soon as he realized that he was in another environment he tried to see his father but he could not reach him. His father was so busy with the duties in the office that he could not respond to his call; therefore, he had come to his mother and he said to her, "You tell Father that all is well with me. I want you to not mourn anymore."

Then President McKay said that the point he had in mind was that when we are relaxed in a private room we are more susceptible to those things, that so far as he was concerned his best thoughts come after he gets up in the morning and is relaxed and thinking about the duties of the day, that impressions come as clearly as if he were to hear a voice and those impressions are right. If we are worried about something and upset in our feelings the inspiration does not come. If we so live that our minds are free from worry and our conscience clear and our feelings are right toward one another, the operation of the spirit of the Lord upon our spirit is as real as when we pick up the telephone; but when they come, note this, we must be brave enough to take the suggested action. . . .

Let that be something to remember—you do likewise. Take time to meditate. Many times you will be wrestling with problems, the solution of which can be spiritually discerned.[9]

Don't get so busy that you don't have time to meditate. Take the time. The most important testimony does not come by sight, but by the inner witness. Christ may be nearer than we have knowledge. "I am in your midst, but you do not see me. The Holy Ghost bears the sure witness. Mine eyes are upon you. The day cometh when ye shall know that I am." [See D&C 38:7–8.][10]

Suggestions for Study and Discussion

- Why must we take time to nurture ourselves spiritually? What can we do each day to develop our spirituality?

- What can interfere with our efforts to nurture ourselves spiritually?

- How can we make our home a place that nurtures the spirituality of each family member?

- In what ways has honoring the Sabbath day helped you to grow spiritually? What activities on the Sabbath help you and your family to maintain a spirit of worship throughout the day? When we violate the Sabbath, why are we "losing a soul full of joy in return for a thimble full of pleasure"?

- What blessings come to those who fast? (See Isaiah 58:8–11.) How have you seen these blessings fulfilled?

- What do we learn from the story of Bishop John Wells about the importance of taking time to meditate on spiritual things? In what ways have you been able to incorporate meditation on spiritual things into your life?

Notes

1. *Decisions for Successful Living* (1973), 149–50.

2. *Decisions for Successful Living*, 145.

3. "Learning the Gospel by Living It," address to 52nd annual Primary conference, 3 Apr. 1958, Historical Department Archives, The Church of Jesus Christ of Latter-day Saints, 5–7.

4. *The Teachings of Harold B. Lee*, ed. Clyde J. Williams (1996), 264.

5. *Stand Ye in Holy Places* (1974), 333.

6. *Decisions for Successful Living*, 146–50.

7. "Fast Offerings and the Welfare Plan," *Relief Society Magazine*, Dec. 1952, 799–801.

8. *The Teachings of Harold B. Lee*, 130.

9. "With Love Unfeigned," address to regional representatives' seminar, 3 Apr. 1969, Historical Department Archives, The Church of Jesus Christ of Latter-day Saints, 5–6.

10. Address to meeting of Provo Temple workers, 9 July 1972, Historical Department Archives, The Church of Jesus Christ of Latter-day Saints, 10.

Living the Law of Chastity

*What can we do to safeguard the chastity of
ourselves and our families?*

Introduction

"If you want to have the blessings of the Spirit of the Lord to be with you, you must keep your body, the temple of God, clean and pure," said President Harold B. Lee.[1]

He used a sorrowful letter from a man who had violated the law of chastity to illustrate the importance of this counsel: "When I was enjoying the Spirit of the Lord and was living the gospel, the pages of scripture would stand open to me with new understanding and the meaning of the pages of scripture would just leap into my soul. Now since the sentence of excommunication, I no longer read with understanding; I read with doubt the passages that before I thought I understood clearly. I formerly enjoyed performing the ordinances of the gospel for my children, to bless my babes, to baptize them, to confirm them, to administer to them when they were sick. Now I must stand by and witness some other man performing those ordinances. I used to enjoy going to the temple, but today the doors of the temple are closed against me. I used to complain a bit about the contributions the Church asks, paying tithing, paying fast offerings, contributing to this and contributing to that, and now as an excommunicant, I am not permitted to pay tithing; the heavens are closed to me now because I can't pay tithing. I shall never in all my life complain again of the requests of the Church to make sacrifice of my means. My children are very kind to me, but I know that deep down in their souls, they are ashamed of the father whose name they bear."[2]

Said President Lee, "That man or that woman who has his eye ever fixed upon that eternal goal of eternal life, is rich indeed, because his whole soul is charged with a fire that comes to him who has kept his life worthy."[3]

Teachings of Harold B. Lee

Why is it essential to obey the law of chastity?

To the end that man and woman might be brought together in this sacred marriage relationship, whereby earthly bodies are prepared as tabernacles for heavenly spirits, the Lord has placed within the breast of every young man and every young woman a desire for association with each other. These are sacred and holy impulses but tremendously powerful. Lest life be valued too cheaply or these life processes be prostituted to the mere gratification of human passions, God has placed foremost in the category of serious crimes against which we are warned in the Ten Commandments, first, murder, and second only to that, sexual impurity. "Thou shalt not kill! Thou shalt not commit adultery!" (See Exodus 20:13–14.) . . . The Church counsels you to be modest in your dress and manner and to forbid the evil thoughts that would prompt your lips to obscenity and your conduct to be base and unseemly. To gain the highest bliss in holy wedlock, the fountains of life must be kept pure.[4]

Be virtuous. This is one of the greatest of the commandments.

"Let thy bowels also be full of charity towards all men, and to the household of faith, and let virtue garnish thy thoughts unceasingly; then shall thy confidence wax strong in the presence of God; and the doctrine of the priesthood shall distil upon thy soul as the dews from heaven.

"The Holy Ghost shall be thy constant companion, and thy scepter an unchanging scepter of righteousness and truth; and thy dominion shall be an everlasting dominion, and without compulsory means it shall flow unto thee forever and ever." (D&C 121:45–46.)

But never in the world will we have that dominion, that power, that companionship of the Holy Ghost unless we have learned to be virtuous in thought, in habit, and in our actions.[5]

Clothe yourself with the armor of righteousness. Don't give way in a moment of weakness. Safeguard that citadel of purity. Your body is the temple of the Holy Ghost, if you will keep it clean and pure.[6]

Live the law of chastity more perfectly than you have ever done it before, by thinking pure thoughts. Remember what the Master stated, "It was said by them of old time, Thou shalt not commit adultery: but I say unto you, That whosoever looketh on a woman to lust after her hath committed adultery with her already in his heart" (Matthew 5:27–28). Now, our thoughts must be pure. Overcome any habits that you may have that have a tendency to immoral acts, and forbid the immorality that otherwise would blight your lives.[7]

What are the consequences of violation of the law of chastity?

Never before has there been such a challenge to the doctrine of righteousness and purity and chastity. The moral standards are being eroded by powers of evil. There is nothing more important for us to do than to teach as powerfully, led by the Spirit of the Lord, as we can in order to persuade our people in the world to live close to the Lord in this hour of great temptation.[8]

Satan's greatest threat today is to destroy the family, and to make a mockery of the law of chastity and the sanctity of the marriage covenant.[9]

One of our stake conferences closed on an interesting note some while ago. . . . As the stake president got up to close the conference, he looked up to the balcony filled with youngsters and said, "There is something I want to say to you young people up in that balcony. Perhaps while I am your stake president, every one of you will come to me for an interview—advancement in the priesthood, or for some position to which you are to be called, or for temple recommends—and among other things I am going to ask you one soul-searching question. Are you morally clean? If you can answer honestly, 'Yes, President, I am morally clean,' you will be happy. If you have to answer, 'No, I'm not,' you will be sad; and if you lie to me, bitterness will fill your soul as long as you live." . . .

One day [we] will have to meet our Maker and as Moroni put it—and this is pretty strong language—he said, "Do you think that you could be happy in the presence of the Holy One of Israel with a sense of guilt of your own uncleanness?" He said, "You would be happier to live with the damned souls in hell than in the presence of the Holy One of Israel with your uncleanness and your filthiness still upon you." [See Mormon 9:3–4.][10]

When we break commandments, we hurt ourselves and others too. The error usually results in sadness, depression, hostility, or withdrawal, if we do not repent. We, in effect, diminish our self-esteem; we downgrade our roles as sons and daughters of God; we may even try to run away from the ultimate reality of who we really are!

When we sin we become less effective members of the human family. . . . We may damage others; we may even strike back at the human family in a twisted way for our own failures, and thus human suffering is multiplied. The unchastity of parents can send forth a chain reaction that can span the generations, even though the resentment and rebellion of disappointed children may take a different form. The absence of love at home causes ripples of reaction that roll across all of us; mankind pays an awful price for this kind of failure. What could be more relevant to the needs of the human family than for us to be chaste, to develop love at home—in fact, to keep every commandment?[11]

There is never a man or a woman of station in this church who falls below the standards he is expected to live without dragging down with him many who have had faith in him. He has wounded their conscience; he has dragged down those of weaker faith, and many count the day of their disaffection in this church when someone in whom they had faith fell below that standard they expected him to maintain.[12]

I have pointed out the awfulness of sin; that the wages of sin is death and that through the atonement of the Lord Jesus Christ, you who have sinned may by true repentance find forgiveness and the way to joy in this life and a fulness in the life to come.[13]

What is the responsibility of priesthood bearers in connection with the law of chastity?

Brethren, we must ourselves resolve anew that we are going to keep the law of chastity: and if we have made mistakes, let's begin now to rectify these mistakes. Let's walk towards the light; and for goodness sake, brethren, don't prostitute the wonderful opportunity you have as men, as those who may link hands with the Creator in the procreation of human souls, by engaging in a kind of unlawful relationship that will only go down to disgrace and break the hearts of your wives and your children. Brethren, we plead with you to keep yourselves morally clean, and walk the path of truth and righteousness, and thereby gain the plaudits of a Heavenly Father whose sons you are.[14]

I want to warn this great body of priesthood against that great sin of Sodom and Gomorrah, which has been labeled as a sin second only in seriousness to the sin of murder. I speak of the sin of adultery, which, as you know, was the name used by the Master as He referred to unlicensed sexual sins of fornication as well as adultery; and besides this, the equally grievous sin of homosexuality, which seems to be gaining momentum with social acceptance in the Babylon of the world, of which Church members must not be a part.

While we are in the world, we must not be of the world. Any attempts being made by the schools or places of entertainment to flaunt sexual perversions, which can do nothing but excite to experimentation, must find among the priesthood in this church a vigorous and unrelenting [opposition] through every lawful means that can be employed.[15]

For a child of God, and particularly one bearing the priesthood and having been active in the Church, to consider his God-given gift of creative powers as a mere plaything or that his association with his sweetheart is primarily for the satisfying of his lustful appetite is to play the game of Satan, who knows that such conduct is the sure way to destroy in one the refinement necessary to receive the companionship of the Spirit of the Lord.[16]

How can parents teach their children to understand and live the law of chastity?

Now the most effective teaching in the church is done in the family where the responsibility upon the father and the mother in the home is to teach their children while they're yet small the basic principles of faith, repentance, belief in the Savior, those early principles of chastity, virtue, honor, and so on. The greatest strength that children can have in holding away from these things of the world will be the fear of losing their place in the eternal family circle. If they've been taught in their childhood and youth to love the family and revere the home, they would think twice before they'd ever want to do something that would forever bar them from belonging to that eternal family home. To us, marriage, bearing of children, chastity, virtue are some of the most precious truths we have—the most vital things.[17]

Have we made sure that in the development of that little soul entrusted to our care, that we never left her without the benefit of our maturity of years to teach her the "how" of all we know? Did we, in her growing-up years, lay the foundation and framework for a strong, successful, and happy life, or did we leave it all to the hit and miss of trial and error, and hope somehow that Providence would protect our darling while she gained experience?

Perhaps a true-to-life incident will impress the thought I am trying to introduce. . . . A young pilot in a solo flight high above the airport in a training routine . . . suddenly shouted over the radio communicating system to the officer in the control tower: "I can't see! I have gone blind." Should panic have prevailed in the control tower as well, disaster to the young pilot and to the valuable plane would have been certain; but, fortunately, he was a seasoned officer who, from experience, knew that under certain circumstances temporary blindness could come to a young novice under great tension. Calmly the officer talked to the youth up there, directing him in the process of circling to lose altitude slowly while at the same time ordering emergency equipment to be brought, at once, should there be a crash. After breath-taking minutes which seemed interminable to all who watched, the blinded pilot touched the wheels of his plane to the runway and rolled to a stop on the landing field. The ambulance attendants hastily rushed the boy to the base hospital for treatment.

What would have happened if the officer in the control tower had become excited or had been shirking his duty, or hadn't known how to deal with this kind of an emergency? The answer is that the same thing would have happened which could happen to [a youth] were she bereft of the wise counselor of experience when she is faced with a shocking crisis with which she is unaccustomed. In both instances, a life would be maimed, if not destroyed, and the opportunity for highest attainment blighted. . . .

I wish all mothers could have heard the heart-cries and the questions of a dear, sweet girl who, when it seemed that her girlhood dream of a temple marriage was almost within her grasp, had broken the law of chastity and now . . . lived in the torture chamber of an accusing conscience. Her questions were: "How was I to know that I was in danger? Why didn't I have the strength to resist?" Like the blinded pilot, she had been flying blind, but, unfortunately for her, there was no control tower attendant to guide her to a safe landing in her crisis. Oh, that she could have talked out her problem with a wise mother!

Had mother been too busy with Church work or her housework or with socials or clubs to have cultivated the comradeship which would have invited from her daughter the most intimate confidences on such sacred matters? Perhaps here was a mother who was content to have her daughter instructed in academic courses on these delicate subjects which, all too often, but encourage the students to experiment. Maybe she didn't realize that into her very living room, daily, by radio, magazines, and television were coming the distorted, and yet cleverly disguised ideas of love and life, and marriage that, all too often, are mistaken by youth as the path to happiness.[18]

You mothers, stay close to your daughters. When they're little children, don't let someone else tell them about the so-called facts of life. As soon as your little children begin to ask you questions, little tots about little intimate things, sit down and talk to them about the things to the limit of their intelligence. They will then say, "All right, Mother, that's fine." And then a little later when they get in their teenage, they'll come again a second time, this time a little more sophisticated. Then they begin to date, and where will they come for counsel? If you've done your job, they'll come to ask Mother about her counsel on this and that, and on the night of her marriage, she'll seek counsel from her mother, not from the women on the street.

And you fathers, be companionable with your boys. Never turn your boy aside when he wants to have your counsel about the things that he wants a father to talk to him about. Therein is the safety in the home. There's the safety of your young people. Don't deny them that safety, you fathers and you mothers.[19]

One of the things we must do in teaching our young people is to condition them on how to meet a temptation that comes in an unguarded moment. . . .

The one who has the chief responsibility is the father of the boy. This doesn't mean that the father should wake up some morning and call his boy to his bedside and in fifteen minutes tell him all the facts of life. That isn't what the boy needs. He needs a father to answer when he wants to ask questions of a delicate nature. He is hungering to know; he is curious about things.

If his father will be frank and honest, and tell him up to the limit of his intelligence as he grows up, that father will be the one to whom the son will return for counsel in the years that follow. That father will be an anchor to that boy's soul, as the father takes from his book of experience lessons that he can give to his son to help condition him against the possibility of falling into that fatal trap in an unguarded moment.[20]

How I wish I could impress you today, who must daily walk out on the swaying bridge [over the] worldliness and sin which flows as a turbulent stream below you, how I wish that when you have twinges of doubt and fear that cause you to lose the rhythm of prayer and faith and love, may you hear my voice as one calling to you from further along on life's bridge, "Have faith—this is the way—for I can see further ahead than you." I would to God that you today could feel the love flowing from my soul to yours, and know of my deep compassion toward each of you as you face your problems of the day. The time is here when every one of you must stand on your own feet. The time is here when no man and woman will endure on borrowed light. Each will have to be guided by the light within himself. If you do not have it, you will not stand.[21]

Suggestions for Study and Discussion

- Why must we think pure thoughts if we are to live the law of chastity?

- What blessings come to those who are chaste and virtuous?

- How does being unchaste represent running away "from the ultimate reality of who we really are"?

- What is the responsibility of priesthood holders in safeguarding themselves and their loved ones from the dangers of unchastity?

- What should fathers and mothers teach their children about sexual purity? What can parents do to ensure that their children feel confident enough to share intimate matters with them?

- What influences in the world today can lessen our ability to resist temptations to be immoral? Why is the counsel that "no man and woman will endure on borrowed light" particularly applicable to keeping the law of chastity in today's world?

Notes

1. In Conference Report, Mexico and Central America Area Conference 1972, 103.

2. *The Teachings of Harold B. Lee,* ed. Clyde J. Williams (1996), 105.

3. *By Their Fruits Shall Ye Know Them,* Brigham Young University Speeches of the Year (12 Oct. 1954), 8.

4. *The Teachings of Harold B. Lee,* 213–14.

5. *Stand Ye in Holy Places* (1974), 215.

6. *The Teachings of Harold B. Lee,* 215.

7. *The Teachings of Harold B. Lee,* 608.

8. *The Teachings of Harold B. Lee,* 85.

9. *The Teachings of Harold B. Lee,* 227.

10. Address to Ricks College student body and student leaders, 3 Mar. 1962, Historical Department Archives, The Church of Jesus Christ of Latter-day Saints, 19–20.

11. *The Teachings of Harold B. Lee,* 226–27.

12. *The Teachings of Harold B. Lee,* 504.

13. *Decisions for Successful Living* (1973), 219.

14. *The Teachings of Harold B. Lee,* 218.

15. *The Teachings of Harold B. Lee,* 232.

16. *The Teachings of Harold B. Lee,* 224.

17. Interview with Tom Pettit for NBC, 4 May 1973, Historical Department Archives, The Church of Jesus Christ of Latter-day Saints, 22–23.

18. "My Daughter Prepares for Marriage," *Relief Society Magazine,* June 1955, 348–49.

19. *The Teachings of Harold B. Lee,* 227–28.

20. *The Teachings of Harold B. Lee,* 228.

21. "Fortifying Oneself against the Vices of the World," baccalaureate address given at Ricks College, 6 May 1970, Historical Department Archives, The Church of Jesus Christ of Latter-day Saints, 18–19.

Striving for Perfection

*How can we strive to fulfill the commandment
"Be ye therefore perfect"?*

Introduction

President Harold B. Lee taught the importance of following the example of the Savior as we strive for perfection:

"I am convinced that the Master was not merely thinking relatively when he said, 'Be ye therefore perfect, even as your Father which is in heaven is perfect.' [Matthew 5:48.] . . . Would you suppose the Savior was suggesting a goal that was not possible of attainment and thus mock us in our efforts to live to attain that perfectness? It is impossible for us here in mortality to come to that state of perfection of which the Master spoke, but in this life we lay the foundation on which we will build in eternity; therefore, we must make sure that our foundation is laid on truth, righteousness and faith. In order for us to reach that goal we must keep God's commandments and be true to the end of our lives here, and then beyond the grave continue in righteousness and knowledge until we become as our Father in Heaven. . . .

". . . [The Apostle Paul] pointed to the course by which perfection comes. Speaking of Jesus, he said, 'Though he were a Son, yet learned he obedience by the things which he suffered; and being made perfect, he became the author of eternal salvation unto all them that obey him.' (Hebrews 5:8–9.) . . .

". . . Let then no day pass but that we learn from the great lesson book of [Christ's] life his way to a perfect life and walk therein to our eternal goal."[1]

Teachings of Harold B. Lee

How does an understanding of what we lack help us become perfect?

[There are] three essentials that are necessary to inspire one to live a Christlike life—or, speaking more accurately in the language of the scriptures, to live more perfectly as the Master lived. The first essential I would name in order to qualify is: There must be awakened in the individual who would be taught or who would live perfectly an awareness of his needs.

The rich young ruler did not need to be taught repentance from murder nor from murderous thoughts. He did not have to be schooled in how to repent from adultery, nor from stealing, lying, defrauding, or failing to honor his mother. All these he said he had observed from his youth; but his question was, "What lack I yet?" [See Matthew 19:16–22.]

The Master, with His keen discernment and the power of a Great Teacher, diagnosed the young man's case perfectly: His need and his lack were to overcome his love for worldly things, his tendency to trust in riches. And then Jesus prescribed the effective remedy: "If thou wilt be perfect, go and sell that thou hast, and give to the poor, and thou shalt have treasure in heaven: and come and follow me." (Matthew 19:21.)

In the Apostle Paul's dramatic conversion, when he was physically blinded by the light while on his way to Damascus . . . , he heard a voice that said to him: "Saul, Saul, why persecutest thou me?" [Acts 9:4.] And from the depths of this humbled Saul's soul there came the question that is always asked by the one who senses that he needs something: "Lord, what wilt thou have me to do?" [Acts 9:6.] . . .

Enos, the grandson of Lehi, tells of the wrestle he had before God, before he received a remission of his sins. We are not told what his sins were, but he apparently confessed them very freely. And then he said, "And my soul hungered. . . ." [Enos 1:4.] You see, that awareness and feeling of great need, and that soul-searching, brought him face to face with his lack and his need.

This quality of sensing one's need was expressed in the great Sermon on the Mount when the Master said, "Blessed are the poor in spirit: for theirs is the kingdom of heaven." (Matthew 5:3.) The poor in spirit, of course, means those who are spiritually needy, who feel so impoverished spiritually that they reach out with great yearning for help. . . .

Every one of us, if we would reach perfection, must one time ask ourselves this question, "What lack I yet?" if we would commence our climb upward on the highway to perfection. . . .

How does being born again help us become perfect?

The second essential for perfection that I would name is found in the conversation the Master had with Nicodemus. He discerned as Nicodemus came to Him that he was seeking to have the answer to what many others had asked Him: "What must I do to be saved?" And the Master answered, "Verily, verily, I say unto thee, Except a man be born again, he cannot see the kingdom of God." Then Nicodemus said, "How can a man be born when he is old? . . ." Jesus answered, "Verily, verily, I say unto thee, Except a man be born of water and of the Spirit, he cannot enter into the kingdom of God." (John 3:3–5.)

A man must be "born again" if he would reach perfection, in order to see or enter into the kingdom of God. And how is one born again? That is the same question that Enos asked. And you remember the simple answer that came back: "Because of thy faith in Christ, whom thou hast never before heard nor seen. And many years pass away before he shall manifest himself in the flesh; wherefore, go to, thy faith hath made thee whole." [Enos 1:8.]

Brother Marion G. Romney and I were sitting in the office one day when a young man came in. He was getting ready to go on a mission, and he had been interviewed in the usual way and had made confessions of certain transgressions of his youth. But he said to us, "I'm not satisfied by just having confessed. How can I know that I have been forgiven?" In other words, "How do I know that I am born again?" He felt he could not go on a mission in his present state.

As we talked, Brother Romney said: "Son, do you remember what King Benjamin said? He was preaching to some who had been pricked in their hearts because of 'their own carnal state, even less than the dust of the earth. And they all cried aloud with one voice, saying: O have mercy, and apply the atoning blood of Christ that we may receive forgiveness of our sins, and our hearts may be purified; for we believe in Jesus Christ, the Son of God, who created heaven and earth, and all things; who shall come down among the children of men. And it came to pass that after they had spoken these words the Spirit of the Lord came upon them, and they were filled with joy, having received a remission of their sins, and having peace of conscience, because of the exceeding faith which they had in Jesus Christ. . . .' " (Mosiah 4:2–3.)

Brother Romney said to him, "My son, you wait and pray until you have the peace of conscience because of your faith in Jesus Christ's atonement, and you will know that your sins then have been forgiven." Except for that, as Elder Romney explained, any one of us is impoverished, and we are wandering in a fog until we have had that rebirth. . . .

You cannot have a Christlike life . . . without being born again. One would never be happy in the presence of the Holy One of Israel without this cleansing and purifying. . . .

How does living the commandments more completely help us become perfect?

And then finally the third essential: to help the learner to know the gospel by living the gospel. Spiritual certainty that is necessary to salvation must be preceded by a maximum of individual effort. Grace, or the free gift of the Lord's atoning power, must be preceded by personal striving. Repeating again what Nephi said, "By grace . . . we are saved, after all we can do." [2 Nephi 25:23.] . . .

. . . Now, [this] is one of the essentials if you would live a perfect life. One must "make up his mind" to live the commandments.

The Master answered a question of the Jews as to how they could be certain as to whether His mission was of God or whether

He was just another man. He said: "If any man will do his will, he shall know of the doctrine, whether it be of God, or whether I speak of myself." (John 7:17.)

The testimony of truth never comes to him who has an unclean tabernacle. The Spirit of the Lord and uncleanliness cannot dwell at the same time in a given individual. "I, the Lord, am bound when ye do what I say; but when ye do not what I say, ye have no promise." (D&C 82:10.) ". . . Except ye abide my law ye cannot attain to this glory." (D&C 132:21.) Again and again that truth is repeated in the scriptures.

All the principles and ordinances of the gospel are in a sense but invitations to learning the gospel by the practice of its teachings. No person knows the principle of tithing until he pays tithing. No one knows the principle of the Word of Wisdom until he keeps the Word of Wisdom. Children, or grownups for that matter, are not converted to tithing, the Word of Wisdom, keeping the Sabbath day holy, or prayer by hearing someone talk about these principles. We learn the gospel by living it. . . .

May I say in summary: We never really know anything of the teachings of the gospel until we have experienced the blessings that come from living each principle. "Moral teachings themselves," someone has said, "have only a superficial effect upon the spirit unless they are buttressed by acts." The most important of all the commandments in the gospel to you and to me is that particular commandment which for this moment requires in each of us the greatest soul-searching to obey. Each of us must analyze his needs and begin today to overcome, for only as we overcome are we granted a place in our Father's kingdom.[2]

How are the Beatitudes "the constitution for a perfect life"?

You want to know the "steps" by which one can have his life patterned to that fulness that makes him a worthy citizen or "saint" in God's kingdom. The best answer may be found by a study of the life of Jesus in the scriptures. . . . Christ came not only into the world to make an atonement for the sins of mankind but to set an example before the world of the standard of perfection of God's law and of obedience to the Father. In his Sermon on the Mount the Master has given us somewhat of a revelation of his own character, which was perfect, . . . and in so doing has given us a blueprint for our own lives. . . .

In that matchless Sermon on the Mount, Jesus has given us eight distinct ways by which we might receive . . . joy. Each of his declarations is begun by the word "Blessed." . . . These declarations of the Master are known in the literature of the Christian world as the Beatitudes. . . . They embody in fact the constitution for a perfect life.

Let us consider them for a few moments. Four of them have to do with our individual selves, the living of our own inner, personal lives, if we would be perfect and find the blessedness of that inward joy.

Blessed are the poor in spirit.

Blessed are they that mourn.

Blessed are they that hunger and thirst after righteousness.

Blessed are the pure in heart. [See Matthew 5:3–4, 6, 8.]

To be poor in spirit

To be poor in spirit is to feel yourselves as the spiritually needy, ever dependent upon the Lord for your clothes, your food and the air you breathe, your health, your life; realizing that no day should pass without fervent prayer of thanksgiving, for guidance and forgiveness and strength sufficient for each day's need. If a youth realizes his spiritual need, when in dangerous places where his very life is at stake, he may be drawn close to the fountain of truth and be prompted by the Spirit of the Lord in his hour of greatest trial. It is indeed a sad thing for one, because of wealth or learning or worldly position, to think himself independent of this spiritual need. [Being poor in spirit] is the opposite of pride or self-conceit. . . . If in your humility you sense your spiritual need, you are made ready for adoption into the "Church of the First Born, and to become the elect of God." [See D&C 76:54; 84:34.]

In the Sermon on the Mount, the Savior gave us
the "constitution for a perfect life."

To mourn

To mourn, as the Master's lesson here would teach, one must
show that "godly sorrow that worketh repentance" and wins for
the penitent a forgiveness of sins and forbids a return to the
deeds of which he mourns. [See 2 Corinthians 7:10.] It is to see,
as did the Apostle Paul, "glory in tribulations . . . : knowing that
tribulation worketh patience; and patience, experience; and experience, hope." (Romans 5:3–4.) You must be willing "to bear
one another's burdens, that they may be light." You must be willing to mourn with those that mourn and comfort those that stand
in need of comfort. (Mosiah 18:8–9.) When a mother mourns in
her loneliness for the return of a wayward daughter, you with
compassion must forbid the casting of the first stone. . . . Your
mourning with the aged, the widow and the orphan should lead
you to bring the succor they require. In a word, you must be as

the publican and not as the Pharisee. "God be merciful to me a sinner." [See Luke 18:10–13.] Your reward for doing [this] is the blessedness of comfort for your own soul through a forgiveness of your own sins.

To hunger and thirst

Did you ever hunger for food or thirst for water when just a crust of stale bread or a sip of tepid water to ease the pangs that distressed you would seem to be the most prized of all possessions? If you have so hungered then you may begin to understand how the Master meant we should hunger and thirst after righteousness. It's that hungering and thirsting that leads those away from home to seek fellowship with saints in sacrament services and that induces worship on the Lord's Day wherever we are. It is that which prompts fervent prayer and leads our feet to holy temples and bids us be reverent therein. One who keeps the Sabbath Day holy will be filled with a lasting joy far more to be desired than the fleeting pleasures derived from activities indulged in contrary to God's commandment. If you ask with "a sincere heart, with real intent, having faith in Christ, he will manifest . . . truth . . . unto you, by the power of the Holy Ghost," and by its power you "may know the truth of all things." (Moroni 10:4–5.) . . .

To be pure in heart

If you would see God, you must be pure. . . . Some of the associates of Jesus saw him only as a son of Joseph the carpenter. Others thought him to be a winebibber or a drunkard because of his words. Still others thought he was possessed of devils. Only the righteous saw him as the Son of God. Only if you are the pure in heart will you see God, and also in a lesser degree will you be able to see the "God" or good in man and love him because of the goodness you see in him. Mark well that person who criticizes and maligns the man of God or the Lord's anointed leaders in his Church. Such a one speaks from an impure heart.

But in order to gain entrance into the Kingdom of Heaven we must not only be good but we are required to do good and be good for something. So if you would walk daily toward that goal of perfection and fulness of life, you must be schooled by the remaining four "articles" in the Master's Constitution for a perfect life. These beatitudes have to do with man's social relations with others:

Blessed are the meek.

Blessed are the merciful.

Blessed are the peacemakers.

Blessed are they which are persecuted. [See Matthew 5:5, 7, 9–10.]

To be meek

A meek man is defined as one who is not easily provoked or irritated and forbearing under injury or annoyance. Meekness is not synonymous with weakness. The meek man is the strong, the mighty, the man of complete self-mastery. He is the one who has the courage of his moral convictions, despite the pressure of the gang or the club. In controversy his judgment is the court of last-resort and his sobered counsel quells the rashness of the mob. He is humble-minded; he does not bluster. "He that is slow to anger is better than the mighty." (Proverbs 16:32.) He is a natural leader and is the chosen of army and navy, business and church to lead where other men follow. He is the "salt" of the earth and shall inherit it.

To be merciful

Our salvation rests upon the mercy we show to others. Unkind and cruel words, or wanton acts of cruelty toward man or beast, even though in seeming retaliation, disqualify the perpetrator in his claims for mercy when he has need of mercy in the day of judgment before earthly or heavenly tribunals. Is there one who has never been wounded by the slander of another whom he thought to be his friend? Do you remember the struggle you had to refrain from retribution? Blessed are all you who are merciful for you shall obtain mercy!

To be a peacemaker

Peacemakers shall be called the children of God. The trouble-maker, the striker against law and order, the leader of the mob, the law-breaker are prompted by motives of evil and unless they desist will be known as the children of Satan rather than God. Withhold yourselves from him who would cause disquieting doubts by making light of sacred things for he seeks not for peace but to spread confusion. That one who is quarrelsome or con-tentious, and whose arguments are for other purposes than to re-solve the truth, is violating a fundamental principle laid down by the Master as an essential in the building of a full rich life. "Peace and goodwill to men on earth" was the angel song that heralded the birth of the Prince of Peace. [See Luke 2:14.] . . .

To endure persecution for righteousness' sake

To be persecuted for righteousness' sake in a great cause where truth and virtue and honor are at stake is god-like. Always there have been martyrs to every great cause. The great harm that may come from persecution is not from the persecution itself but from the possible effect it may have upon the persecuted who may thereby be deterred in their zeal for the righteousness of their cause. Much of that persecution comes from lack of under-standing, for men are prone to oppose that which they do not comprehend. Some of it comes from men intent upon evil. But from whatever cause, persecution seems to be so universal against those engaged in a righteous cause that the Master warns us, "Woe unto you, when all men shall speak well of you! for so did their fathers to the false prophets." (Luke 6:26.)

. . . Remember that warning when you are hissed and scoffed because you refuse to compromise your standards of abstinence, honesty and morality in order to win the applause of the crowd. If you stand firmly for the right despite the jeers of the crowd or even physical violence, you shall be crowned with the blessed-ness of eternal joy. Who knows but that again in our day some of the saints or even apostles, as in former days, may be required to give their lives in defense of the truth? If that time should come, God grant they would not fail!

Gradually as we ponder prayerfully all these teachings, we will make what may be to some the startling discovery that after all, God's measure of our worth in his kingdom will not be the high positions we have held here among men nor in his Church, nor the honors we have won, but rather the lives we have led and the good we have done, according to that "Constitution for a Perfect Life" revealed in the life of the Son of God.

May you make the Beatitudes the Constitution for your own lives and thus receive the blessedness promised therein.[3]

Suggestions for Study and Discussion

- How can we learn daily from the "great lesson book" of Christ's life?

- As we strive to become Christlike, why is it important for us to frequently ask ourselves what we lack?

- What experiences have helped you understand that we learn the teachings of the gospel by living them?

- When we realize that we are dependent on the Lord for all the blessings of our lives, how are our attitudes and behaviors affected?

- What are some of the meanings of the statement, "Blessed are they that mourn"?

- How can the love of worldly things dull our hunger and thirst for spiritual things?

- How does being pure in heart help us see the goodness in others?

- How does meekness help us to be strong?

- In what ways can we show mercy to others in our daily lives?

Notes

1. *Decisions for Successful Living* (1973), 40–41, 44.
2. *Stand Ye in Holy Places* (1974), 208–16.
3. *Decisions for Successful Living*, 55–62.

Peace Be unto Thy Soul

Why is adversity necessary to fulfill the Lord's eternal purposes?

Introduction

"All who live upon this earth are to be tested by the winds of adversity," said Harold B. Lee.[1] No stranger to adversity, Harold B. Lee lost his wife, Fern Tanner Lee, and his daughter Maurine Lee Wilkins to death during the 1960s. He also suffered severe health problems throughout his years as a General Authority. He acknowledged in general conference in 1967: "I have had to submit to some tests, some severe tests, before the Lord, I suppose to prove me to see if I would be willing to submit to all things whatsoever the Lord sees fit to inflict upon me, even as a little child does submit to its father." [See Mosiah 3:19.][2]

But President Lee offered comfort in the face of affliction: "The one who confidently looks forward to an eternal reward for his efforts in mortality is constantly sustained through his deepest trials. When he is disappointed in love, he does not commit suicide. When loved ones die, he doesn't despair; when he loses a coveted contest, he doesn't falter; when war and destruction dissipate his future, he doesn't sink into a depression. He lives above his world and never loses sight of the goal of his salvation."[3]

"The path to [exaltation] is rugged and steep. Many stumble and fall, and through discouragement never pick themselves up to start again. The forces of evil cloud the path with many foggy deterrents, often trying to detour us in misleading trails. But through all this journey," assured President Lee, "there is the calming assurance that if we choose the right, success will be ours, and the achievement of it will have molded and formed and created us into the kind of person qualified to be accepted into the presence of God. What greater success could there be than to have all that God has?"[4]

Teachings of Harold B. Lee

How does adversity help us become more like God?

There is a refining process that comes through suffering, I think, that we can't experience any other way than by suffering. . . . We draw closer to Him who gave His life that man might be. We feel a kinship that we have never felt before. . . . He suffered more than we can ever imagine. But to the extent that we have suffered, somehow it seems to have the effect of drawing us closer to the divine, helps to purify our souls, and helps to purge out the things that are not pleasing in the sight of the Lord.[5]

Isaiah said: "But now, O Lord, thou art our father; we are the clay, and thou our potter; and we all are the work of thy hand." (Isaiah 64:8.)

I've read that verse many times but had not received the full significance until I was down in Mexico a few years ago at Telacapaca, where the people mold clay into various kinds of pottery. There I saw them take clay that had been mixed by crude, primitive methods, the molder wading in the mud to mix it properly. Then it was put upon a potter's wheel and the potter began to fashion the intricate bits of pottery, which he was to place on the market. And as we watched, we saw occasionally, because of some defect in the mixing, the necessity for pulling the whole lump of clay apart and throwing it back in to be mixed over again, and sometimes the process had to be repeated several times before the mud was properly mixed.

With that in mind, I began to see the meaning of this scripture. Yes, we too have to be tried and tested by poverty, by sickness, by the death of loved ones, by temptation, sometimes by the betrayal of supposed friends, by affluence and riches, by ease and luxury, by false educational ideas, and by the flattery of the world. A father, explaining this matter to his son, said:

"And to bring about his eternal purposes in the end of man, after he had created our first parents, and the beasts of the field

207

and the fowls of the air, and in fine, all things which are created, it must needs be that there was an opposition; even the forbidden fruit in opposition to the tree of life; the one being sweet and the other bitter." [2 Nephi 2:15.]

It was the Prophet Joseph Smith who said, speaking of this refining process, that he was like a huge, rough stone rolling down the mountainside, and the only polishing he got was when some rough corner came in contact with something else, knocking off a corner here and a corner there. But, he said, "Thus I will become a . . . polished shaft in the quiver of the Almighty." [*History of the Church,* 5:401.]

So, we must be refined; we must be tested in order to prove the strength and power that are in us.[6]

Guided by faith taught by the word of God, we view life as a great process of soul-training. Under the ever-watchful eye of a loving Father, we learn by "the things which we suffer," we gain strength by overcoming obstacles, and we conquer fear by triumphant victory in places where danger lurks [see Hebrews 5:8]. By faith, as the word of God teaches, we understand that whatever contributes in life to the lofty standard of Jesus—"Be ye therefore perfect, even as your Father which is in heaven is perfect" (Matthew 5:48)—is for our good and for our eternal benefit even though into that molding may go the severe chastening of an all-wise God, "For whom the Lord loveth he chasteneth, and scourgeth every son whom he receiveth." (Hebrews 12:6.)

Thus schooled and drilled for the contest with the powers of darkness and with spiritual wickedness, we may be "troubled on every side, yet not distressed; we are perplexed, but not in despair; Persecuted, but not forsaken; cast down, but not destroyed." (2 Corinthians 4:8–9.)[7]

One who has a testimony of the purpose of life sees the obstacles and trials of life as opportunities for gaining the experience necessary for the work of eternity. . . .

If face to face with death, such a one will not fear if his feet have been "shod with the preparation of the gospel of peace," [Ephesians 6:15] and those who lose their loved ones will have the faith of Moroni, the captain of the army, who declared, "For the Lord suffereth the righteous to be slain that his justice and judgment may come upon the wicked; therefore ye need not suppose that the righteous are lost because they are slain; but behold, they do enter into the rest of the Lord their God." (Alma 60:13)[8]

Listen to the Master's lesson in human horticulture—"Every branch that beareth fruit must be purged [or pruned] that it might bring forth more fruit" (see John 15:2). . . .

Rarely, if ever, is there a truly great soul except he has been tried and tested through tears, and adversity—seemingly pruned by the hand of a master gardener. By applying the knife and the pruning hook the branch is shaped and fashioned to God's omnipotent design, in order that its full fruitage may be realized.

Every one of you must endure trials, and hardships, heartaches and discouragements. When in sorrow and in despair if you will remember, you will be comforted if you learn this lesson: "For whom the Lord loveth he chasteneth, and scourgeth every son whom he receiveth" (Hebrews 12:6)—and again: "My son, despise not the chastening of the Lord; neither be weary of his correction: for whom the Lord loveth he correcteth; even as a father the son in whom he delighteth" (Proverbs 3:11–12).[9]

The Prophet Joseph [Smith] . . . was worried because of depredations against the Saints and in the midst of his troubles you remember he cried out, "O God, how long shall it be before thine eyes shall see and thine ears hear the piteous cries of the Saints and avenge their wrongs on the heads of their enemies?" [See D&C 121:1–6.] And it was as though the Master had taken a frightened child into his arms and said:

"My son, peace be unto thy soul; thine adversity and thine afflictions shall be but a small moment;

"And then, if thou endure it well, God shall exalt thee on high; thou shalt triumph over all thy foes." (D&C 121:7, 8)

Then he said a stunning thing:

". . . know thou, my son, that all these things shall give thee experience, and shall be for thy good." (D&C 122:7)

. . . Then the Master said:

While the Prophet Joseph Smith was facing great adversity in
Liberty Jail, he received the comforting revelations that became
sections 121 and 122 of the Doctrine and Covenants.

"The Son of Man hath descended below them all. Art thou
greater than he?

"Therefore, hold on thy way. . . . Fear not what man can do,
for God shall be with you forever and ever." (D&C 122:8, 9)

I came to a time in life when I had to apply that to myself. The
Son of Man went through all of these.[10]

The purpose of our being here is clearly spelled out in the
Lord's revelation to Moses. He said, "This is my work and my
glory—to bring to pass the immortality and eternal life of man."
[Moses 1:39.] "Eternal life of man" means a return back to the
presence of God the Father and His Son to live eternally with
Them. Now, He didn't say it was His purpose that all His children
should live here upon the earth in the lap of luxury, with wealth
and ease and they should have no pain and no sorrow. He didn't
say that. For sometimes, as Isaiah put it, from out of the briar
bush may come forth a beautiful myrtle tree [see Isaiah 55:13].
. . . What may seem for the moment to be a tragedy may, as we
see the whole picture from the beginning to the end, in the wisdom of our Father, be for one of the great blessings instead of a
tragic ending as we have supposed.[11]

How can we find inner strength and peace in times of trouble?

Every soul that walks the earth, you and I, all of us—whether rich or poor, whether good or bad, young or old—every one of us is going to be tested and tried by storms of adversity, winds that we must defend ourselves against. And the only ones who won't fail will be those whose houses have been built upon the rock. And what's the rock? It's the rock of obedience to the principles and teachings of the gospel of Jesus Christ as the Master taught.[12]

I make no apologies . . . in asking you this morning, to believe with me in the fundamental concepts of true religion—of faith in God and in His Son Jesus Christ as the Savior of the world and that in His name miracles have been and are being wrought today and that only by a full acceptance of these truths can you and I be anchored to unfailing moorings when the storms of life rage about us.

I invite you therefore, to humble yourselves . . . and with prayerful hearts dare to believe all that the holy prophets have taught us of the gospel from the Holy Scriptures from the beginning.[13]

So the all-important thing in life isn't what happens to you, but the important thing is how you take it. That's the important thing. In the closing of the Sermon on the Mount, you remember, the Master gave a parable. He said:

"Therefore whosoever heareth these sayings of mine, and doeth them, I will liken him unto a wise man, which built his house upon a rock:

"And the rain descended, and the floods came, and the winds blew, and beat upon that house; and it fell not: for it was founded upon a rock. . . ." [Matthew 7:24–25.]

What was he trying to impress? He was trying to say that the winds of adversity, the floods of disaster, the difficulties, are going to beat upon every human house upon this earth; and the only ones who will not fall—when the bank fails, when you lose a loved one, in any other disaster—the only thing that will hold us through all these storms and stresses of life is when we've built upon the rocks by keeping the commandments of God. . . .

Wait patiently on the Lord in the season of persecution and deep affliction. The Lord said,

"Verily I say unto you my friends, fear not, let your hearts be comforted; yea, rejoice evermore, and in everything give thanks;

"Waiting patiently on the Lord, for your prayers have entered into the ears of the Lord of Sabaoth, and are recorded with this seal and testament—the Lord hath sworn and decreed that they shall be granted." (D&C 98:1–2)[14]

What can we say to those who are yearning for an inward peace to quiet their fears, to ease the aching heart, to bring understanding, to look beyond the sordid trials of today and see a fruition of hopes and dreams in a world beyond mortality? . . .

The Master indicated the source from which ultimate peace would come when he said to his disciples, "Peace I leave with you, my peace I give unto you: not as the world giveth, give I unto you. Let not your heart be troubled, neither let it be afraid." (John 14:27.)[15]

"Keep the commandments of God," for therein is the one course that brings that inward peace of which the Master spoke when He bid farewell to His disciples: "These things I have spoken unto you, that in me ye might have peace. In the world ye shall have tribulation: but be of good cheer; I have overcome the world." (John 16:33) So may each of you, in the midst of the turmoil all about you, find that heavenly assurance from the Master who loves us all, which puts to flight all fears when, like the Master, you also have overcome the things of the world.[16]

Where is there safety in the world today? Safety can't be won by tanks and guns and the airplanes and atomic bombs. There is only one place of safety and that is within the realm of the power of Almighty God that he gives to those who keep his commandments and listen to his voice, as he speaks through the channels that he has ordained for that purpose. . . .

Peace be with you, not the peace that comes from the legislation in the halls of congress, but the peace that comes in the way that the Master said, by overcoming all the things of the world. That God may help us so to understand and may you know that I know with a certainty that defies all doubt that this is his work, that he is guiding us and directing us today, as he has done in every dispensation of the gospel.[17]

Today, as prophesied, the whole world seems to be in commotion and men's hearts are failing them. We truly must expect to live with that inner peace born from applying the gospel of Jesus Christ in the world of trouble and calamity. Failure of the heart may come upon men in part out of despair and significantly it will come in a time when the love of men shall wax cold. The power of the priesthood in us today must be called upon and we must even love those who despitefully use us and keep our minds sound as the Apostle Paul advised Timothy. [See 2 Timothy 1:7.] If we do not, we will be rendered ineffective. We will receive inadequate assurances. Then the adversary would not need to get us to break the commandments or to apostatize. We will have already dawdled away our strength.[18]

A businessman in Atlanta, Georgia, with whom I have been associated . . . was trying to comfort me through a devastating loss; he took me aside and he said to me, "Now, I want to tell you something. I'm a much older man than you. Thirty-four years ago the telephone rang at the bank where I was the president. The message was that my wife had been critically injured in an automobile accident. Immediately I said, 'Oh, God wouldn't let anything happen to this sweetheart of mine—she is so wonderful, so lovely, so beautiful.' But within an hour word came again that she was dead. And then my heart cried out, 'I want to die; I don't want to live; I want to hear her voice.' But I didn't die, and I didn't hear her voice. And then I sat down to try to speculate. What can be the meaning of such loneliness and such tragedy that stalks the path of all of us? And the thought came to me that this is the most severe test you'll ever be required to face in life. And if you can pass it, there isn't any other test that you won't be able to pass."

Somehow, as I rode home on the plane that night, there was peace, and for the first time I began to walk out of the shadows.

And there came to me what the Apostle Paul said of the Master, "Though he were a Son"—meaning the Son of God—"yet learned he obedience by the things which he suffered; and being made perfect, he became the author of eternal salvation unto all them that obey him" (Hebrews 5:8–9). Now, if you will think about that, that through the refining processes of separation, of loneliness, of devastation, I suppose there comes something that has to be before we are ready to meet some of the other tests of life.[19]

We have been called to difficult tasks in a difficult age, but this could be for each of us a time of high adventure, of great learning, of great inner satisfaction. For the converging challenges posed by war, urbanization, dilution of doctrine, and domestic decay surely provide for us the modern equivalent of crossing the plains, enduring misunderstanding, establishing a kingdom throughout the world in the midst of adversity. I pray that we may do our part during the journey, and be with, and leading, the caravan of the Church as it enters the final chosen place— His presence.[20]

Suggestions for Study and Discussion

- What are our sources of safety and peace during times of adversity? What has strengthened you and given you peace during the trials in your life?

- Why is everyone—both the righteous and the unrighteous— subjected to trials and adversities?

- In what ways is adversity a blessing in our lives? In what ways can trials help us to become stronger and better able to serve the Lord?

- Why must we put our trust in the "omnipotent design" of our Father in Heaven? What does it mean to be like clay in the hands of the Lord?

- What does it mean to wait patiently on the Lord in times of trial? What have you learned as you have done this?

- In what ways does God grant us peace to sustain us through times of adversity?

Notes

1. Address given at Brigham Young University Freedom Festival, 1 July 1962, Harold B. Lee Library Archives, Brigham Young University, 6.

2. In Conference Report, Oct. 1967, 98; or *Improvement Era,* Jan. 1968, 26.

3. *The Teachings of Harold B. Lee,* ed. Clyde J. Williams (1996), 171.

4. *The Teachings of Harold B. Lee,* 69–70.

5. *The Teachings of Harold B. Lee,* 187–88.

6. *Stand Ye in Holy Places* (1974), 114–15.

7. *Stand Ye in Holy Places,* 339.

8. In Conference Report, Oct. 1942, 72–73.

9. *The Teachings of Harold B. Lee,* 191.

10. *Education for Eternity,* address given at Salt Lake Institute of Religion "Lectures in Theology: Last Message Series," 15 Jan. 1971, Historical Library files, The Church of Jesus Christ of Latter-day Saints, 6.

11. Address given at funeral of Mabel Hale Forsey, 24 Oct. 1960, Historical Department Archives, The Church of Jesus Christ of Latter-day Saints, 6.

12. Devotional address given at Brigham Young University, 15 Nov. 1949, Historical Department Archives, The Church of Jesus Christ of Latter-day Saints, 10.

13. " 'I Dare You to Believe': Elder Lee Urges USAC Graduates Seek Spiritual Facts," *Deseret News,* 6 June 1953, Church News section, 4.

14. *Education for Eternity,* 7–8.

15. "To Ease the Aching Heart," *Ensign,* Apr. 1973, 2.

16. "A Message to Members in the Service," *Church News,* 2 Dec. 1972, 3.

17. In Conference Report, Oct. 1973, 169, 171; or *Ensign,* Jan. 1974, 128–29.

18. Address to regional representatives' seminar, 3 Apr. 1970, Historical Department Archives, The Church of Jesus Christ of Latter-day Saints, 4.

19. *The Teachings of Harold B. Lee,* 54.

20. *The Teachings of Harold B. Lee,* 408.

The Resurrection, an Anchor to the Soul

How does a testimony of the Resurrection of Jesus Christ and of our own forthcoming resurrection strengthen us in our earthly trials?

Introduction

President Harold B. Lee had an abiding testimony of the Resurrection of Jesus Christ, which was further strengthened shortly after his call to the Quorum of the Twelve Apostles in April 1941. He recalled: "One of the Twelve came to me and said, 'Now we would like you to be the speaker at the Sunday night service. It is for Easter Sunday. As an ordained apostle, you are to be a special witness of the mission and resurrection of the Lord and Savior Jesus Christ.' That, I think, was the most startling, the most overwhelming contemplation of all that had happened.

"I locked myself in one of the rooms of the Church Office Building and took out the Bible. I read in the four Gospels, particularly the scriptures pertaining to the death, crucifixion, and resurrection of the Lord, and as I read, I suddenly became aware that something strange was happening. It wasn't just a story I was reading, for it seemed as though the events I was reading about were very real as though I were actually living those experiences. On Sunday night I delivered my humble message and said, 'And now, I, one of the least of the apostles here on the earth today, bear you witness that I too know with all my soul that Jesus is the Savior of the world and that he lived and died and was resurrected for us.'

"I knew because of a special kind of witness that had come to me the preceding week. Then someone asked, 'How do you know? Have you seen?' I can say that more powerful than one's sight is the witness that comes by the power of the Holy Ghost bearing testimony to our spirits that Jesus is the Christ, the Savior of the world."[1]

Teachings of Harold B. Lee

How is the reality of the resurrection a "cheering promise"?

"Now upon the first day of the week, early in the morning, the women came unto the sepulchre. . . . They found the stone rolled away from the sepulchre. And they entered in, and found not the body of the Lord Jesus. And it came to pass that as they were much perplexed thereabout, behold two men stood by them in shining garments! And as they were afraid, and bowed down their faces to the earth, the angel said unto them, Why seek ye the living among the dead? Fear not ye, be not affrighted; for I know that ye seek Jesus of Nazareth, which was crucified.

"He is not here, for He is risen, as He said. Come, see the place where the Lord lay—where they laid him.

"And go quickly and tell his disciples and Peter that He is risen from the dead—that He goeth before you into Galilee; there ye shall see Him. Remember how He spoke unto you while He was yet in Galilee saying: The Son of Man must be delivered into the hands of sinful men and be crucified and the third day rise again. Lo, I have told you." [See Luke 24:1–7; Matthew 28:5–7; Mark 16:5–7.]

Thus do the writers of the gospels of Matthew, Mark, and Luke, record the greatest event in the history of the world, the literal resurrection of the Lord Jesus Christ, the Savior of mankind. Dramatically had been demonstrated the greatest of all the divine powers of an incarnated Son of God. He had declared to the sorrowing Martha, at the time of the death of her brother Lazarus: "I am the resurrection, and the life: he that believeth in me, though he were dead, yet shall he live." (John 11:25.)

To the Jews with murderous intent, His pronouncement of His divine power was even more explicit and meaningful. "Verily, verily, I say unto you, The hour is coming, and now is, when the

The resurrected Savior appeared to Mary at the tomb.
Through the witness of the Holy Ghost, we can each receive the
comforting assurance that the Savior has risen from the dead and broken
the bands of death for all mankind.

dead shall hear the voice of the Son of God: and they that hear shall live.

"For as the Father hath life in himself; so hath he given to the Son to have life in himself;

"And . . . to execute judgment also, because he is the Son of [God]." [John 5:25–27.]

Following swiftly His own resurrection, there came an evidence of a second transcendent power to raise from the grave, not only Himself, but others "who though dead, had believed in Him." Matthew makes this simple, forthright record of the miraculous resurrection of the faithful, from mortal death, "And the graves were opened; and many bodies of the saints which slept arose, And came out of the graves after his resurrection, and went into the holy city, and appeared unto many." [Matthew 27:52–53.]

Nor was this to be the end of the redemptive powers of this illustrious Son of God. Down through the ages, in every dispensation, has come the cheering promise: "For as in Adam all die, even so in Christ shall all be made alive," (I Cor. 15:22), ". . . they that have done good, unto the resurrection of life; and they that have done evil, unto the resurrection of damnation." (John 5:29.) Time is rapidly moving on to a complete consummation of His divine mission.

If the full significance of these thrilling events were understood in this day when, as the prophets foretold: The wicked are preparing to slay the wicked; and "fear shall come upon every man" (D&C 63:33), this understanding would put to flight many of the fears and anxieties which beset men and nations. Indeed if we "fear God and honor the king" [see 1 Peter 2:17] we can then lay claim to the glorious promise of the Master: "If you strip yourselves from jealousies and from fear, you shall see Me" [see D&C 67:10].[2]

The purpose of life was to bring to pass immortality and eternal life [see Moses 1:39]. Now, immortality means to eventually gain a body that will no longer be subject to the pains of mortality, no longer subject to another mortal death, and no longer disillusioned, all these former things having passed away.[3]

How does a knowledge of the resurrection sustain us in times of suffering or death?

Have you ever felt yourself spiritually devastated by an inconsolable grief?

May I take you to a sacred scene portraying one whose all seemed slipping from her grasp and let you feel her strength in a fateful hour! Huddled at the foot of the cross was the silent figure of a beautiful middle-aged mother with shawl drawn tightly about her head and shoulders. Cruelly tormented on the cross above her was her first-born son. One can but feebly understand the intensity of the suffering of Mary's mother-heart. She now faced in reality the import of old Simeon's doleful prediction as he had blessed this son as a tiny infant child, "He shall be as a sign for to be spoken against; Yea, a sword shall pierce thine own heart also." [See Luke 2:34–35.]

What was it that sustained her during her tragic ordeal? She knew the reality of an existence beyond this mortal life. Had she not conversed with an angel, a messenger of God? She undoubtedly had heard of her son's last recorded prayer before His betrayal as it has been written by John: "And now, O Father," he had prayed, "glorify thou me with thine own self with the glory which I had with thee before the world was." (John 17:5) This sainted mother with bowed head heard His last prayer murmured from the cross through tortured lips: "Father, into thy hands I commend my spirit," (Luke 23:46) thus inspiring her with resignation and a testimony of reassurance of a reunion shortly with Him and with God her Heavenly Father. Heaven is not far removed from him who, in deep sorrow, looks confidently forward to a glorious day of resurrection.[4]

Is there any assurance of reunion and a fulfilment of our dreams in the hereafter? That is the cry of a mother's grief as she lays away her infant child in death. Such is the whispered but often inaudible inquiry of the sick and the aged when life's sands are running fast. What strength and comfort must come to him in any of these circumstances, who hears the glorious promise of the Lord:

"Thy dead men shall live, together with my dead body shall they arise. Awake and sing, ye that dwell in dust: for thy dew is as the dew of herbs, and the earth shall cast out the dead." (Isaiah 26:19.)

The heavy hand of death becomes lighter, the pall of gloom is pierced and throbbing wounds are soothed as faith lifts us beyond the sordid trials and sorrows of mortal life and gives a vision of brighter days and more joyous prospect, as has been revealed, when "God shall wipe away all tears from their eyes; and there shall be no more death, neither sorrow, nor crying, neither shall there be any more pain: for the former things are passed away" (Rev. 21:4) through the atonement of the Lord Jesus Christ. With such faith and understanding you who may be called upon to mourn can sing as it has been written, "Death is swallowed up in victory. O death, where is thy sting? O grave, where is thy victory?" (I Cor. 15:54–55.)[5]

You, too, can know that your Redeemer lives, as did Job in the midst of his temptation to "curse God, and die," [see Job 2:9; 19:25] and know also that you, too, can open the door and invite Him in "to sup with you." [See Revelation 3:20.] See also yourselves one day as resurrected beings claiming kinship to Him who gave His life that the rewards to mortal men for earthly struggle and experience will be the fruits of eternal life even though as measured by human standards one's life's labors seemed to have been defeated.[6]

How is an understanding of the resurrection an anchor to our souls?

Let us look at the example of Peter, [who] . . . denied the Master thrice on the night of the betrayal. Compare this fear-torn Peter with the boldness in him manifested shortly thereafter before those same religious bigots who had so recently demanded the death of Jesus. He denounced them as murderers and called them to repentance, suffered imprisonment, and later went fearlessly to his own martyrdom.

What was it that had changed him? He had been a personal witness to the change which came to the broken, pain-racked body taken from the cross, to a glorified resurrected body. The plain and simple answer is that Peter was a changed man because he knew the power of the risen Lord. No more would he be alone on the shores of Galilee, or in prison, or in death. His Lord would be near him.[7]

I know . . . what it means to have the shattering devastation of loneliness with the snatching away of a loved one. Over my years, I have been called and tried to comfort those who mourn, but until I had to repeat those very things to myself that I have been saying to others, then only did I come to sense something that was far beyond words, that had to reach down to the touchstone of the soul before one can give real comfort. You have to see part of you buried in the grave. You have to see the loved one die and then you have to ask yourself—Do you believe what you have been teaching others? Are you sure and certain that God lives? Do you believe in the Atonement of the Lord and Master—that He opened the doors to the resurrection in the more glorious life? Sometimes when we stand in the stark nakedness all alone, it's then that our testimony has to grow deep if we are not going to be shattered and fall by the wayside.

As the wife . . . of Job said, "Why don't you curse God and die." [See Job 2:9.] But in the majesty of Job's suffering, he gave expression to something that I think no funeral service is quite complete without repeating. He said, "I know that my redeemer liveth, and that he shall stand at the latter day upon the earth: and though after my skin worms destroy this body, yet in my flesh shall I see God: whom I shall see for myself, . . . and not another; though my reins be consumed within me." [Job 19:25–27.] You folks today, if you know that you have anchored your souls in that divine testimony that He lives and that at the latter day He will stand upon this earth and you will meet Him face to face—if you know that, no matter what the risks and the responsibilities and the tragedies may be—if you build your house upon the rock, you won't falter. Yes, you'll go through the terrifying experience of sorrow over a lost loved one, but you won't falter; eventually you'll come through with even greater faith than you ever had before.[8]

The more complicated our lives and world conditions become, the more important it is for us to keep clear the purposes and principles of the gospel of Jesus Christ. It is not the function of religion to answer all the questions about God's moral government of the universe, but to give one courage, through faith, to go on in the face of questions he never finds the answer to in his present status.[9]

Today in commemoration of the world's greatest victory I invite the honest in heart everywhere in deep humility to rise above their human fears and frustrations and rejoice as did the apostle to the Gentiles "Thanks be to God, which giveth us the victory through our Lord Jesus Christ." (I Cor. 15:57.)[10]

Suggestions for Study and Discussion

- What did the Savior mean when He said, "I am the resurrection, and the life"? (John 11:25). How do you feel when you think about the Resurrection of the Savior?

- How has an understanding of the reality of the resurrection affected your daily life?

- In what ways does a testimony of the resurrection sustain us when someone we love dies? In what other situations does a testimony of the resurrection bring us comfort and help us overcome fear?

- What can we do to gain a greater understanding and testimony of the resurrection?

Notes

1. *Ye Are the Light of the World* (1974), 26–27.
2. CBS "Church of the Air" broadcast, in Conference Report, Apr. 1958, 133–34.
3. *The Teachings of Harold B. Lee*, ed. Clyde J. Williams (1996), 30.
4. CBS "Church of the Air" broadcast, 134–35.
5. *Decisions for Successful Living* (1973), 179–80.
6. In Conference Report, Apr. 1958, 136.
7. *The Teachings of Harold B. Lee*, 63.
8. Address given at the funeral of David H. Cannon, 29 Jan. 1968, Historical Department Archives, The Church of Jesus Christ of Latter-day Saints, 5–6.
9. In Conference Report, Oct. 1963, 108; or *Improvement Era*, Dec. 1963, 1103.
10. In Conference Report, Apr. 1958, 136.

Safely Home at Last

Are we safely on the path that leads to our eternal home and life in the presence of the Father?

Introduction

Throughout his ministry, Harold B. Lee emphasized this teaching: "The thing for which we are striving is to so keep ourselves and to so live that one day we can go back home to that God who gave us life—back into the presence of that eternal Heavenly Father."[1]

He recalled: "Some time ago I read an article written by a famous newspaper journalist who explained how he went about arranging for a meaningful conversation with some person whom he wished to interview. He would ask a question similar to this: 'Would you mind telling me the inscription you would have written on your tombstone?' He reported that many would give answers like 'have fun,' 'gone to another meeting,' and so on. Then the journalist was asked what he himself would have written on his tombstone. He replied very quietly and sincerely, 'Safely home, at last.'

"When the full significance of this statement is impressed upon us, we might well ask ourselves, 'After all, what is life all about, and what is our hope beyond this life, believing, as we do, in a life after this one?' Almost everyone, no matter what his religious faith may be, looks forth to an existence that may be defined in various ways. If my assumption is correct, then, we would all wish to have written on our tombstones, as an epitaph to our life's work, that we were 'safe at home, at last.' "[2]

Teachings of Harold B. Lee

What is the purpose of our mortal life?

What is the purpose of life . . . ? The only answer can be found in one scripture which reveals the purpose of God in giving life at all, and that purpose was explained in a revelation to the prophet Moses: "This is my work and my glory—to bring to pass the immortality and eternal life of man." [Moses 1:39.] If one were to breathe but a moment in mortal life and then were to be taken away, or should he live to the age of a tree, the purpose of our Father would have been accomplished so far as having gained immortality. And this thing called eternal life is to have so lived that one would, by his living, have been counted worthy of eternal life in the presence of God the Father and the Son.[3]

Man in the spirit world was the offspring of Deity. The earth was created and organized as the dwelling place of heaven-born spirits in mortal bodies to "prove them herewith, to see if they will do all things whatsoever the Lord their God shall command them." [See Abraham 3:25.] God's purpose in so doing was "to bring to pass immortality and eternal life" or, in other words, as a result of a successful mortal life, to bring each soul back into the presence of "that God who gave him life" and with a resurrected body not subject to death and thus perfected, to live eternally in the presence of the Lord our Master and the Father of us all.[4]

[President George F. Richards] related this story, a story of a young man who was very desirous of getting an education. His parents were unable to send him to college, so he walked to the college city, and after diligent inquiry he succeeded in finding a place [where] he could pay his board and lodging. Later one of the college professors gave him a job cutting wood to pay for his tuition. Others, learning of his success as a woodchopper, employed him to chop wood for them. He soon found that he had no time to go to college, and he became content with his success as a woodchopper.

This represents a condition which obtains with many of us. We came to earth for a specific purpose—that of working out our own salvation, or in other words, to prepare for the life which is to come, which is everlasting. Some of us seem to have forgotten the purpose we had in view, and have become content with our search for the wealth and fame which life affords, in other words, content with merely "chopping wood."[5]

May we who have the testimony [of Jesus] . . . from our hearts cry out to our Father: "Lord, what wilt thou have me to do?" [Acts 9:6.]

And if we pray in real sincerity and faith, there will come back to us from out of the scriptures the answer to that prayerful inquiry. The answer has come oft repeated, time and time again, that all that we do should be done "with an eye single to the glory of God." [D&C 82:19.] What is the glory of God? The Lord told Moses that:

". . . this is my work and my glory—to bring to pass the immortality and eternal life of man." (Pearl of Great Price, Moses 1:39.)

With that goal always before us, seeing every act of our lives, every decision we make as patterned toward the development of a life that shall permit us to enter into the presence of the Lord our Heavenly Father, to gain which is to obtain eternal life, how much more wisdom there would be in the many things of life.[6]

From the scriptures, from the writings of inspired Church leaders, and from secular commentaries, eternal life may be defined as life in the presence of those eternal Beings, God the Father and His Son Jesus Christ. To shorten that definition, we might then say that eternal life is God's life. . . .

To eventually attain to this celestial excellence should be the never-ending quest of all mortal beings.[7]

Are we ready to stand before the judgment seat of God?

Every one of you . . . must stand before "the judgment-seat of the Holy One of Israel . . . and then must . . . be judged according to the holy judgment of God." (II Nephi 9:15.) And according to the vision of John, "The books were opened: and another book was opened, which is the book of life: and the dead were judged out of those things which were written in the books, according to their works." (Rev. 20:12.) The "books" spoken of refer to the

President Harold B. Lee taught that our efforts in mortality
should be focused on "living life to its full abundance here and . . .
preparing for the celestial world."

"records [of your works] which are kept on the earth. . . . The book of life is the record which is kept in heaven." (Doc. and Cov. 128:7.) Those of you who have lived a righteous life and die without having become the servants of sin, or who have truly repented of your sins, will enter into the "rest of the Lord," which rest "is the fulness of the glory of the Lord." [See D&C 84:24.][8]

We are told from inspired writings that "our words will condemn us (or exalt us), our works will condemn us (or uplift us) . . . [see Alma 12:14], as we are brought face to face with the Great Judge of us all, hopefully to receive the Master's plaudits: "Well done, thou good and faithful servant." [Matthew 25:21.] Contrary to the usual concept of religionists, that the Apostle Peter is the keeper of the gateway to the life beyond this, we are told that "the keeper of the gate is the Holy One of Israel; and he employeth no servant there." (II Nephi 9:41.)[9]

The greatest hell that one can suffer is the burning of one's conscience. The scriptures say his thoughts will condemn him, he'll have a bright recollection of all his life (see Alma 12:14; 11:43). You'll remember that in the scriptures they speak of the Lamb's book of life, which is a record kept of man's life which is kept in heaven. . . . Men will be judged according to the records that have been kept of our lives. (See D&C 128:6–7.) Now, when we fail of that highest degree of glory and realize what we've lost, there will be a burning of the conscience that will be worse than any physical kind of fire that I assume one could suffer.[10]

When we pass through the portals of death . . . He's going to say to us, "Now you took upon yourselves my name. What have you done with my name? Have you ever brought disgrace to the name of the Lord Jesus Christ, as a member of my church?" Imagine a frown, imagine He shakes His head and turns and walks away. . . . But imagine when we meet Him that a smile lights up His face. He puts out His beckoning arms to us, and says to us, "My son, my daughter, you've been faithful on earth. You've kept the faith. You've finished your work. There's now a crown prepared for such as you in my kingdom." [See 2 Timothy 4:7–8.] I can't think of any ecstasy in all the world that will transcend that kind of a reception into the presence of the Almighty, in that world to come.[11]

How do we prepare to meet the Lord?

The Lord has granted us a few more days or a few more weeks or a few more years as the time goes—it matters not how long— for in the accounting of the Almighty, every day of preparation is precious. One prophet has put it, "This life is the time for men to prepare to meet God; yea, behold the day of this life is the day for men to perform their labors. . . . For behold, if ye have procrastinated the day of your repentance even until death, . . . the devil . . . doth seal you his." (Alma 34:32, 35.)[12]

We need to remember that it doesn't make so much difference whether we die early in life or in middle age, the all-important thing is not when we die, but how prepared are we when we do die. This is a day of preparation for men to prepare to meet their God. How great and merciful He was in allowing us a period of probation during which time man should be perfecting himself.[13]

Today is the day for us to begin to search our souls. Have you discovered which is the most important of all the commandments to you today? . . . Are you going to begin working on it today? Or are you going to wait until it is too late? The little boy says, "Well, when I get to be a big boy, then I'm going to do so and so." And what is that? When he gets to be a big boy, . . . then he says, "When I get married, then I'll do so and so." And then after he gets married, it all changes, and "Well, when I retire." And then after he is retired, a cold wind sweeps down over him and suddenly he realizes too late that he has lost everything. And it is too late. And yet all his life he has had all the time that there was. He just hasn't taken advantage of it. Now, today, this is the day for us to begin to do something about it, before it is too late.[14]

[I am reminded] of a story that I was told over in the Hawaiian Islands last summer about a little girl who had taken her friend to her home. They were playing about, and the elderly grandmother in the home spent much of her time while they were there reading the Bible. Every time this little neighbor girl came, the grandmother was reading the Bible, and she said finally, to the little granddaughter, "Why does your grandma spend so much time reading the Bible?" And the little granddaughter replied, "Oh, Grandma's cramming for the final examination."

Well, she wasn't so far wrong. And I think it would be well if all of us would be a little more mindful of the importance of cramming for the final examination.[15]

How long have you postponed the day of a repentance from your own misdeeds? The judgment we shall face will be before the Righteous Judge who will take into account our capacities and our limitations, our opportunities and our handicaps. One who sins and repents and thereafter fills his life with purposeful effort may not lose as much in that day of righteous judgment as one who, though not committing serious sin, falls down miserably by omitting to do that which he had capacity and opportunity to do but would not.[16]

As we sit here today, contemplating our lives, suppose that something should happen as we leave this congregation, and our lives are stopped in their course. Is there any unfinished business that you have to do yet before that time comes to you? . . . Do you have some wrongs that need to be righted before that time comes? Do you have any folks on the other side that are waiting for you that you will be proud to meet if you do certain unfinished things that you have to do today? Are you ready to meet the folks over there, having done all you can for the happiness of their future prospects? Have you any sins that need to be repented of before you go home to Him who gave you life?[17]

Here and now in mortality, each one of us is having the opportunity of choosing the kind of laws we elect to obey. We are now living and obeying celestial laws that will make us candidates for celestial glory, or we are living terrestrial laws that will make us candidates for . . . terrestrial glory, or telestial law. The place we shall occupy in the eternal worlds will be determined by the obedience we yield to the laws of these various kingdoms during the time we have here in mortality upon the earth.[18]

How do you prepare to meet the Lord? . . . The Lord said, "Therefore, sanctify yourselves that your minds become single to God, and the days will come that you shall see him; . . . and it shall be in his own time, and in his own way, and according to his own will." (D&C 88:68.) Here was the formula that he gave us in a revelation . . . , "Verily, thus saith the Lord: It shall come to pass that every soul who forsaketh his sins and cometh unto me, and calleth on my name, and obeyeth my voice, and keepeth my commandments, shall see my face and know that I am." [D&C 93:1.][19]

What is the reward for one who lives "worthy of a testimony that God lives and that Jesus is the Christ"?

Heaven, as we have usually conceived it, is the dwelling place of the righteous, after they have left this earth life, and the place where God and Christ dwell. Of this happy state the Apostle Paul said, "Eye hath not seen, nor ear heard, neither have entered into the heart of man, the things which God hath prepared for them that love him" (1 Corinthians 2:9).[20]

Success is many things to many people, but to every child of God it ultimately will be to inherit his presence and there be comfortable with him.[21]

There is only one objective so far as our Father's work is concerned, and that is that in the end when we shall have finished our work here on earth, whether after a short space of time or a long, we too shall have overcome the world and have earned the right to that place called the Celestial Kingdom.[22]

One who lives . . . worthy of a testimony that God lives and that Jesus is the Christ, and who is willing to reach out to Him in constant inquiry to know if his course is approved, is the one who is living life to its full abundance here and is preparing for the celestial world, which is to live eternally with his Heavenly Father.[23]

May I remind you to ponder the marvelous promise of the Lord to all who are faithful:

"And if your eye be single to my glory, your whole bodies shall be filled with light, and there shall be no darkness in you; and that body which is filled with light comprehendeth all things." (D&C 88:67.)

That each one who seeks thus may earnestly gain for himself that unshakable testimony which will place his feet firmly on the pathway which leads surely toward the glorious goal of immortality and eternal life is my humble prayer.[24]

Suggestions for Study and Discussion

- In what ways are we sometimes like the young man who chopped wood?
- What can help us keep focused each day on the goal of returning safely to our Father in Heaven?
- In what ways are you now choosing the place you will occupy in the eternal worlds? What are the consequences of procrastinating your preparation to stand before the judgment seat of God?
- What can we do with one more day from God?
- What does it mean to live with an eye single to the glory of God? (See D&C 88:67–68.)
- What has it meant to you to take upon yourself the name of the Lord Jesus Christ? What can we do to honor His name?
- What has your study of the teachings of President Harold B. Lee taught you about how to return safely home to God?

Notes

1. *Be Loyal to the Royal within You,* Brigham Young University Speeches of the Year (20 Oct. 1957), 10–11.

2. *Ye Are the Light of the World* (1974), 261–62.

3. Address given at the funeral of Aldridge N. Evans, 7 Jan. 1950, Historical Department Archives, The Church of Jesus Christ of Latter-day Saints, 4.

4. "The Sixth Commandment: Thou Shalt Not Kill," in *The Ten Commandments Today* (1955), 87.

5. "Elder Lee Recalls Counsel Given by Pres. Richards to Family, Associates," *Deseret News,* 16 Aug. 1950, Church section, 2, 4.

6. In Conference Report, Oct. 1946, 145.

7. "Eternal Life," *Instructor,* Oct. 1966, 378.

8. *Decisions for Successful Living* (1973), 186–87.

9. "The Greatest Need in the World Today," Utah State University baccalaureate address, 5 June 1970, Historical Department Archives, The Church of Jesus Christ of Latter-day Saints, 6.

10. *The Teachings of Harold B. Lee,* ed. Clyde J. Williams (1996), 67.

11. Address given at the Detroit Stake conference, Aug. 1958, Harold B. Lee Library Archives, Brigham Young University, 6–7.

12. Address given at the funeral of Irene Tolman Hammond, 18 Mar. 1968, Historical Department Archives, The Church of Jesus Christ of Latter-day Saints, 5.

13. Address given at the funeral of William G. Sears, 13 Mar. 1943, Historical Department Archives, The Church of Jesus Christ of Latter-day Saints, 14.

14. Address given to Ricks College student body and leaders, 3 Mar. 1962, Historical Department Archives, The Church of Jesus Christ of Latter-day Saints, 20–21.

15. *The Teachings of Harold B. Lee,* 65–66.

16. *The Teachings of Harold B. Lee,* 67–68.

17. Address given at the Detroit Stake conference, 4–5.

18. In Conference Report, Apr. 1947, 46.

19. "Preparing to Meet the Lord," *Improvement Era,* Feb. 1965, 124.

20. *The Teachings of Harold B. Lee,* 77.

21. *Decisions for Successful Living,* 2.

22. Address given at the funeral of Aldridge N. Evans, 8.

23. *The Teachings of Harold B. Lee,* 614.

24. *Stand Ye in Holy Places* (1974), 319.

List of Paintings

Index

W

Wayward children, loving, 134–36

Welfare work

beginnings of, xvi–xvii, 165–66

food storage, 172–73

foundation principles of, 166–69

Harold B. Lee leads, xvi–xvii, 165–66

individual and family responsibility, 169–73

role of priesthood quorums and Relief Society, 170–71

role of storehouses, 170–71

self-reliance essential to, 168–73

Wells, Bishop John, experience with deceased son, 182–83

Wives. *See* Marriage, eternal

Women

who do not have an eternal marriage, 114–15

See also Mothers

Woodchopper, story about, 225–26

Work

necessity of, 168–69, 171–73

teaching value of, 124

Worthiness

necessary for temple work, 105–7

See also Obedience

Y

Youth

preparing for eternal marriage, 115–17

teaching about chastity, 190–93

teaching in the home, 119–27

wayward, never give up on, 134–36